Looking In, Looking Out

Redefining Child Care and Early Education in a Diverse Society

Authors/Researchers

Hedy Nai-Lin Chang
Amy Muckelroy
Dora Pulido-Tobiassen

Editor

Carol Dowell

Contributing Editor & Writer

Julie Olsen Edwards

A California Tomorrow Publication
1996

California Tomorrow
Fort Mason Center, Building B
San Francisco, CA 94123
telephone (415) 441-7631
fax (415) 441-7635

The photographs in this book were taken by the California Tomorrow Early Childhood Project staff or provided to us by the child care programs and families connected to the project. Many thanks to all who provided the images.

Funding for *Looking In, Looking Out: Redefining Child Care and Early Education in a Diverse Society* and the California Tomorrow Early Childhood Project has been generously provided by the Miriam and Peter Haas Fund, the James Irvine Foundation, The Danforth Foundation, The David and Lucile Packard Foundation, the Trio Foundation and the A.L. Mailman Family Foundation. California Tomorrow general support is provided by the Gap Foundation.

Printed in the U.S.A by Coast Litho

ISBN 1-887039-12-0

Book design: Elaine Joe Design

California Tomorrow

Mission

California Tomorrow is a nonprofit organization working to help build a strong and fair multiracial, multicultural, multilingual society that is equitable for everyone. We believe creating such a society involves promoting equal opportunity and participation—social, economic and educational—and embracing our diversity as our greatest strength.

California Tomorrow's primary focus is on people, organizations and communities in California. Since our work is connected to national trends, we also share lessons learned from the California experience, draw upon the knowledge of colleagues working on similar issues across the United States, and join with others to influence national policies or practices which impact our respective work.

California Tomorrow seeks to:

- Promote the transformation of public and private institutions so that they support the healthy development of children, youth and families in a racially, culturally and linguistically diverse society.
- Build public awareness, knowledge and will about the benefits of diversity and the approaches, policies and investments needed to create a strong and fair multicultural, multiracial, multilingual society.
- Partner with organizations and people working to strengthen the ability of families and communities to hold institutions accountable, to build upon their assets, and to forge alliances within and across differences in race, culture, language, age and class.
- Model a positive approach to diversity through our own organizational policies and practices.

Table of Contents

uting to our analysis and writing. When the rest of us were ready to sign off on written pieces, Amy pointed out deeper complexities we hadn't yet tackled or ways we could enhance the substance. She continually reminded us not to skip steps that could mean missing important pieces of the picture. She was very adept at putting our interviewees at ease, so that we could ask sensitive questions that greatly informed our findings. Amy also taught us to pay closer attention to the racial experiences and identity development of biracial/bicultural people, so as not to perpetuate the invisibility of those issues.

We are also deeply indebted to many individuals whose time, energy and wisdom have influenced this book. Most significantly, this report bears the mark of our gifted editor, Carol Dowell. Since the beginning of the writing, through draft after draft, Carol worked with us to shape our book's structure, content, tone and message. A skillful listener, Carol is adept at balancing multiple concerns and perspectives in the editing process. During this long collaboration, her insights and humor helped keep the work moving. She is extremely respectful and encouraging to individual writers, and she labors to preserve their voices. Her careful editing, questioning and grasp of the nuances have been key to ensuring our words are accessible. A white woman, Carol's work is a testimony to

Advisory Committee Members

Parker Anderson, *National Association for the Education of Young Children*
Ruby Brunson, *Oakland Licensed Day Care Association*
Maria Casey, *Urban Strategies Council*
Richard Cohen, *Pacific Oaks College*
Ardella Dailey, *Alameda Unified School District*
Lynn De Lapp, *Policy Analysis of California Education*
Louise Derman-Sparks, *Pacific Oaks College*
Lourdes Diaz Soto, *Pennsylvania State University*
Julie Olsen Edwards, *Cabrillo Community College*
Eugene Garcia, *University of California, Berkeley*
Jackie Garcia, *former director, Native American Child Development Center*
Janet Gonzalez-Mena, *Napa Valley City College*
Neal Halfon, *University of California, Los Angeles*
Carollee Howes, *University of California, Los Angeles*
Sharon Lynn Kagan, *Bush Center in Child Development and Social Policy, Yale University*
Fran Kipnis, *California Resource and Referral Network*
Antonia Lopez, *National Council of La Raza*
Alice Paul, *University of Arizona*
Yolanda Torres, *Pacific Oaks Children's School*
Vivian Weinstein, *Pacific Oaks College*
Marcy Whitebook, *National Center for the Early Childhood Workforce*
Lily Wong Fillmore, *University of California, Berkeley*
Norman Yee, *Wu Yee Children's Services*
Greta Yin, *Kai Ming Head Start*

her years helping to frame the voice of California Tomorrow and other organizations working for equity.

We owe a tremendous debt to Julie Olsen Edwards, director of the Early Childhood and Family Life Education Department at Cabrillo Community College in Santa Cruz. In addition to being a member of our advisory board, Julie was invaluable in helping us analyze our findings and conceiving the structure of the book. It was critical to have a "veterana" of the child care field and anti-bias movement lending her experience and expertise to our thinking. Julie also co-facilitated our meetings with community colleges. Then when we circulated the second rewrite, Julie not only pushed us to make it better but she guided us through critical pieces with her superb editing and writing skills. In order to do this, Julie volunteered precious weeks of her sabbatical from Cabrillo, where she has been a faculty member for 25 years and is the founding director of the campus Child Care and Lab School. Her touch has made a huge difference in the delivery of our message.

Looking In, Looking Out has the great fortune of bearing important contributions from a number of pioneers working for equity in early childhood education. We thank Marcy Whitebook, senior research policy advisor and founding executive director of the National Center for Early Childhood Workforce, and Dan Bellm, early childhood education advocate, editor and author, who helped us design and carry out the interviews of trainers. Their knowledge and rich interviewing skills gleaned tremendous information for our book and created the basis for our Workforce chapter. We would like to express our appreciation to Sharon Hawley, director of the Child Development Training Consortium, who arranged focus groups and provided us with a range of information about how community colleges currently address issues of race, culture and language. We greatly thank Phyllis Brady of the Leadership in Diversity Project for her eloquent and risk-taking article about the journey to anti-racist identity. And we thank authors Janet Gonzalez-Mena, a member of our advisory committee and instructor at Napa Community College, and Lisa Lee of the Parent Services Project for their insightful articles on provider-family relations in Chapters 3 and 5.

We thank Louise Derman-Sparks, not only for her pioneering early childhood anti-bias work, but for the wisdom, encouragement and excellent editing suggestions she offered as a member of our advisory committee. Knowing that Louise believed in our project was a source of great inspiration. We thank her and the Anti-Bias Curriculum Task Force for motivating so many of us in this work and for allowing us to reprint the article on self reflection in Chapter 2.

All of our project advisors, whose names appear on page 7, broadened our knowledge and sharpened our thinking throughout the project. We thank them for their support and for devoting the time to react to two major report drafts. We were fortunate to have such a tremendous range of perspectives and disciplines contributing to our analysis. We also thank our many other readers throughout the country who took the time to review the second manuscript. Their ideas and expertise have strongly impacted our final book.

We thank Elaine Joe, the designer of our book, for her sense of beauty and aesthetics, her patience and unfailing encouragement during our crazy production process, her brownies, and for bringing her own gifted editorial instincts to the book. The parent of two young children, she cared as much about our message as we did, and worked hard to make it as inviting to readers as possible. She is truly a master at burning the midnight oil and still turning out exquisite work.

We thank Julie Jeeves Li-Wong, who came and basically gave us her life for the final weeks of production. Without Julie's precise editorial eye, humor and support, we would never have survived the grueling production process. Coming in at the end, Julie gave us hope that our book could do what we had intended—prompt people to reflect on their own experiences regarding family, culture, language and experiences living in a society that still perpetuates racism.

Our California Tomorrow colleagues were a source of strong support throughout the two-and-a-half years of this project. We especially thank Laurie Olsen, co-director of California Tomorrow and the visionary who has spearheaded our organization's work in educational equity. Always a teacher, Laurie forced us to clarify what we meant and shared her deep knowledge regarding cultural issues, anti-racism work and the history of movements to change educational practice. Laurie's confidence in our team was critical during the low points. And, she carried a huge load of work for us—on top of her already massive responsibilities—so we could devote the time necessary to bring the book to the quality we sought. Now in her second decade with California Tomorrow, Laurie's passion for equity as a parent, educator and advocate continues to set the tone for the work of our organization.

We thank our other terrific California Tomorrow co-workers for cheering us on and giving us critical feedback: Cecelia Leong, Katherine Sussman Cheng, Jaimee Karrol, Jacqueline Alamilla, May Li and Gilberto Arriaza. Extra special appreciation to Oleg Pravdin who was critical to our dissemination process and always helpful in countless other ways. And thanks to our former co-workers: Nancy Belton, who was a great early supporter, and Lisa Raffel, who was important in the design and beginning research phase of the project before she set off to teach in Ghana. We are lucky to work with such a committed and fun group of colleagues.

We thank Lew Butler, the founder and president of California Tomorrow, whose commitment to a more egalitarian future has made our work possible. Lew constantly reminded us that our message about the future of young children was not only important to early childhood educators but to everyone in our society. We also thank the other members of the California Tomorrow board of directors: Lily Wong Fillmore, Bob Friedman, Bong Hwan Kim, Marty Krasney, Stewart Kwoh, Antonia Lopez and Joyce Germaine Watts. Special thanks to Hugo Morales for the maguey harvest and for taking care of Carol while she edited three books at once.

We thank our funders for their belief in the Early Childhood Project and the resources to carry out the work: the Miriam and Peter Haas Fund, the James Irvine Foundation, the Danforth Foundation, the David and Lucile Packard Foundation, the Trio Foundation, the A. L. Mailman Family Foundation and the Gap Foundation.

We thank our families—our parents for the values and beliefs they taught us when we were young and that they continue to model for us as adults. We thank our partners Jack Chin, Frank Tobiassen and Greg McClain—for their terrific support, for putting up with our long hours at the office and on the road, for allowing their homes to be invaded for weekend marathons of writing and production, and for their contributions to the book, from Frank's computer expertise to Jack's editorial skills to Greg's empathy, having been through a process this intense himself as an author for California Tomorrow.

Finally, we owe our greatest debt to the child care providers, parents, program administrators, resource and referral staff, trainers and community college faculty whose knowledge and practices form the heart of this book. Throughout the process we have been inspired by their insights and commitment to promoting the well-being of children in a diverse society. Often they were moving forward even in the face of severe limitations of time and other resources. We deeply appreciate their willingness to talk about their accomplishments, hopes and struggles. They opened up a remarkable window into the world of early childhood care and education. Their commitment gives us hope to continue to work for an equitable multiracial, multicultural, multilingual society.

Hedy Nai-Lin Chang   *Amy Muckelroy*   *Dora Pulido-Tobiassen*

August 1996

Introduction

There were no mirrors in my Nana's house
No mirrors in my Nana's house
And the beauty that I saw in everything
The beauty in everything was in her eyes
There were no mirrors in my Nana's house
No mirrors in my Nana's house
So I never knew that my skin was too Black
I never knew that my nose was too flat
I never knew that my clothes didn't fit
And, I never knew there were things that I missed
And the beauty in everything was in her eyes

—© Ysaye Maria Barnwell

These lyrics from the song "My Nana's House" by Ysaye Maria Barnwell of the singing group "Sweet Honey in the Rock" portray a reality that most of us can see if we reflect upon our childhoods . . .

As "My Nana's House" reminds us, the people who took care of us when we were very young had a tremendous impact on how we think about ourselves and interpret the world. Our sense of self worth and the worth of others closely mirrors what we saw in their eyes. They laid the foundation for our values and beliefs, just as we were learning to connect to other human beings, develop bonds of trust and communicate our first words.

This book is about the impact of people who care for young children on their social well-being. It especially focuses on how adults can help children develop positive racial and cultural identities, respect for differences among people, and the ability to resist racism and prejudice. Although many adults would identify a parent or relative as the person who most strongly influenced their youngest years, this book is about another caregiver. It is about the professional child care providers with whom children today spend many, and sometimes most, of their waking hours. Society now entrusts to these caregivers a tremendous responsibility—the shared fostering of the next generations.

Profound demographic shifts are changing—virtually within a few generations—the nature of how young children are raised and socialized. Unlike their parents, many children today live in families where either both parents or the single head of the household works outside the home. In 1993, 59 percent of all women with children under age six worked in paid jobs, compared to 11 percent in 1947-48. These working parents must find other adults to help them care for their children. Almost 40 percent of children of working parents are now being cared for in a child care center, in a family day care home or by an in-home caregiver. Perhaps most

striking, children are being placed at earlier and earlier ages and spending longer hours in child care (Willer, et al., 1991).

The shift in who is caring for children coincides with another major demographic transformation. By the middle of the next century, it is predicted that there no longer will be a dominant racial group in the United States, a shift moving fastest among children under five. In some states, such as California and many urban areas nationally, there is no racial majority within the younger populations. In California, whites will cease to be the majority overall by approximately the year 2000. The children of California collectively speak more than 100 languages. Their families represent cultures from all over the world. According to California Tomorrow's *Affirming Children's Roots*, published in 1993, demographic shifts in California are profoundly impacting child care facilities. In a random survey of 435 centers in five California counties, we found 96 percent caring for children from more than one racial group, and 80 percent caring for children from more than one language group.

The combination of these profound demographic changes—more racially, culturally and linguistically diverse children than ever before, and more children in child care than ever before—presents amazing responsibilities and challenges to our society and to early childhood professionals. Child care providers now share with parents the responsibility for socializing children to be members of their family, their community and the larger society. In this book, we explore the roles child care providers do—and can—play in helping the next generations to thrive in a multiracial, multicultural, multilingual society.

What happens in care during the earliest years of life can shape whether children become open to or fearful of people with different skin colors, customs and languages. It shapes whether children learn to feel proud of their culture, or ashamed because of adult messages that their family ways are inferior and should be discarded. It lays the foundation for children to grow up excited and able to speak languages in addition to English.

Racial, cultural and linguistic diversity is the reality within and outside of the borders of the United States. The question is, will we raise children who can live and work together respectfully and equitably? Our own adult generations have not achieved this vision. The future of our society depends on fostering children better equipped than ourselves for the task. To begin, we must work to change ourselves and our interactions with children.

Exploring the Implications of Diversity for Early Care and Education

To find out whether and how child care programs are taking on these powerful responsibilities, California Tomorrow conducted in-depth research for the past two years. We conducted site visits to 23 centers and 10 family child care homes, selected for their noted efforts to address cultural, linguistic and racial diversity, and for their representation of a cross-section of the field in terms of geography, racial composition and auspices. Some programs built their curriculum around a specific racial, ethnic, cultural or linguistic group and placed a heavy emphasis on affirming the heritage of children of those backgrounds. A few programs explicitly sought a multicultural population in order to create an environment where children would meet peers of other backgrounds. Still others were adjusting their curriculum to respond to the cultures and languages of the families who walked through the doors. During our visits we spoke with parents, providers and administrators. We observed program activities and interactions between providers and children and between providers and parents.

We also researched staff development and recruitment issues related to diversity, seeking to learn how staff at centers and family day care programs had entered the field, their perceptions of barriers to advancement and recruitment, and the nature of their professional development opportunities. We interviewed an additional 28 trainers and documented key programs aimed at either recruitment or professional development of early childhood professionals. We used regional meetings of the California Child Development Training Consortium to hold discussions about the implications of diversity with community college instructors throughout the state. Finally, as part of our effort to learn how greatly diversity issues come into play when parents select care for their children, we interviewed staff members of 33 resource and referral agencies.

The question is, will we raise children who can live and work together respectfully and equitably?

These interviews and site visits provided us with a wealth of information. We were inspired by the energy and commitment we found among practitioners up and down the state. We saw individuals and programs working hard to use their limited resources to foster the well-being of children and promote attention to diversity. At the same time, our visits and discussions also gave us a much deeper appreciation for the challenges of moving an agenda of equity and diversity forward.

The Book

Based upon the voices and the promising efforts we identified through our research, ***Looking In, Looking Out*** offers a vision of how child care must be redefined in order to support the development of a next generation with the skills and capacities to thrive in an increasingly multicultural world.

It opens with parents, providers and trainers describing their hopes and fears about the role of child care in a diverse society. Parents talk about their desire for children to learn to appreciate differences, to resist internalizing the racist messages in society and to combat racism. They talk about their desire for their children to know their family cultures and languages, as well as to be prepared academically and socially to function competitively within the dominant society. Practitioners talk about the beliefs underlying their chosen approaches to child care, such as creating programs to affirm the racial and cultural backgrounds of specific groups of students, or programs to expose diverse students to a multicultural, multilingual world.

Taking into account these diverse perspectives, California Tomorrow developed a set of common "Principles of Quality Care in a Diverse Society." The principles are the heart of our book, based on the most inspiring of what we saw in the field and our analysis of what we and others identified as still missing. The principles are:

- One: Combat racism and foster positive racial identity in young children.
- Two: Build upon the cultures of families and promote respect and cross-cultural understanding among children.
- Three: Preserve children's family languages and encourage all children to learn a second language.
- Four: Work in partnership with parents to respond to issues of race, language and culture.
- Five: Engage in dialogue and reflection about race, language and culture on an ongoing basis.

Each principle is presented in its own chapter, including a discussion of its importance, and strategies and challenges we observed for implementation. We believe the principles draw upon already existing strengths of the child care profession. For example, child care programs have proven to be flexible and innovative in their ability to tailor curricula to specific children, families, communities, ethnicities, language groups and neighborhoods. Likewise, the proposed principles can hold true across different types of care settings—family child care or center-based—whether they serve a single racial/cultural group or children across a variety of backgrounds.

The principles draw upon the pioneering work of many child care organizations and individuals who have raised understanding among professionals of the implications of diversity and the need to change practice. There have been some very hopeful developments—for example, the widespread dissemination of books on reducing bias in the classroom, cross-cultural differences in child rearing, and the importance of support for children's home languages. A growing number of articles on issues of race, language or culture are appearing in professional magazines. Major organizations such as Head Start and the National Association for the Education of Young Children, as well as some individual centers, have developed policies and guidelines on diversity. And the implications of diversity for staff development are receiving greater focus within the field. Our principles seek to expand upon and knit together the exciting and important information already being generated.

Also deeply ingrained in the profession is the assumption that children are, first and always, members of families. Working closely with parents to address issues of race, language and culture, then, can become a natural outgrowth of providers' already known commitment to partnering with parents. No other social institution has the daily contact with parents that is the hallmark of most child care programs. Not only is there contact, but many parents report a strong sense of support from "their" child care person. Many also say they learn important skills in managing their children and find programs an effective antidote to the isolation so common with families of young children.

Finally, our principles build upon the fact that much of child care work, particularly if it takes place in a center-based facility or a large family child care home—is done in teams. Head teachers, assistants, aides—and often parents—work side by side in the classroom with the children. This offers great possibilities for dialogue and mutual revelation that is daily, informal and closely connected to real experiences with children and families. It offers the opportunity for child care providers to draw upon each other as cultural resources and to talk about the implications of race, language and culture in their work.

Of course, in order for the Principles of Quality Care in a Diverse Society to be realized, we must develop a workforce with the ability to implement them. Chapter 7 calls for support of an early childhood workforce which reflects the racial backgrounds of children and families. We focus on improving the early childhood education workforce through recruitment, training, retention and professional development.

The extent to which any particular program employs staff from a diversity of backgrounds will vary, but the field as a whole needs to reflect the overall demographics of families with young children. When staff speak the languages of families, they are better able to establish strong communication with children and their parents and to support the continued development of children's home languages. Staff who share families' cultural backgrounds are invaluable because of their knowledge of the values and practices of families and communities. And although the larger society may not pay the respect due to child care workers, in the eyes of children they are important and influential figures. When children see providers from their same racial group, it helps validate their identity. When providers are from a different racial group than the children it can help to break down stereotypes.

Simply having a diverse workforce is, however, not enough. Practitioners from every cultural, linguistic or racial background also need opportunities for gaining a deeper understanding of how to provide quality care in a diverse society. Our book discusses the types of professional development needed at all levels of the system from the women and men who have direct caregiving responsibilities to the individuals involved in pre-service and in-service professional development.

While these Principles of Quality Care in a Diverse Society describe what we believe should be taking place in programs which work directly with families, we emphasize that implementation can only be achieved if providers and programs are supported with the appropriate resources and policies. While the dependence upon child care has grown exponentially, resources for the provision of quality care remain painfully limited. The development of a skilled, demographically reflective

workforce requires confronting the appalling lack of investment of resources. It requires confronting head on the painfully low wages which discourage providers from continuing with their education or even remaining in the field. It involves grappling with the fragmentation and lack of coordination of professional development opportunities.

The final chapter of this book calls for a new research agenda which will expand the existing knowledge base about the implications of diversity for early care and education. A key issue is broadening the available information beyond research on white middle class children which currently forms the basis for most child development theory.

The Imperative of Moving Forward

The current political context only makes it more important to be willing to take a stand for equity and diversity. While some politicians are seeking to establish English as the one and only language of the country, this book calls for supporting bilingualism among all young people and ensuring that language minority children do not lose the ability to speak their family languages while learning English. At a time when people of color, immigrants and the poor are being scapegoated for the nation's economic woes, our book calls for standing against racism and prejudice. At a time when social and political volatility are silencing crucial discussions, our book calls for engaging in dialogue about how to best draw strength from our diversity. At a time when the largely white voting public appears reluctant to invest in the future generations that will be the majority children of color, we are calling for resources to support quality care and education for children of all backgrounds, beginning from birth.

The field of early care and education can serve as a model for other professionals and institutions grappling with how to redefine themselves to build a better future. Redefining the quality of child care may be important especially for serving low income families, more and more of whom will need to place their children in care if proposed welfare policies pass. Low income families currently do not have the choices of child care available to higher socioeconomic families. A movement to address race, language and culture issues in child care must assure the inclusion of the needs and desires of families of every circumstance.

Moving forward will require action on the part of individuals as well as groups. It will require the development of a more coherent advocacy voice calling attention to issues of race, language and culture as central to the role of early care and education. We hope that this book serves as a tool and a resource for such efforts. We seek to present a vision to California and the nation that offers unity without uniformity, and that challenges and inspires.

We hope that our principles, taken collectively, offer the field a comprehensive vision of what could and should happen.

Defining Terms

CLEAR DEFINITIONS OF TERMS are essential to discussions about diversity issues. Given this concern, we offer the following definitions we use for key terms related to race, language and culture in this book. The relationships between these concepts will be explored throughout the book.

DIVERSITY: In the field of early childhood care and education, "diversity" is typically used to refer to a wide range of dimensions, around which people may differ. These dimensions include race, language, culture, class, age, gender, sexual orientation and physical or mental ability/disability. Because of the mission, experience and organizational strengths of California Tomorrow, in this report the term diversity primarily refers to differences among racial, cultural or linguistic backgrounds. In some cases we will point out interconnections with related concerns about gender, class, sexual orientation, religious background and physical ability, but the emphasis remains with these three concepts. Our definition of diversity encompasses people of all races, languages and cultures, including white English-speaking Americans of European ancestry.

RACE: "Race" refers to the way our society currently categorizes people based upon skin color and general appearance. Although often used as a biological distinction, race is in fact a socially constructed label, as is evident in the inconsistent and biased ways in which racial terms are often applied. At the same time, a person's race profoundly affects his or her status and prospects in this society. The contradictions of race have become even more apparent with the increasing numbers of interracial births, transracial adoptions and immigrants with mixed racial heritage.

HOME LANGUAGE: "Home language" refers to the language a child develops and learns through interaction with his or her family members. Children in families where more than one language is regularly used may acquire more than one home language. Once acquired, a home language is also a vehicle for communication with a broader community which speaks the same language.

CULTURE: "Culture" refers to the values, beliefs and traditions of a particular group. It is the set of rules that, to varying degrees, guide the behavior of individuals who are members of that group, whether that group is defined in terms of national origin, racial experience, linguistic experience, religious background, socioeconomic status, age, etc. Rather than being static in nature, the culture of any given group is constantly evolving in response to what is occurring in the environment. Individuals and families are often members of more than one cultural group at the same time. Culture is defined in more detail in Chapter 3.

DOMINANT CULTURE: The "dominant culture" refers to the culture of the group in power. Because people originating from Europe, particularly Britain, have held power since the founding of this country, the Anglo European Christian culture is the dominant culture of the United States. Scholars Lynch and Hanson suggest that values contained within the dominant culture of the United States are:

– the importance of individualism and privacy;

– a belief in the equality of individuals;

– informality in interactions with others;

– an emphasis on the future, change and progress;

– belief in the general goodness of humanity;

– an emphasis on time and punctuality;

– high regard for achievement, action, work and materials; and

– pride in being direct and assertive.

ETHNICITY: "Ethnicity" refers to a group identity defined by a common political, historical and social experience and which people use to categorize themselves and others. Ethnicity is shaped by race, language and culture, but the extent to which each of these forms salient factors varies by group. For example, the Latino/Hispanic population includes people who are fair as well as dark skinned, but members of the group are bound together by a common political experience in the United States and past colonization by the Spanish while in their countries of origin. Italian Americans are another example of an ethnic group. This group differentiates because of its unique cultural and linguistic heritage, even though it shares a white racial background. Most ethnic groups encompass a number of different cultural groups, although these groups may also share some broad characteristics. Some ethnic groups tend to share a common language; other ethnic groups encompass a wide variety of languages. A person may still identify as being from a particular ethnic group even if s/he has ceased to speak the language typically spoken by members of that group. ❧

Redefining "Quality Care"

OVER THE YEARS, "quality care" has become a widely recognized term and concept in the early childhood profession. A variety of different dimensions are used to assess program quality, including staffing ratios, group size, the educational levels of providers, as well as adherence to the Developmentally Appropriate Practice curriculum of the National Association for the Education of Young Children (NAEYC). Some have also attempted to define quality in terms of the impact of child care services on children's development.

The fact that "quality care" has become a concept so central to the early childhood profession is a tribute to the advocates, practitioners and researchers who have striven for many years to generate greater public attention to the quality of care. Their efforts grew out of several concerns. First, policymakers and the public continue to fail to invest sufficient resources toward program development in early childhood education. Too often, early care is viewed primarily as a support for working parents, while the potential benefits of care to children's development go unappreciated and unrealized. The Cost, Quality and Outcomes Study and other recent projects have clearly demonstrated the importance of our country investing strongly in the programs and people to whom we are entrusting the well-being of the next generation.

A second major concern feeding the movement for quality care has been the growing tendency of many programs to focus on academics in early care without properly informed consideration for whether activities are age appropriate. NAEYC's Developmentally Appropriate Guidelines were developed in response to this concern, offering a definition of quality care to help practitioners and policymakers understand how education for preschool-aged children should be different than education for older children. These guidelines have strongly influenced the curriculum of the majority of early childhood programs in the United States.

To date, however, the definitions and measures of quality care are, for the most part, missing an analysis of the implications of racial, cultural and linguistic diversity in child development and in child care. Some practitioners believe certain definitions of quality care are inappropriate for children and families not from the dominant culture and language of the United States.

Our Principles of Quality Care in a Diverse Society proposed in this book seek to offer a framework to help the early childhood field begin to redefine what fully constitutes quality care. Given the changing nature and demographics of care, a redefinition is timely and essential. Of course, this would raise many questions and challenges for the field. Would redefining quality care entail starting from scratch or building upon what already exists? Our book seeks to begin the dialogue needed to answer these questions. Chapter 8 also delves into some of many further questions we need to research if we are ever to realize the best quality child care for a diverse society. ❧

Chapter 1
Perspectives on the Role of Care in a Diverse Society

"I want her to grow up in an environment which reflects the diversity of the world . . . A place where you can find children of different races and languages . . . where she can feel free and proud of who she is . . . "

"What my son needs now is a sense of belonging . . . "

"If parents and teachers want children to appreciate and value diversity, they have to introduce it to counteract the negative bias that these kids are going to be exposed to . . . "

"I think it is critical for children in California to speak more than one language . . . "

—Voices of child care providers and parents of young children

Child care plays many roles in the lives of children and their families. At a minimum, families rely on child care to provide a safe and caring place for their children while the adults are at work or school. Families often look to the child care program for information and guidance on child development, family services or schools in the area. Many programs become a supportive center of community for the families who attend. And, child care programs provide educational environments in which children are encouraged and guided in developing their motor, social, cognitive and language skills.

All of these functions are widely accepted as appropriate for child care programs. But within such functions, many questions remain unanswered about how child care should support and prepare children and families for a *diverse society*. For example, fostering language development is clearly a role of child care, but what about fostering second language development? Similarly, it is well recognized that young children are socialized to the norms and expectations of our society while in care, but when families and child care providers are from different cultures with different norms and expectations, what socialization process should occur? Given the context of our society, where often people are judged and opportunities afforded on the basis of race, what is the role of child care in preparing young children to interact with people who look different from themselves? Or, what is the role of child care in preparing children for the racism and prejudice they will encounter in society?

These were the kinds of questions California Tomorrow sought to answer in our visits to child care centers and family child care homes throughout the state. We interviewed parents, providers and directors, as well as trainers, community college instructors and researchers of many racial, cultural and linguistic backgrounds. All expressed a range of expectations, hopes and fears for the future of children and their ability to thrive in a diverse society.

Despite the wide spectrum of views, a few central issues emerged that most people interviewed agreed upon. Clearly, interviewees recognized the tremendous diversity of our society—the many races, cultures and languages represented in our people. And, they tended to agree that there are certain attitudes, knowledge and skills that children should learn at a young age to help them thrive in this diverse society: high self esteem and self confidence; respect for themselves and for others; pride in their cultural and linguistic heritage; appreciation and ability to learn from people of different racial, cultural and linguistic backgrounds; and the ability to recognize and resist racism, prejudice and bias in themselves and others.

People's views differed, however, about how to instill these values and skills in children and about what role child care programs should play in the process. The following categories capture most of the variety of points of view that we found. However, it is important to note that the categories were not mutually exclusive—many people believed that child care should play more than one of the roles described as follows:

- Teach children to appreciate and respect differences among people, and to resist racism and prejudice.
- Help children to resist internalizing the effects of racism.
- Support the development of a positive racial identity for biracial children.
- Preserve and support children's cultural identity.
- Preserve and support children's home language skills.
- Teach a second language to children whose home language is English.
- Teach English to children whose home language is not English.
- Teach behavioral norms promoted and expected by the dominant U.S. culture.

In documenting these viewpoints, we realized how seldom it is that parents, providers and others have the opportunity to express their hopes and fears for young children growing up in a diverse society and the role child care can play in supporting this positively. Rarely do we take the time to listen and understand why we hold different viewpoints, or why children may have different individual needs in order to thrive in a multiracial, multicultural, multilingual society. Some of the views are contradictory, but closer examination—which we attempt to do throughout this book—reveals overlapping aspirations for young children on the part of adults who care for them. Only by striving for a deeper understanding of the range of perspectives can we begin to find common ground.

While we may not have captured every possible perspective, we hope that in reading others' thoughts on the roles child care can play, readers will find that some of these voices ring true and spark imagination about the potential and possibilities of early care and education.

Perspective

Teach children to appreciate and respect differences among people, and to resist racism and prejudice toward others.

> *There is cultural diversity at home and that is why I wanted Iara to grow up in an environment which reflects the diversity of the world...a place where you can find children of different races and languages...where Iara could feel free and proud of who she is.*
>
> —Angela Roa, mother of a Chilean-Brazilian daughter

Some parents, providers and trainers looked to child care as a place where young children could be exposed to peers and adults who look different, come from different cultural backgrounds or speak a different language than themselves. Of these, many expressed the hope that through such exposure and interaction, children would begin to view themselves as part of a larger community and become better able to interact with others. "Diversity is the real world," many said. "Isolation from people who are different will put children at a disadvantage."

Hilltop Nursery is a center in Los Angeles with a multicultural philosophy and curriculum. Siv Roeder, a white teacher at Hilltop, talked about the importance of the diversity of the families and teachers at the center:

> *The diversity gives kids an excellent start. They are at the beginning of their lives—they will start out in a wonderful, rich, complex environment. It's the best way. They won't end up with a sheltered mind.*

Adan Maciel is a Mexican father whose child attended Las Casitas in San Jose, one of the Santa Clara Head Start programs:

> *I feel that preschool programs provide children with a valuable lesson about living with others. Children learn to interact with other cultures in the environment, that there isn't one that dominates, and that all should be treated with equal consideration. In this world, there are many cultures, and it is very important for us to try to understand each other as best as possible, now and for the future.*

Avoa Henry is an African American parent and teacher at Step One School in Berkeley, a multicultural program with a strong anti-bias philosophy. She chose Step One in part due to her belief that exposing children to others who are different helps them learn to comfortably interact with a variety of people. She reflected on her own experience growing up in a primarily Black neighborhood. Unlike many of her friends and neighbors who attended a mostly African American school, Avoa went to a very diverse school. She felt that this better prepared her for later encounters in life:

> *It helped in reinforcing my pride and my belief in my potential. It also encouraged a positive and tolerant attitude towards my peers of a differ-*

> *ent race and helped me to value the differences and sameness of other children. My positive experience of a diverse community helps me to problem-solve and resist and reduce racist attitudes and stereotypes.*

Agnes Chan, Asian outreach coordinator for the BANANAS Resource and Referral Agency in Oakland and an instructor at City College of San Francisco, described an incident that caused her to believe that child care must teach children about human diversity through a diverse staff and enrollment:

> *What got me thinking about it 18 years ago was when I was working in a center and I noticed the children talking to somebody who was delivering lunch. He was a Black man. The children asked him why his hands were so dirty on the outside and clean on the inside. We realized that we had to start with the staff—to diversify the staff so the children would be exposed to different people. Then, if possible, we would diversify the children.*

What is the role of child care in preparing children for the racism and prejudice they will encounter in society?

Many interviewed thought child care had a responsibility to proactively address racism and prejudice on the part of children and adults in the program through program design and curricular activities.

Liz Spencer, a white parent, enrolled her daughter in Marin Learning Center, a program with an African American cultural focus that serves mostly African American children. She chose the program because she wanted her daughter to be able to resist racism and prejudice when she encounters it as she gets older. Liz grew up in a homogenous environment—an all-white town in Pennsylvania—where racist attitudes and comments were commonplace among her friends and their families. As a young person, she felt strongly that their attitudes were wrong, yet she did not know what to say to them or how to respond. But she hoped that her daughter, who was learning that "everyone is different and that is a positive thing," will know how to resist racism in herself and others when she grows up.

PERSPECTIVE

Help children to resist internalizing the effects of racism.

> *If parents and teachers want children to appreciate and value diversity, they have to introduce it in order to countervail the negative bias that these kids are going to be exposed to.*
>
> —CAROL BRUNSON PHILLIPS, EXECUTIVE DIRECTOR OF THE COUNCIL FOR EARLY CHILDHOOD PROFESSIONAL RECOGNITION

Some of the parents, providers and trainers reflected on the power of racism in our society and how every one of us is inundated with racist stereotypes and images about non-white people. Unless *all* children are "armed" to resist the racist messages that permeate their world, they will adopt the messages by developing prejudices, or internalize the messages into a negative self image. They looked to the child care setting to help prevent this.

Carol Brunson Phillips said all programs, even if they are homogenous or predominantly of one ethnic group, must act to prevent children from internalizing racist messages coming at them from all sides. She talked about the forces at work leading children to develop distorted self images and images of others:

> *Children's attitudes about other racial/cultural groups are influenced by the prevailing attitudes in the society to a much greater extent than by the children's actual contact with the people. Kids, to the extent they are exposed to the society's prevailing attitudes about race and culture, are not in an environment where that influence is neutral...the images they are exposed to on television, newspapers and in the larger community may well carry a tremendous amount of bias.*

One of the reasons Linwood Fenderson enrolled his daughter in Drew Child Development Corporation was because it was predominantly African American. He had been strongly impressed with how the Drew program equipped his older son to resist internalizing racist comments and behavior:

> *My son had a bad experience in the 6th grade in an almost all-white school—he was being called names because he was Black. But he knew how to handle it because he had gone to Drew. He knew that Black is beautiful and valuable. I want my daughter to have the same foundation when she faces name calling.*

Perspective

Support the development of a positive racial identity for biracial children.

> *I want my daughter to be proud of her uniqueness. I want her to understand as much as she can about the different cultures that are brought together in her family and then take that out into the world and value the differences of the kids around her. I want her to know that we are lucky to live in a world where there are different people of different colors and family traditions that we can learn from.*
>
> — Celesta Cheney-Rice, mother of a biracial daughter (African American and European American)

The growing population of biracial and multiracial families can be perhaps most evidenced in today's child care settings. But in a society which categorizes people by race, some biracial families interviewed expressed fears that their children would be misunderstood or discriminated against because they did not easily fit into one racial group or another. These parents believed that the child care program played an important role in helping their children to develop a positive racial identity.

When Honor Galloway and her husband were choosing care for their son, they knew that they did not want him to feel that being biracial was negative. She was pleased with Rancho de Los Amigos:

> *Here at Rancho they incorporate and encourage many different cultures and nationalities—whether they are represented in the families of the center or not.*

Because the Rancho program was very diverse and acknowledged differences, the Galloways felt that their son would not be singled out and could learn to take pride in his uniqueness.

Kristi Terrell sent her three-year-old son Sykes to Marilyn Allen's family child care program in Torrance. Kristi appreciated the concern and support Marilyn gave to her and how nurturing and loving she was with Sykes. Kristi recalled an experience with a former neighbor, whose daughter was Sykes' age, that reinforced her desire to find an affirming care environment for her son:

> *The two children would play and play. Everything was fine until [the friend's] mother found out that Sykes' father is Black and she wouldn't let [her daughter] play with Sykes anymore. I remember Sykes asking, "Why can't she play with me?" To explain this to a three-year-old child was heartbreaking...Luckily we haven't had any more experiences like that. I'm sure there are more to come just because that, unfortunately, is the way our society is. It is the blessing of society [that someday] there will be so many mixed children that people won't know any different. But it is such a long time coming.*

Perspective

Preserve and support children's cultural identity.

> *Knowing who you are is important for attaining an education, because knowing who you are gives you a base for learning everything.*
>
> —Anthony Behill, grandfather, member of the Chumash Tribe

Some parents and providers desired a child care program that instilled connection and pride in the child's family culture. They also emphasized the belief that the better children know and respect themselves, the better they will be able to appreciate the languages and cultural heritage of others. The interviewees who fell into this group placed a high value on grounding children in their home culture as a way of preparing them for a diverse society. Through personal experience, people

in this group had witnessed the process of cultural assimilation, and strongly felt the danger facing many minority communities of losing their cultural and linguistic heritage.

Anthony Behill's grandson attended a center in Fresno in which the teachers and families were predominantly of Native American tribal backgrounds, and the curriculum strongly emphasized the traditions, music and dance of the tribes in the region:

> *I was looking for a program that provided an education, and also a place where there was an understanding of where he came from and who he is...where he would know that his culture would be reinforced.*

Ann Yee is a Chinese American parent whose son Anthony attended the family child care program operated by Anita Surh in Oakland. Ann appreciated that Anita's program is primarily attended by Chinese families, that both Chinese and English are spoken in the program, and that Chinese culture is celebrated in the curriculum:

> *Right now what he needs is a sense of belonging. I like that there are other Chinese kids that he can identify with and learn the language. I look at his bigger brother who also went to Anita's. He is confident about being a Chinese person even if he goes to another school where there aren't a lot of people his same race. He is very comfortable with who he is. I want Anthony to have that same sense of himself.*

Liz Forge-Chapman is the African American director of Drew Child Development Corporation, an organization which runs six child care programs in the Watts and Bellflower areas of Los Angeles. She expressed the importance of stressing children's own culture:

> *You need to provide some exposure to other cultures, but the focus is the children's own background. The kids need to know who they are. Children have to know about themselves before they can know about others.*

In light of the commanding influence of the dominant culture and language in this country, most represented in this group of interviewees said concerted efforts were needed to protect and nurture the heritage of children of non-dominant backgrounds. Many parents and teachers felt that being immersed in one's own culture was a valuable, but rare, opportunity. They recognized that children, as they grew older and attended public school, would have fewer and fewer opportunities for this. Janet Rothschild, the director of Simcha, a Jewish center in Santa Cruz, talked about this:

> *Simcha is the one place where children have an opportunity to be around Judaic curriculum, feel Jewish and be surrounded by Jewish children. Such opportunities are scarce once the child enters elementary school, though schools are becoming increasingly multicultural. All of the Jewish children leave Simcha feeling very Jewish because they have had so many Jewish experiences.*

Perspective

Preserve and support children's home language skills.

> *The risk of not learning English is small. On the other hand, the risk of losing Spanish is high.*
>
> —Gilberto Diaz, teacher, Centro de Niños, bilingual program in Riverside

Several parents and teachers talked about the pain of losing the ability to speak their family language. As a young child, the only language Alicia Flores spoke was Spanish. But once she entered public school and began to speak English, she stopped speaking Spanish altogether. At this early age, she lost her language, a critical piece of her identity and culture as a Mexican American. It was very important to her that her own children not experience this same loss. Her first criterion for a program was that it be bilingual and that it focus on Latino culture.

For Daniel Yang, who immigrated from China 14 years ago, finding a Chinese bilingual child care program for his children was very important:

> *I have cousins who were born in the U.S. and living in the state of Washington. Even though their parents speak Chinese, they don't speak Chinese. Now they are all grown up—24 and 30 years old. All they can say is "How are you?" in Chinese and nothing else. I don't want to see this happen to my kids.*

Daniel's children attended Discoveryland in San Francisco, a church-based Chinese bilingual center. There as well as at home, he said, his children would be exposed to Chinese while learning English.

Janet Gonzalez-Mena, author of *Multicultural Issues in Child Care*, agrees with many in the field of bilingual education that children can lose their home language with alarming speed, and along with it their connections to non-English-speaking family and community members. Therefore, intensive exposure to their primary language in their early years is critical:

> *Children should hear their own language from the beginning. If a second language comes into play it shouldn't do anything in any way to detract from the first language...I have been swayed by Lily Wong Fillmore's strong view that English should start later so that the home language doesn't disappear. It is easy to see that many people's home language does disappear. It's gone in one generation. It used to take longer than that. It goes fast now. I think we should be doing everything we can to change that situation. Otherwise the parents and the children can't talk to each other. The parents lose their authority if the child is translating English and the child doesn't even speak the parents' language anymore. It's a terrible thing.*

The better children know and respect themselves, the better they will be able to appreciate the languages and cultural heritage of others.

Guadalupe Rodriguez, a Mexican teacher at Live Oak Migrant Head Start, also stressed the importance of language in connecting families. Her daughters went to Live Oak, which incorporates three languages: English, Spanish and Punjabi:

> *At home my daughters only speak Spanish. I intentionally chose a bilingual school for them because I wanted them to be slowly exposed to English. Now, my daughters speak and write English and Spanish well. Kids need parents to help them with their homework. How can they if they don't share a common language?*

Other parents focused on the economic and social value of their children becoming bilingual. Maura Blanco knew her children would learn English by the very nature of living in an English-speaking society, but she wanted to ensure that they maintained their home language as well. She had sent her two children to Centro VIDA, a Spanish bilingual program in Berkeley with a multicultural focus:

> *My children are going to speak Spanish and I want them to speak it well. I want them to learn it not only because it is their first language, but because they will have better opportunities in life by being bilingual.*

In many communities, parents whose primary language is not English fear that their children will lose the home language because of the pressures to learn English early and because of the higher status English holds in our society. Additionally, families of many Native American tribal backgrounds want their children to learn the indigenous languages that they themselves were not allowed to retain or learn; generations of Native peoples well into this century were forced to attend English-only boarding schools in order to be "Americanized," "civilized" and "assimilated." This severing from home, land, family and community contributed to the systematic destruction of scores of indigenous North American languages. Tribal members are anxious to preserve those languages that do still exist. Children, grandchildren and great-grandchildren of boarding school students who are now parents themselves want their own children to be able to speak the native languages even if they cannot. Nancy Johnson, director of Management Services of the Greater Minneapolis Day Care Association, talked about this:

> *The Native American community here has been reclaiming their language. I think the tragedy is that there are so few speakers of Native American languages because of the history of today's parents not being allowed to use their language when they were children. Most Indian children aren't hearing it at home. So it isn't an issue of being connected with the home language, it's almost like rediscovering the home languages to reclaim the strengths and values of their cultural heritage.*

Perspective

Teach a second language to children whose home language is English.

> *I think it is critical raising children in California to speak another language, especially Spanish.*
>
> —Michelle Harris, African American parent at Centro VIDA, bilingual program in Berkeley

Some parents, like Michelle Harris, wanted their children to go beyond exposure and appreciation of differences to an in-depth experience of a second culture and second language. The main reason Michelle chose Centro VIDA for her daughter was that it was bilingual. Michelle believed that her daughter would benefit immensely—academically and socially—from exposure to a second culture and proficiency in a second language.

Centro VIDA serves a number of families whose first language is English. The director, Beatriz Leyva-Cutler, said about these families:

> *Our families come in feeling very strong in their home culture. They come in saying they want their children to learn a second language, to be exposed to a second culture...There are few programs like this and parents will tell you they think there is a definite value in their child learning a second language.*

One child development specialist agreed with those parents:

> *Creating a generation of very comfortably bilingual children—bilingual, bicultural, biliterate children—I think should be our goal. I think that as we do that, it shouldn't only be the children that we would label "language minority" children, but it should be the language majority children that are having that experience too...As people begin to see English-speaking children learning Spanish and seeing that valued, it would begin to*

> *erase those prejudices and stereotypes which make it difficult for the Spanish-speaking children to hold only their language. I just used Spanish as an example, but I realize we have many, many other languages.*

Angela Kwok was a Chinese parent at Discoveryland. At home with her children, she said, she spoke Chao Zhou, their first language. At the time of the interview, the children were in a bilingual Chinese program, but no one there spoke her family's dialect—nor did she think that this would be necessary. She wanted the children to learn both Cantonese and English at the center because she felt strongly that it is a great advantage to be able to speak many languages—a societal survival skill. She did not think it would be a problem for her children to learn English later, when they were in grade school. To learn Cantonese, however, was important now because the children might never have another opportunity to be so surrounded by this language.

PERSPECTIVE

Teach English to children whose home language is not English.

> *When new families come in each year, the part that is really important to them is that they are here in this country and they want their child to learn English—for survival. They think that the only way their children will succeed is by learning English, and that they will get the Spanish at home.*
>
> —BEATRIZ LEYVA-CUTLER, DIRECTOR OF CENTRO VIDA

> *The children learn English at school, which is what we wanted.*
>
> —GUSTAVO ROMERO, PARENT

While it was very important to Gustavo Romero that staff at Centro de Niños spoke Spanish so that his children's culture would be supported and respected, he felt that the primary responsibility of the center was to teach his children to speak English. This was a feeling echoed by many immigrant parents who did not feel that they could provide the English skills to their children.

Juanita Mora is a teacher at Plaza Child Observation and Development Center in East Los Angeles. She agreed that children should become proficient in their family language (at home with her own children she spoke only Spanish), but she believed that the language at the center should be English:

> *If we don't emphasize English at the center, we are cheating the child. I don't want them to be confused when they get to school.*

A Punjabi parent at Live Oak Migrant Head Start wanted her children to be able to speak Punjabi so that she could communicate with them, and also:

> *We are going to live in America so the children should learn English.*

She didn't feel that the staff needed to speak Punjabi with her children, because she believed the youngsters already knew enough Punjabi for her to communicate with them in that language.

A trainer with many years in child care settings talked about the concerns of non-English-speaking parents:

> *When we get into issues of...primary and secondary language acquisition, it raises controversies for parents..."I want my child to be able to be successful in the mainstream culture," and "What do you mean, telling me my child should hold only their home language? If they do, they're going to be ridiculed, not accepted, and they won't be able to communicate."*

On first consideration, it may seem that there is no common ground between adults who wish to focus on preserving the non-English home languages of children and adults who believe the emphasis should be on teaching children English. However, as our Principle on Language will discuss later, a deeper understanding of language issues and language development reveals these two groups are not so far apart in philosophy, nor in their desire to do what is best for children.

Perspective

Teach behavioral norms promoted and expected by dominant U.S. culture.

> *It's beyond language. It's about being able to succeed in the future.*
>
> — Gustavo Romero, parent

Another role of programs described by parents, providers and trainers was to help in children's transition between the home culture and the dominant American culture. Learning English was part of this transition for some families, but not all. And even if the child's first language was not English, there was more to the transition than language. Many families who are not from the dominant Euro-American culture, whether born in the United States or immigrants, feel that child care programs can play a role in teaching their children the behavioral and cultural expectations they will face in school so that they will be better prepared to interact, behave and achieve along with their white or U.S. born peers.

Dr. Olivia Thompson-Green, an African American family child care provider in Los Angeles, said:

> *I see the whole early childhood experience as a necessity. It is not something that should be optional. Because...we are global, and children must be taught how to interact with other people and not be afraid to want to learn.*

Some parents looked to the center to teach their children academic skills and knowledge of cultural expectations in order to start kindergarten with an advantage, or at least on par with children who grew up in households of the dominant culture. Some recently immigrated parents looked to the program for information about U.S. cultural norms and expectations as well. Some Latino and African American parents and providers placed a high emphasis on ensuring that children graduated from programs with the ability to recite the letters of the alphabet, count, recognize colors and to know behaviors they will need in school, such as sitting still and raising hands. This may have been in part due to the all-too-common fear that children of color who could not exhibit such skills would be falsely labeled as remedial or unintelligent once they reached kindergarten and grade school. Parents interviewed worried that if their children did not know "how to act" when they got to kindergarten, they would be judged slow or mislabeled as learning disabled. Given the disproportionate number of children of color who are quickly relegated to remedial and special education classes, these fears are well grounded.

The Interview Sample

It is important to clarify that the interviews from which the perspectives presented here were collected were not conducted with a random sample of parents, providers and trainers. While our experience leads us to believe that the views represented here are shared by others outside of our interviewees, our research methodology does not allow us to predict their overall prevalence in society at large.

As described in our introduction and methodology chapter, the interviews took place during program site visits to 23 child care centers and 10 family child care homes specifically nominated for their efforts to address racial, cultural or linguistic diversity. We sought a collection of programs that would represent a cross-section of the field in terms of auspices, geography within California, ages of children served and racial, cultural and linguistic composition. Trainers interviewed for this project were selected because of their experience and knowledge about the implications of diversity for staff development.

Clearly, the nature of the child care setting where we found the parents and providers influenced the types of viewpoints we heard expressed. A program's overall approach to diversity had a significant impact on its entire operations, from mission, to curriculum, to enrollment policies, to hiring practices—and ultimately to families served and providers employed. The varying approaches included:

- Programs attempting to address diversity issues in response to the children and families of the community served (the largest group);
- Programs committed to affirming the racial, cultural and linguistic heritage of a specific ethnic group of children (the second largest group); and
- Programs committed to creating diverse multicultural environments for children (the third largest group).

Generally, programs practicing variations on these approaches tended to attract people who shared similar perspectives on the role of care. Viewpoints were likely to have been shaped over time as a result of the benefits and drawbacks parents and providers experienced from having children in a particular type of environment.

For example, the programs in our samples that focused on affirming the heritage of specific groups included those that targeted African American, Native American, Chinese, Latino and Jewish communities. Promoting awareness and understanding of the group's culture, language and social values was central throughout the curriculum and daily caregiving routines. These programs tended to attract providers and families already very much in tune with the philosophy, or the programs became very influential in shaping individuals' opinions about the importance of promoting such values in care. Similarly, for programs purposely creating ethnically diverse environments for children, this mission was central and therefore key in recruitment presentations to potential new families. Parents were expected to support and buy into the center's multicultural focus. Anti-bias types of activities were a major focus of the curriculum, and staff were sought who could collectively reflect the diversity of our society and also who felt harmonious with the philosophy.

Parents who had at least one older child or a past experience with child care tended to have thought more about the implications of diversity in care.

It was evident that interviewees who had previous opportunities to think and talk about how race, language and culture impacted their lives and their child care practices were more ready to talk about issues of diversity. In programs or communities which were relatively diverse, both parents and providers had experienced more such opportunities. Also, parents who had at least one older child or a past experience with child care tended to have thought more about the implications of diversity in care. These parents had watched their sons' and daughters' transition into kindergarten or school, and so had a longer perspective on the possibilities for a child care program to prepare children for the larger world.

In the categories of perspectives presented earlier, we only quote opinions related to the role of care in addressing issues of race, language and culture. Not every person (although most) interviewed articulated a role for child care in a diverse society. Parents who were younger and had children in child care for the first time often seemed to have uncertain expectations for child care in general, and even less concrete views regarding diversity issues in care. Other parents did not think programs should attempt to address their children's racial or cultural identity or home language development because there was no one at the program who shared their same background. Some providers said that they did not believe it was ever appropriate to focus on racial or cultural differences, and that they themselves did not in any way recognize skin color or other distinctions among people. Other interviewees were simply uncomfortable or unaccustomed to talking about race, language or culture at all. All in all, however, those who did not believe that child care had a role to play in preparing children for a diverse society were by far a smaller group than those who did.

Multiple Perspectives/Multiple Roles

Finally, while we have presented these perspectives as separate categories, it is important to keep in mind that they are not mutually exclusive. One family may believe that a child care program can and should play more than one of these roles. And, some programs have chosen to take responsibility for a combination of some or all of the roles. For example, Annie Ip, a parent at Discoveryland, appreciated both that the center was developing her child's cultural identity and primary language while at the same time giving her the skills she needs to succeed in the dominant culture. Conversely, families and providers connected to the same program may have chosen that program for very different reasons. Liz Spencer, a white mother at Marin Learning Center, a predominantly African American center, wanted a program where her daughter would be exposed to people who were different from herself, whereas African American parents at the same program looked to it to support their children's African American cultural identity.

We hope that some of the views expressed here will ring true to our readers as they did for us as researchers, and highlight the value of finding out about our fellow colleagues' and community members' fears and dreams for children in a diverse society. We also hope that these perspectives spark the imaginations of providers and parents about the exciting contributions child care can make in our diverse world. The Principles of Quality Care in a Diverse Society that begin in the next chapter seek to offer a unifying vision for the child care field to begin this journey.

Chapter 2
Principles of Quality Care in a Diverse Society

Principle One: Combat Racism and Foster Positive Racial Identity in Young Children

At Centro VIDA, a multicultural child care center in Berkeley with a strong focus on supporting Latino culture and language, teaching assistant Carmen Madrid recalled the following story:

"I heard a child say, 'I hate brown.' I asked, 'Why?' She said, 'Kids don't like me because I am Black.' I told her, 'All colors are beautiful. I'm not ashamed of my skin color. My skin color is like yours. Your skin color is beautiful.' Afterwards I overheard the same child telling her classmate, 'You know what! The teacher says that I am beautiful, my color is beautiful and I am happy about it.'"

Racial identity and racial bias begin to develop in children at a very early age, at least by two or three years old. Children learn to identify themselves, figure out how they are the same and different from others, and begin to figure out which of those differences matter in the world. These are the years children begin to develop their sense of self pride, self esteem and their basic approach to feeling open to, or fearful of, others. Child care providers can address the development of bias in young children, before bias either turns into racism or is internalized into a negative self image. When child care providers are equipped with the skills to respond to incidents such as the one described above, they can intervene at key moments and help a child sort through the confusing messages they are receiving about human difference. They can create an environment and curriculum which support children to develop a healthy and positive sense of racial identity and comfortable acceptance of other racial backgrounds.

What is Racism?

If providers are to play a role in preventing the development of racism in children, they must first understand racism and its various expressions. The *Anti-Bias Curriculum*, developed by Louise Derman-Sparks and the Anti-Bias Task Force, explains:

> *Although race is not a scientifically valid way to categorize people, racism endows "race" with very significant social meaning. The physical characteristics all humans share are far more biologically important than the variations in skin color, hair texture and eye shape that originally were adaptations to different environmental demands. [In today's soci-*

> *ety] access to economic resources, political power and cultural rights is still very much determined by a person's membership in a specific racial group. Stereotyping and prejudice based on race remain a powerful part of prevailing social practice.*

Physical differences between human beings are not the cause but the excuse for racism. In other words, although "race" is not real, the power of racism is, and racial identity becomes a key definer in the lives of children.

A person exhibits racism or racial prejudice when he or she discriminates against someone of a particular racial background, through actions or words, out of a belief that all people of that racial group are somehow inferior. If a provider refused to work with a child, or avoided talking or interacting with a child, because of the color of the child's skin, these would be very clear incidents of racial prejudice.

People also exhibit racial prejudice when, through misinformation, fears and/or obliviousness, they treat other human beings based on assumptions about membership in a racial group. Racial prejudice exists when a caregiver assumes that all Latino children are Catholic, or that a Japanese American child will love the math manipulatives, or that all African American children have "natural rhythm."

"Institutional" or "systemic" racism is another prevalent form of racism. Institutional racism reflects the practices, policies or norms of an organization, institution or society which, intentionally or not, lead to or justify one racial group receiving better treatment or opportunities. For example, if opportunities for leadership in a program are based on staff development, and only white providers can afford to pay for staff development, then staff of color will be excluded from power in the center. Then, if the voices and opinions of staff of color regarding caregiving practices are not taken into account, based on the belief that only providers with a certain level of education have credibility, institutional racism must be addressed. A person who believes in the equality of all people may still unknowingly uphold racism by supporting a racist practice or participating in a racist institution.

In *Affirming Diversity: The Sociopolitical Context of Multicultural Education*, Sonia Nieto writes:

> *Institutional racism is manifested through established laws, customs and practices that reflect and produce racial inequalities in society...We need to understand the role that power plays in institutional racism. It is primarily through the power of the people who control these institutions that racist policies and practices are reinforced and legitimized.*

"Internalized racism" is one of the most damaging results for children of color living in a society where "white is right." Many children of color internalize the messages that they are not intelligent, that they are unattractive, and that authority and power are not available to them. When dark skinned children want to play only with the light skinned dolls, this is internalized racism. When Mexican farmworker children feel ashamed to have their parents visit their school, that too is internalized oppression.

Children pick up racist messages, whether overt (such as a provider saying, "You Black boys always give me so much trouble at circle time.") or more covert ("I know you can't sit still for long, but please try just this once."). If these injuries continue uncontradicted, too often the child comes to believe they are true. Internalized oppression can build over the years to a profound sense of self worthlessness, "badness" and stupidity. When continually fed by institutional racism, internalized racism becomes a self monitoring device, where the child's damaged self image may stop her or him from trying new behaviors.

In order to protect children from racial fear or shame about themselves and their families, racism must be combated at all levels. Racist attitudes must be changed in ourselves and others through education, self reflection, dialogue, action and, often, confrontation. Institutional racism can be dismantled by our learning to analyze practices, policies and norms of an institution or society in order to identify racist aspects as well as potential solutions. Racist behavior can be unlearned by helping individuals understand how they can stop unwittingly participating in perpetuating racism. And, children of color must be supported with the skills to resist internalizing racism through caring, strength building, pride enhancing, collective experiences, as well as opportunities to express their anger, cry and "unlearn" the misinformation. Understanding how racism is internalized, and helping children to counter this, is essential if child care staffs are to truly support internal strength in young children.

In order to protect children from racial fear or shame about themselves and their families, racism must be combated at all levels.

Understanding the Development of Racial Awareness in Children

From the very beginning, human infants pull in information about their world and actively try to make sense of it. Infants gaze and observe closely; within the first days of life they begin to make distinctions between sounds of different languages, voices of individuals, smells, the already recognized stimuli and the new. Before they are a year old they have figured out who is familiar and who is a stranger, and have developed selective responses to the different styles of their various caregivers. A main source of learning for infants is social referencing: paying close attention to the adult's sometimes quite subtle responses to new and different people and situations. Does my mother hold me tighter when that dark man approaches? Does my caregiver's face relax when someone speaks in that language?

Toddlers are by nature curious. They observe their caretakers' actions and interactions and listen to their words. They notice difference just as "difference," something interesting to explore. Toddlers make early observations of racial cues: looking back and forth between dark skinned and light skinned faces; patting (or sometimes pulling!) differently textured hair; looking from the picture of an Asian child to the eyes of an Asian child in the room.

When toddlers notice difference, they also pay close attention to the emotional response of adults. The toddler's development of rudimentary concepts is supported by an interested, matter-of-fact response. A young girl may notice that a little boy in a picture has eyes like one of the other Asian children in her child care center. The provider might then say to the girl, "Let's look in the mirror and see what your eyes look like." The child begins to conceptualize, "We all have eyes. Eyes look different." By ignoring a child's cues of interest, adults may convey that they feel uneasy and that the child has stumbled upon something potentially unspeakable. What adults do not talk about, do not name, becomes dangerous. For the child, the rudimentary concept becomes tainted with, "There is something worrisome, scary about different shapes of eyes."

Three-, four- and five-year-olds are very aware of the many aspects of a person's physical being. How we look is concrete, touchable, "real." What we are like as people is more abstract, subjective and harder to define. One of the developmental tasks for these children is to create comparative categories. A child might say, "I'm brown and you're Black." Or, a child might ask one Latino child if a Latino person working at the center is his or her mother. Again, the adult response to children's observations will cue children to the societal judgements of physical differences. The adult's silence, or nervousness, or over-politeness, are indicators of discomfort, anger and fear. These feelings can, and very often do, become part of the child's early concept development around racial categories.

As the *Anti-Bias Curriculum* has described, during the preschool years children are developing a sense of themselves as individuals, trying to figure out the central aspects of who they are. They question, "What parts of me are the same as others—and what parts will change or stay the same?" About gender they wonder, "Will I always be a girl or boy? If I like to climb trees do I become a boy? If I like to play with dolls, do I become a girl?" Young children also notice and question racial characteristics: "How come my skin is this color? Can I change it? Why is my hair different from yours?"

Around ages four and five, children begin to figure out the irrevocability of some cues. People get bigger and older, but gender, skin color, eye shape do not change. Although this seems obvious to adults, it is very confusing to children. Particularly confusing is figuring out the racial categories people are defined by. Why are some people called "white" when their skin is pinkish tan? Why are some people who are called "Black" lighter than some who are called Jewish? How come someone who is called Chinese has a father who looks Asian but her mom looks just like my teacher, who is called white? As racial categories are socially constructed and do not reflect real differences between humans, and as these categories are laden with feelings of confusion, fear and distrust amongst adults, it is very difficult for children to understand which physical cues matter and which do not.

It is in this atmosphere that young children develop self identity and recognition of others as members of the same or different identification groups. By age five, children have already learned that in our society skin color matters and is as important to how we are perceived as being a boy or a girl.

Trying to understand race and racial categories takes on another layer of complexity when the child and each parent all look different from one another. Children of parents of different racial backgrounds—biracial or multiracial children—develop their racial self identity in a unique context. Often, the biracial child will look different than all of the other children in the child care program, even among other biracial children. A biracial child is affected by racism in the same manner as all children of color. Yet the child's development of group identification presents an additional challenge, as our common application of racial categories does not easily allow for a child who is not "one" or "the other" but "both" or "many."

Young children, of course, do not understand the social or political context of race or racism, nor that there is no biological basis for racial categories. But they are developing opinions and judgements about people based on skin color and other characteristics. Louise Derman-Sparks and the Anti-Bias Task Force call this "pre-prejudice," which is not yet racism, but can lead to racism as the child grows older.

Beginning ideas and feelings in very young children may develop into real prejudice through reinforcement by prevailing societal biases. Pre-prejudice may be misconceptions based on young children's limited experience and developmental level, or it may consist of imitations of adult behavior. More serious forms are behaviors that indicate discomfort, fear or rejection of differences.

Derman-Sparks told us a story illustrating how young children categorize and assimilate information about racial characteristics. She was drawn to anti-bias work because of her own personal struggles about how to best raise her son:

> *When my son was about 18 months old, we lived in a white community where the only African American person we had contact with was the garbage man. I noticed that when we went to the park or zoo, he would see African American men and say, "There's the garbage man!" I panicked and thought he was learning all the wrong stuff. So we took him to see the Persuasions (a famous a cappella soul group). He loved the singing and at the intermission said in a loud voice, "When are the garbage men going to sing again?" I realized this demonstrated exactly what I knew about developmental theory. I had hoped this concrete experience would enlarge his category, but he just assimilated the singers into the category he already had.*

Caregivers Can Make a Difference

Child care providers working with young children are in a crucial position to support the development of positive racial identity, and to combat the development and internalization of racism in children. Caregivers have many opportunities throughout the day to counteract the development of prejudice and to affirm

a child's growing sense of racial identity.

When a child asks, "Why is your skin darker than mine?" or "Will the color wash off?" or "My skin isn't really white, it's tan," a provider is presented with a chance to make a difference. But, adults often respond by ignoring the question or hushing the child, and the child learns from these kinds of interactions that the subject of skin color is bad, shameful and unspeakable. After many such interactions a child may eventually internalize a sense of shame because she or he has dark skin, a certain hair texture or other characteristics. Children begin to believe that dark skinned people have something to be ashamed of, which leads to a poor self image or light skinned children's beginning prejudice.

But if child care providers are prepared to actively respond to children's questions and observations about racial characteristics, they can help children to be proud of who they are and appreciate the different skin tones, eye colors and shapes, and hair textures that they see around them. By "active" we don't assume that simply exposing children to people of different racial backgrounds is sufficient. The classroom environment, the curriculum, staff and family relationships all must incorporate an understanding of how racism is absorbed in young children and must specifically counter such hurtful learnings. Caregivers need skills and strategies to respond to incidents as they arise, and most importantly, they must be willing to step in when they see an opportunity rather than let an incident pass by because they are not sure how to respond.

Anti-Bias Curriculum offers many suggestions for how to take an active approach to addressing race and bias in young children. An anti-bias approach does not only deal with race but also with gender, physical ability, language and sexual orientation. In this chapter, we concentrate on race and racial bias, although it is important to acknowledge the interconnection of racism with other expressions of bias—and that each bias feeds the others. The strategies outlined below are derived from our research for this publication and from California Tomorrow's experience facilitating dialogue among individuals concerned about race, racism and bias in young children. Following each strategy, we discuss the related challenges involved.

Promising Strategies and Challenges

Strategy 1

Create an environment which reflects positive images of different racial groups.

> *Marilyn Allen operates a family child care home in the city of Torrance. African American herself, she is strongly committed to fostering the self esteem of the ethnically mixed children in her care. Her home is full of pictures, books, dolls, paper, paint and other materials which support the learning of appreciation for all skin colors and racial characteristics. During circle time, she leads the activities using ethnically diverse puppets. Marilyn also has a personal connection to Japanese culture, after working with that community for many years now. This is visible in her collection of Japanese textiles, screens, ceramics and dolls. She knows this not only cultivates the pride of the Japanese American children in her program, but exposes all the children to an international perspective.*

As child care workers know, an effective learning environment is essential to quality care. A diversity of human images in the overall environment can both support a child's development of a positive racial identity and expose him or her to people of different racial backgrounds.

Virtually every program California Tomorrow visited sought to decorate and equip the classroom with pictures, toys, books and other materials mirroring the ethnic backgrounds of the children in the program. Some also made an effort to reflect groups not represented among the children in care.

Classroom materials came from many sources. Teachers sought out supplies from libraries, museums and local ethnic stores, as well as companies which produce educational materials. In some cases, parents or community groups donated traditional costumes, games or other items which reflected the racial background of the children in care or groups not represented at the program.

When such materials couldn't be found, caregivers often came up with other solutions. Some made their own materials and books or modified existing materials to be more representative of people of different racial backgrounds. Many centers displayed children's own artwork depicting their lives, families and communities. We were told of a migrant farmworker center where staff gave the parents Polaroid cameras to take on visits to Mexico so that they could photograph their home villages, relatives, the stores, houses, people and landscapes. The parents brought the photographs back to be displayed in the center. The same idea worked nicely for a center serving children in Oakland, where the families photographed their neighborhoods, relatives and friends to decorate the center.

Challenges to Strategy 1

Challenge: Limited resources for purchasing materials

Resources for purchasing classroom materials are, almost without fail, very limited. Staff frequently spend their free time locating or constructing materials and, on occasion, even used their own resources to purchase the supplies. Often, programs had to think creatively about how to obtain in-kind donations of appropriate supplies.

Challenge: Lack of information about how to locate materials

We found that while staff members at some programs, especially in less urban areas, are hungry for more resources to create multiracial/multicultural environments, finding access to the appropriate materials presents a real challenge. Michelle DeLury, a young white teacher working at Alpine, a center in a rural area of Northern California that serves children of the Washoe Tribe and white children, noted:

> *The story books are all white. If children never see anyone who looks like them, then they can't recognize themselves in it. But I don't know where to get other books.*

Staff at other programs also observed that books for young children in non-English languages, especially Southeast Asian languages, are often even harder to obtain, either because they are expensive or they aren't sold by local stores or through mainstream publishers. In spite of the recently growing networks of multicultural resource publishers and materials for educators, the staff in sites we visited needed better access to these. We offer a small sampling of resources at the end of this book on pages 233-234.

When toddlers notice difference, they also pay close attention to the emotional response of adults.

Challenge: Recognition that changing the environment isn't enough

While the visual messages of the physical environment are critical, in and of themselves they cannot combat racism or help children develop positive racial identities. Paying attention to images is an important first step. However, programs also require a more complex understanding of the issues and strategies involved. Providers do not always recognize that they must move beyond the surface and examine their attitudes, actions and policies with young children. Too often, well-intentioned efforts start and end with classroom decorations.

Strategy 2

Looking inward: watch for unintentional ways that one's own actions, beliefs or words can promote bias.

Adults who feel a responsibility to prevent the development of racial bias and to support positive racial identity among children need to start by examining their own biases and misinformation. Often, we do not analyze our ingrained beliefs—which began to form when we were two, three and four years old. Despite our best intentions, we may make assumptions or perpetuate stereotypes about people of certain racial groups. We may exhibit racial biases through our behavior and words, and pass these along to the young children we care for. Does a white provider, for example, tend to tense up when he or she is talking to her African American colleague? Does an English-speaking provider show impatience when needing to communicate with an Asian parent who has difficulty speaking English? Does an African American or Latino caregiver show preferential treatment to lighter skinned children? The key to preventing this from happening is to be aware of our own biases through self reflection. Strategies adults can use for self reflection are discussed in this chapter, in our Principle on Dialogue and in the *Anti-Bias Curriculum*, among other resources.

Avoa Henry, an African American teacher working at Step One School, explained:

> *It is important for us to soul search. Children pick up a lot of things from us. We make a significant impact on their lives. I question my actions and reactions on a daily basis.*

Our society has a long history of racism and racial strife. Often the most difficult aspects of racism to combat are those which are so familiar to us, and so much a part of our traditions, that we do not notice them. An incident at one center we visited reveals how easy it is to perpetuate racist stereotypes until providers take the time to reflect upon their practice. In this case, an African American director of an ethnically diverse center overheard an African American teacher singing the song, "One little, two little, three little Indians." Like many people, the teacher thought of this as a simple counting song that she herself was probably taught as a child. She was not aware of the negative connotations of the words that reinforce a simplistic stereotype of Native Americans, relegating them to counting objects instead of human beings. Some have pointed out that the song's conclusion, "No more Indians," is especially insensitive to the actual destruction of Native American cultures and peoples in this country. Rather than single out the teacher, the director decided to bring a book from her collection of Black memorabilia—much of which chronicles the history of racist images of African Americans—to share at the next staff meeting. She showed her entire staff this book, which illustrated the same well-known song but substituted the word "niggers"[1] for "Indians." The staff members were clearly able to understand how the song was objectionable no matter "who" was used as the diminishing counting object. All of us are susceptible, and make mistakes or assumptions. Although well-meaning, the teacher in this story

[1] We recognize that this word is deeply offensive to many people. Many believe that the word nigger must never be repeated because it is so abhorrently symbolic of racism. Others believe that exactly because it is so symbolic, it must be used in the context of exposing the persistence of racism. Providers must be prepared to talk about the full range of emotions and responses that can arise when discussing these sensitive issues.

Activities for Increasing Self Awareness

Adapted from Anti-Bias Curriculum: Tools for Empowering Young Children
by Louise Derman-Sparks and the Anti-Bias Curriculum Task Force

INTEGRATING AN ANTI-BIAS curriculum into your care setting takes thoughtful personal work. No one escapes learning and believing some of the stereotypes and biases that undergird sexism, racism and handicapism. We all carry scars, whether as initiator or target of unjust acts. Many of us have been both at different times. Few of us have had the opportunity or taken the time to examine deeply and openly the impact on us of these experiences. Instead, we keep them hidden and are reluctant to expose our confusions, frustrations, hurt, anger and guilt. These experiences and feelings daily influence our interactions with children, even if we are not aware of it.

The self-awareness exercises will help you clarify your thinking and identify discomforts and prejudices that would interfere with doing anti-bias work with children. For these exercises to be useful, allow each member to reveal her or his feelings in safety. Do not judge each other. Help each other examine the attitudes which emerge.

As you do the self-awareness activities, you may feel pain. Racism, sexism and handicapism are ugly, so it can hurt as we face their negative image of us. Don't let the pain stop you. Acknowledge it, and then figure out how to turn pain into energy for acting to implement anti-bias curriculum.

Begin with the following:

- Share with your group how you describe or define your racial/ethnic identity. What is important and not important to you about this aspect of yourself? If it is important, why? If not, why not? How do you feel about your racial/ethnic identity? Repeat this exercise two more times, the second talking about your gender identity and the third about differences in physical abilities.
- Share how you learned about your racial/ethnic identity, your gender identity, and your physical abilities and limitations. What are your earliest memories? What was fun or painful as you learned about these aspects of your identity?
- Share how you disagree with your parents' views about race, ethnicity, gender and abledness. If you disagree, how did you develop your own ideas? What and who were significant influences on you? If you are a parent (or plan to be one), what do you want to teach your own children?
- Make a list of what you want other people to know about and what you don't want people to say about your racial and ethnic identity. Share with the group. Discuss what you want a person who knows very little about your group to learn. ❧

had reinforced the stereotype of Native Americans. She probably had not examined the meanings conveyed by the song because it was so familiar to her. The opportunity for examination of our assumptions is very important.

An environment that encourages staff to help each other identify when they may be unintentionally acting in a biased way is critical. Patti Hnatiuk of Wheelock College recalled an incident when she was director of a center and a new teacher joined the staff. The new provider, who was white, was very enthusiastic about working in a multicultural environment:

> *One day while interacting with an African American boy in her classroom, she took the child in front of a mirror and said, "You look just like Curious George." She was delighted—she loved Curious George. Another staff person didn't interrupt her right then, but came to a staff meeting [to discuss the incident]. Many staff were horrified.*

Patti said that the key response to this incident from other staff was a desire to help the new teacher understand why her actions were inappropriate and the implications of her comment to the child:

> *She did it unknowingly, but...in an atmosphere of collegiality and support, she went about remedying the error. The African American staff were very helpful, and actually it couldn't have been resolved without their maturity, self awareness and commitment to change. The staff recommended that she talk first with the child's parents about the incident, which she did. And staff supported her in the process. It was painful at times, but ultimately resolved by collective efforts.*

This story is an example of how important it is for providers to understand the underpinnings of racism and its many expressions—and to be willing to learn and confront the ways one's own actions may feed racism, even unknowingly. Curious George is a small monkey who gets into all sorts of adventures in a popular children's book series that in itself is benign. But comparing an African American child to Curious George can be perceived as perpetuating the long history of African Americans being called "monkeys," "gorillas" or "apes," based on derogatory and racist reasoning: comparing the supposed lack of intelligence and "civilized" habits of African Americans to apes; referring to the African continent as a "jungle" and African Americans as sub-human wild animals, more like apes than people of European descent.

Challenges to Strategy 2

Challenge: Limited opportunities and skills to reflect upon bias

Providers often lack opportunities to think about their own personal bias and how it may be reflected in the care setting. A number of issues contribute to this, including people's fears, lack of resources for staff development, and lack of structured times for staff to meet together about many topics. Time and resources are clearly needed to help directors and staff to develop skills of facilitation, self reflection and dialogue. Without such skills and opportunities for reflection, stereotypes or discriminatory behaviors may all too often be perpetuated in care. For example, on the walls of one center we visited were several "educational" posters about fetal alcohol syndrome which depicted Native American women drinking alcohol or breast feeding. A person from a local Native American tribe in the community commented on the poster, worrying that its message was, "That's all Indians do—have babies and drink." On the walls of the care environment, these posters clearly conveyed the wrong message to the Native American and non-Native American children in the center. If there had been more discussion and reflection, the posters may not have been placed where they were.

Challenge: Moving beyond the "color-blind" perspective

A very common view in our society, which stems in part from American values of equality and fairness, is that we should all be "color-blind." During our interviews, we repeatedly heard expressions such as:

> *We treat all of the kids exactly the same. That is the way that I deal with diversity. I don't see Black faces, Asian faces or Latino faces.*

This approach, again, usually grows from good intentions. Color-blindness arose as a progressive argument against laws and practices which mandated unequal treatment of people of color. But, if adhered to uncritically, this viewpoint does not recognize the reality that people of color are in fact treated differently than white people from the dominant culture. It also fails to acknowledge or value the differences each one of us brings to the world. In her article, "Do You Have Cultural Tunnel Vision?", Janet Gonzalez-Mena explains the down-side of the color-blind approach:

> *Some people go out of their way to emphasize similarities and de-emphasize differences. They claim to be color-blind, or culture blind. My husband, who was born and raised in Mexico, is often told by well-meaning people who wish to compliment him that they never think of him as being Mexican. Since I'm not Mexican, I don't know how that feels, but I do*

know how I would react if some well-meaning person told me in a complimentary way that he or she never thinks of me as being a woman. That would shock me, because being female is a vital part of who I am, and I don't want to be considered genderless. I don't want anyone to hold my gender against me, or treat me unequally, but I don't want a vital part of my identity ignored either.

Talking about race, racism and related issues can be personal and emotional. In an environment that insists on "color-blindness," there is little opportunity for people to practice positively talking about race and difference. People are afraid to make mistakes and say the wrong thing, so they tend to not say, or ask, anything at all. Countering racism requires an active approach, which we further discuss in our Principle on Dialogue.

Strategy 3

Interact and intervene with children to promote positive racial identity and counteract racial prejudice.

Fostering the growth of positive racial identity and counteracting the development of racial prejudice in young children are two different processes which should not be confused. However, many strategies can advance both goals at once. The key is for adults, through interactions and interventions with children, to take an active role in breaking down attitudes which contribute to prejudice. This might take the form of a planned activity, a story or a response to a specific incident.

For example, a teacher may design an activity to help ensure children don't attach a negative value to darker colors. In our society, dark colors and evil or "badness" are often associated. Encouraging children to work with brown colors is a way to lessen their sense that dark is bad and scary. And for the dark skinned child, it fosters confidence that dark colors are as attractive and desirable as any others. Children should have access to plenty of brown and black materials, crayons, paint, photographs, puppets, etc. According to trainer Margie Carter:

It's at a sensory level for kids. Because of all the negative associations with brown and black colors, I work on simple things like putting yummy smelling extracts in black or brown playdough. We don't even talk about it as related to a skin color. The same with making sure the environment and books are full of positive associations with those colors.

Some activities are aimed at helping children understand that humanness is not defined by color. Margaret McCullough is a white teacher at Step One School, a program which up until several years ago served mostly white, upper middle class families. In recent years, Step One has made significant efforts to diversify its enrollment. Margaret created a game where children take on the persona of someone who looks different:

> *I take nylons and stretch them over coat hangers to make masks that children can hold in front of their faces. Nylons come in every color. The children hold the masks up to their faces and look at themselves in the mirror, trying different shades. Everyone gets to use them.*

From Margaret's perspective, this activity helps children to appreciate different skin colors, and learn that a person is still a person regardless of skin color.

Eleanor Wong works at Discoveryland, a predominantly Chinese center operated under the auspices of a Seventh Day Adventist Church in San Francisco. To teach children to accept and appreciate different types of people, Discoveryland teaches the concept that God created all humans equal. Eleanor states:

> *I think my responsibility is to help make sure that they know whoever you are is important. If you are Caucasian, you are important. We tell the children you are important because God made everyone unique. I convey this message through the Bible. I use it to teach that each person is important and we should treat others the same as we would like them to treat ourselves. We shouldn't look down on anybody.*

Intervening when children make racist comments or behave in a prejudiced way toward others can make a lasting difference.

The previous strategies can be adapted to help biracial or multiracial children develop a positive racial identity. Often a biracial child will not easily be identified as fitting into any one racial category, and may feel different from everyone. It is important to address the experience of biracial children directly, when appropriate. For example, when reading a story about a traditional family, a provider might make a point of saying, "Not all mommies and daddies look alike. Some children have a mommy with dark skin and a daddy with light skin."

Teachers need strategies to help children resist internalizing the racism of our society, as well as strategies for addressing the racist attitudes and behaviors they encounter in individual children. In our example from Centro VIDA at the beginning of this chapter, the teacher had the skills to begin to guide the Black child out of her already internalized racism. At the moment the child expressed bad feelings about her skin color, the teacher immediately responded to let her know she loved her own dark skin, just as the child should and could love her own.

Intervening when children make racist comments or behave in a prejudiced way toward others can make a lasting difference. An example of this is described in *Anti-Bias Curriculum*. Jeffrey, a two-and-a-half-year-old Asian American child, exhibited a number of behaviors indicating discomfort with dark skinned children. For example, when he saw pictures of dark skinned children in a book, he said, "Yucky." Another time, Jeffrey wouldn't hold the hand of a Black classmate, saying the child's hand was "dirty." Jeffrey's mother related a disturbing incident at home: after she washed Jeffrey's hair, he said to her, "Now it's white." She responded, "Your hair is black." Jeffrey insisted, "No, it's white, only the dirt is black." The teacher decided it was time to develop a plan together with Jeffrey's parents to help Jeffrey overcome his discomfort with "blackness."

At school over the next two months, the teacher tried a variety of activities with Jeffrey. Together they put dirt on dark skinned and light skinned dolls and then washed them many times. The teacher pointed out that when the dirt came off the dark skin, the skin was still dark; she showed Jeffrey that brown skin was still brown when it was clean. They washed the doll's hair and saw that it was still black. The teacher and Jeffrey also played with brown and black playdough and paint, among other activities, and they spent time examining each other's skin, hair and eyes. One day three months after the first pre-prejudice incident, Jeffrey initiated the following exchange with his teacher: "You're brown," he stated matter-of-factly. "Yes, I'm brown," his teacher replied. "You're my friend," Jeffrey said next. "Yes, I'm your friend," she agreed.

Taking the *time* to develop strategies for dealing with different situations helps providers respond appropriately. Through discussions, staff can identify and practice strategies, ensuring they will have consistent responses across the program.

Challenges to Strategy 3

Challenge: Lack of dialogue skills/fear of stereotyping

Many providers are afraid or unsure of how to discuss differences between children or groups without accidentally promoting a stereotype. As described in the previous discussion of "color-blindness," the following typifies the sentiment of many interviewed:

> *I say everybody is different but we all can be friends, like a family. It's the only thing they can understand and I can say without offending certain groups. I'm not going to talk about Black, white, Asian. People are so sensitive.*

In her book *Developing Roots and Wings*, Stacey York writes:

> *Time and time again I meet teachers who want to do what's right, who don't want to make a mistake. Teachers don't want to offend parents or co-workers and they don't want to hurt children's feelings. For this reason, they choose to ignore the differences and teach children that everyone is the same.*

Challenge: Insufficient staff development opportunities

Although the anti-bias approach has gained greater acceptance in the field, California Tomorrow found that there is much need for greater staff development opportunities about these issues and practices. Many providers in the field are familiar with the *Anti-Bias Curriculum* and *Developing Roots and Wings*. The National Association for the Education of Young Children's distribution of *Anti-Bias Curriculum* has been instrumental in promoting awareness of these concepts throughout the nation.

Through our research, however, we found that the opportunities to develop an in-depth understanding of anti-bias concepts remain limited and inconsistent. Opportunities for such training in non-English languages are essentially non-existent. And, for most English-speaking providers, exposure had been limited to one-shot workshops at a conference or to brief discussions within the child, family and community class required to receive a children's center teaching permit in California. Providers were aware that they did not emerge from these experiences with the skills they needed to implement what they learned in the care setting. Professional development trainers expressed great frustration with lack of follow-up support and training for anti-bias work. A former intern with the Leadership in Diversity Program of the California Association of Education of Young Children captured this feeling well:

> *Hour-and-a-half workshops just can't make a significant enough impact. What teachers need is to hear the topic presented, the rationale and what we know from research and development. Then they need time for application—the balance of theory and practice...We actually do a disservice to our profession by giving the message to people that they can learn all of this in 70 minutes.*

Program directors also said it was very difficult to contact qualified and effective trainers in anti-bias or other forms of diversity training, and that they themselves did not feel qualified to lead a discussion or conduct a training with an anti-bias curriculum.

Eleanor Clement Glass, former professor at San Francisco State University and currently a foundation officer at the San Francisco Foundation, commented on the potential impact when training does not emphasize the time and skills for deep self examination:

> *Teachers can get a lot of diversity training, but if they haven't dealt with prejudice or bias in themselves, they are not at all prepared to deal with it in their classroom. I don't care how many books from every land they have in their classroom. They will read the story about an African American boy, but when the African American boy in their class starts wiggling around and gets distracted, they start yelling at him.*

The process of becoming aware of race and bias—and culture and language, class and gender—and how they relate to the child care setting is an ongoing and usually difficult process.

Challenge: Underattention to issues regarding biracial or multiracial experience

During our site visits to family child care homes and centers, we saw many children who were biracial or multiracial. However, there seemed to be very little, if any, discussion, reflection or strategizing around the needs of these children with regard to understanding race and developing a positive self identity. In fact, when asked to describe the populations served by their programs, providers often did not specifically identify the biracial or multiracial children, even when such children and their families were clearly present. The lack of attention paid to the experiences and identity of biracial children among providers mirrors society at large.

Challenge: The cultural embeddedness of approaches to combating racism

Providers need to be aware that their own beliefs about how to combat racism are probably embedded in their cultural belief system and may not align with children's families. While a provider may wish to teach children to challenge biased words when they hear them, the parents may believe that confrontation is inappropriate and instead teach their children to ignore—neither challenging nor condoning—bias. Here it is important for the provider and parents to communicate with one another, to recognize that the goal may be the same but a respectful agreement will need to be reached balancing both the center's and the parents' principles. The following chapter further explores the cultural embeddedness of care and the respectful inquiry and negotiation that need to take place between providers and parents. At present, a conflictual model for acting against racism is prevalent in anti-bias philosophy. More research and work are needed to identify other culturally embedded models for acting against racism.

Children of color have a great need to see adults from their own background in authority. These children can scarcely avoid negative images of people who look like themselves through the media.

STRATEGY 4

Use hiring practices to promote the goals of positive racial self identity and appreciation of racial differences among children.

Live Oak Migrant Head Start serves Mexican and Punjabi families. When Carol Masih started working at the center, she was the only Punjabi staff person. One morning when Carol was out, a Punjabi child enrolled in the program. When Carol came to work that afternoon, she met the child and told her that she was a teacher. The girl's reaction was, "Oh, I thought only white people worked here," and she immediately became much more relaxed. She was clearly noticing the skin color and other features of the adults around her compared to her own, and she was visibly comforted by the presence of a teacher who looked more like herself. Additionally, although the little girl had not seen any Punjabi staff members until Carol arrived at work, in fact, all of the teachers she had met that morning were Mexican immigrants and Mexican Americans—not "white," as we identify the majority racial group in the United States. At her young age, the little girl apparently thought of people in authority who were not from her background as "white." Already, she seemed to have developed an ingrained sense of who had power in her world.

Adults are a crucial ingredient of the environment of the child care program. Children's observations of providers' racial backgrounds and working relationships become core information in the evolution of their own self identity and ability to interact with others.

Most of the programs visited by California Tomorrow sought to hire staff who reflected the backgrounds of the children in care, or who could expose children to people who were of different racial backgrounds. The hiring practices and the racial diversity of teachers varied according to program goals and philosophy. Programs that focused on serving predominantly one racial group (or cultural or language group) hired staff of that background. Programs that purposely served a diverse group of families tried to hire a diverse staff to reflect the children. Some very diverse programs often did not have the capacity to hire one staff person to reflect each child in the program, but hiring practices were guided by the goal of having a diverse staff such that most children would see a teacher who looked like them.

Children of color have a great need to see adults from their own background in authority. These children can scarcely avoid negative images and stereotypes of people who look like themselves through the media and other aspects of society. Hiring staff who reflect children's racial backgrounds can help to counteract the negative messages. For example, at Hintil Kuu Ca, an intertribal Native American Center in Oakland, the majority of staff reflects the Native American background of most of the children in care. The center considers this key to helping children develop positive self identity and self esteem. As in many communities throughout the country, most children from Native American tribes in Oakland seldom experience the sense of possibility which comes from seeing people like themselves work and succeed in professional positions. According to one mother, Hintil has been critical to her children's development:

> *My children know who they are. Before they saw white people of authority, they saw their own people in those kinds of positions.*

Some programs hired a diversity of staff specifically to counter children's fears or ignorance about people who look different from themselves. An African American provider working at a predominantly white center recalled her first day at work when she realized many of the children had never been exposed to dark skinned people. Even now, when the new year starts and a new group of children come in, many are amazed at her skin color, and they will sit on her lap and touch her arm. Once a child said in amazement, "You're brown all over!" She said, "Yes—well, my palms are a little beige." He asked, "Will it wash off?" She said, "No." For this boy, the opportunity to ask the questions on his mind about skin color and to get an honest and caring response was very positive. Other children in the program, who also had never had relationships with African Americans, were able to experience real understanding of the teacher as an individual, as opposed to a stereotypical image based upon what they had heard or seen in children's books or on television.

This example illustrates how white children also benefit from opportunities to see teachers and other authority figures of different racial backgrounds. White children are normally exposed to many white adults in positions of power outside their families. Also, positive images and messages about white children are abundant in society, the media and schooling. For white children—as for all children—an early message that people of all racial backgrounds possess knowledge and leadership is important in the development of unbiased attitudes toward others.

Challenges to Strategy 4

Challenge: Transforming staffing patterns into learning opportunities

Regardless of hiring practices, we found widely varying degrees to which programs drew upon the racial backgrounds, experiences and perspectives of the staff in order to promote understanding among children. Some consciously did this by encouraging staff to openly discuss their own skin color, hair texture or other racial differences with the children. Other programs hired staff of different backgrounds, but did not take advantage of this critical resource as fully as they might have to enrich their programs. They did not develop activities and strategies to ensure that staff were prepared to respond to children's reactions and questions. Or they did not spend time thinking about how they might use the racial composition of staff to model how people of different backgrounds can work harmoniously together.

Challenge: Supporting staff who are in the minority

Programs that hire staff based on a desire to expose children to different backgrounds can unwittingly create a difficult and potentially alienating situation for a staff person. It is easy to feel isolated and unsupported as the only member of a certain background in a program. For example, a program which served large numbers of Asians hired an African American teaching assistant as a step toward preventing the development of prejudice in the children. The African American provider was the only Black person in the program, and often the first Black person the children had ever met. She said:

> *When I first arrived, the Asian children wouldn't even eat with me at my table. They wouldn't approach me. The children had never been exposed to a big Black woman before.*

The provider tried many different approaches with the children but they were hesitant, scared or distrustful of her. She wondered if the children would ever warm to her, and at one point, feeling alienated and ineffective, believed she would have to leave the center. However, she and the director worked together on the problem, and after four months the children overcame their hesitations. The director

of the program said one way she tried to resolve the situation was to make sure the children saw the teaching assistant in a variety of leadership roles. When California Tomorrow interviewed the teaching assistant, she had been at the program for two years. She said she could not have stayed and worked through the difficult situation without the support of the director who believed in her.

Challenge: Addressing concerns about racial considerations in hiring policies

In this polarized social climate, the practice of taking race into consideration when hiring staff may be seen as controversial. Programs need to be prepared to answer internal and external concerns and questions, and they must be clear about the rationale and implications of their approach. Of course, no person should be hired simply because of his or her racial background. Clearly, children need to be placed with adults with the interpersonal and professional skills to foster their healthy development. At the same time, people's racial backgrounds can be great assets in terms of conveying positive messages to children and bringing unique knowledge. The life experiences of a worker who shares the racial identity of a child can make the worker more sensitive to the child's needs and feelings. Parents and families are likely to feel more comfortable with the presence of someone from their background in the center. Directors and providers who decide to take race into account in their hiring policies need to take the time to reflect upon the overall racial composition of staff and children in the program, and assess all the implications for their hiring criteria.

Challenge: Thinking about the desired racial composition of staff

What should a program's goals be in terms of the racial composition of staff? This question is not easily answered. Goals depend upon the demographics of the children served and the philosophy of the program. Policies related to staff racial composition must be balanced with other staffing needs, such as skills for working with different age and language groups, etc. This balance must constantly be negotiated as programs inevitably have a limited number of positions.

Strategy 5

Be aware of the message sent by grouping children, and its power to promote either racial understanding or stereotyping among children.

Who are the children in our center? What are their different backgrounds? How are we responding to their diversity through our grouping policies and practices? Are we placing children based on their best interests? Are we promoting tokenism? What might we do differently? Paying attention to the messages sent by the way children are grouped is essential.

Using enrollment practices to create a program with a particular racial composition is one form of grouping. For example, programs aimed at serving a certain racial minority seek to enroll children from that group. The assumption behind this approach is that children of color will grow more comfortable and proud of their identity by spending targeted time in their early years surrounded by peers who are not likely to question who they are or what they look like. For some children, this will be the only opportunity to build positive relationships with children from their same ethnic community. For example, for the children of various Native American tribes who attend Hintil Kuu Ca, the center is probably the only place they would have such regular interaction together, since they live geographically dispersed throughout Oakland's many neighborhoods. These experiences are partially designed to build the self confidence of children for when they enter multiracial situations.

Another enrollment policy approach is to attract and select children who will collectively create a racially diverse environment. Two centers we visited took this approach because they wanted to create a place where children could regularly interact across races, cultures and languages.

But the overall composition of a program is not the sole grouping consideration. It is also critical to look at the message sent by the placement of children within the program. For example, one program we visited agreed that exposure to a racially mixed group of children was very important at a young age, but through a learning process concluded that every child also needs to be around peers from the same racial (or cultural or language) group. Initially this program, which was one-third children of color and two-thirds white, evenly distributed the children of color throughout the different classrooms so each was as "diverse" as possible. Over time, however, African American parents raised concerns about their children being the "token" people of color in the classrooms, and the center responded by changing its policies. One parent recalled:

> *I didn't think it was good for my daughter to be treated as different all the time. It gave the impression that she was only in the classroom because she was Black and it put her in the position of being the authority on being a Black child.*

This parent's reflections speak to the subtle impact of tokenism, the impact of which can be painful and harmful. Today, the program groups several children of the same background in a classroom. The result is that every classroom has children and adults of different racial backgrounds, but not every classroom has every racial background.

Grouping practices determined by non-racial factors, if unexamined, can lead to potentially distorted messages about different racial groups. One school district child development center noted this and quickly made a change in its grouping practices. The center was 98 percent Chinese until special needs children were integrated into the program. Initially, all of the special needs children recruited were African American. The director became concerned about the potentially negative impact of a context where this was the only contact the Chinese children had with any African American children. She began to diversify the students in the special needs program as well as to recruit African American children for the regular program. Doing so required getting an informal waiver from her administration so she could bypass the existing waiting list. Whatever enrollment or grouping strategies a program uses, the program should analyze the potential messages sent by the compositions of the program.

Paying attention to the messages sent by the way children are grouped is essential.

Challenges to Strategy 5

Challenge: Clarity and articulation of policies for recruitment and enrollment of children from specific racial backgrounds

California Tomorrow's interviews showed that many people still assume that a color-blind perspective is best. Therefore, efforts which take the race of children into consideration are sometimes interpreted as actually perpetuating rather than resolving any problems. Programs must be prepared to answer such concerns. For example, programs aimed at serving a particular minority, racial or ethnic group need to be able to clearly articulate why it is important for children to spend time in an ethnic-specific setting, and how that setting will support the ability of children to eventually participate in multiethnic situations. Observers may question the difference between these kinds of enrollment policies aimed at protecting minority children from racism and racist practices by which the dominant group would exclude children of other backgrounds, which is illegal.

Programs that intentionally create a multiethnic setting may also find their policies questioned. In order to maintain a certain racial balance, such programs might admit one child over another because of his or her racial background, in order to create the desired multiracial care environment. This could easily result in frustration and anger on the part of the parent whose child could not be enrolled. While such scenarios are clearly undesirable, they are likely to occur given limitations in the number of child care slots. Programs must be prepared to explain to disappointed parents the challenge of weighing the needs of the group and the needs of the individual child.

Challenge: Dealing with funding limitations

Decisions about ethnic composition are often not, however, entirely up to the discretion of the staff and director. The way a program is funded can have a significant impact on its ability to enroll an ethnically diverse or ethnically specific population of children. Providers need to understand the implications of their program funding sources. In California, for example, funding for state-subsidized child development programs that meet eligibility guidelines are administered by the California Department of Education. According to these guidelines, programs must give priority to families with the lowest income and highest risk of child abuse and neglect. Race is not considered an appropriate criterion. Given the difficulties of monitoring whether race is being used for the purposes of exclusion, many may view this as an appropriate public policy. At the same time, programs should be aware that this stipulation does not prevent a program from trying to influence the composition of its group through its recruitment activities. Programs can engage in special efforts to encourage families from particular groups to enroll. They can, for example, publicize the program in community-based organizations and churches, develop flyers and brochures in the target home languages, or advertise in the ethnic media. What is prohibited is the use of race/ethnicity as criteria for deciding which families should be allowed to enroll once they have filled out an application.

Program fees can also have an impact on the racial composition of a program. If a program is funded entirely through parent fees, then enrollment will be limited to children from middle and high income families. Given the close intersection between race and class, in many communities this may mean most of the children enrolled in a fee-for-service program will be white. Some programs, such as Step One School in Berkeley, have addressed this issue by offering scholarships to families whose presence will help to diversify their population. Programs which are completely reliant upon subsidized slots may also have problems with diversification if all of the low income families in the immediate vicinity are of a particular ethnic background. Other programs, like Centro VIDA, have some slots funded by the state and others by parents' fees. Some programs, such as the Hilltop Parent Co-op, are able to offer fee reductions and scholarships for parents in exchange for volunteer time. In the case of Hilltop, this is possible in part because the parents conduct a variety of ongoing fundraising activities for the center.

We have described different approaches to distributing children and adults of different racial backgrounds in programs to help children develop positive racial identity and to prevent the development of racism. We believe that there is no one right way. Programs must look at the needs of the communities they are serving, and directors and staff must examine their own beliefs about race and racism to build a program that works for everyone.

Chapter 3
Principles of Quality Care in a Diverse Society

Principle Two: Build Upon the Cultures of Families and Promote Respect and Cross-Cultural Understanding Among Children

At Hintil Kuu Ca, which means "House of Children" in the Pomo Indian language, Native American symbols and images are integrated into all teaching materials. When learning to count, children at this child development center created by parents in Oakland use feathers instead of apples. They play "concentration" (a matching card game) using different Native American tribal symbols and pictures of baskets, pottery and drums. Children glue colored tissue paper on construction paper, recreating the traditional design patterns of the tribe they are currently studying. During circle time, a teacher brings out a drum and gently beats it. The children sing Paiute, Miwok, Hopi and Navajo songs with her.

Culture is core to the life of a child, family and community. Rootedness in the family culture is vital to a child's healthy development. It helps to sustain a sense of connection to family and the larger community during childhood and later in life. Many cultural attributes, especially those which are most subtle, such as the way relationships are built and sustained, are acquired naturally and subconsciously as a child is being raised by family and community members. A strong cultural foundation can also help build a child's capacity to forge relationships across cultures. A strong sense of identity and security within the family/community may lead to openness to new people and ideas.

One of this country's greatest strengths lies in the potential to draw upon the knowledge, skills and insights of the diverse cultural groups living here. Rather than be limited to "one way" of doing things, we have the opportunity to learn many ways of carrying out tasks, solving problems and understanding the world as it grows more and more cosmopolitan.

But we can only benefit from the strengths of the diverse cultures in our midst if the succeeding generations are prepared to do so. We need children who are able to appreciate their own cultures and learn from others, as well as to negotiate the differences they will inevitably encounter. We need to help children recognize what they hold in common, so they can build strong communities across cultural boundaries. We also need to ensure that children learn about and understand the essential elements of their cultural heritage so that they are free as they grow up to make informed decisions about what they will retain and what they will adapt.

WHAT IS CULTURE?

Culture as we use it in this book refers to the values, beliefs and traditions of a group—the set of rules that, to varying degrees, guide the behavior of members of the group. The culture of a group is not static—it is constantly evolving. Cultures adapt and change as a result of how the group is treated—positively or negatively—within the larger society and through exposure to values, practices and traditions of other cultural groups. A group can be defined by many different factors, including racial experience, nation of origin, religion, socioeconomic status, generation in the United States and shared experience speaking a language that is not the dominant one in a society.

Individuals and families often have been shaped or abide by the norms of more than one culture. Marriages across cultural groups, for example, are resulting in a growing number of children being raised by parents with a cultural mix of parenting beliefs and practices. Furthermore, as the lives of parents change during the years of child rearing, the parents' expressions of values, beliefs and family practices may also change, so that even within a child's family, the way culture is experienced may be different at different times.

Some cultural traits are very obvious, such as traditional clothes, foods and celebrations. Other manifestations are more subtle, such as the way culture shapes values, world perspectives and patterns of human interaction. Child rearing beliefs and practices—how a mother feeds and toilet-trains her child, or which learning styles a caregiver emphasizes (rote-memorization or active exploration of materials, etc.)—are deeply rooted in culture. Jayanthi Mistry writes:

> *The way parents arrange the daily routines and schedules at home conveys to children appropriate behaviors, beliefs and attitudes of the family and cultural community that should be learned. Culture has direct impact on the skills children learn from routines.*

Parents and caregivers are often unaware of the countless subtle ways that their actions and beliefs reflect their cultural roots. Julie Olsen Edwards of Cabrillo College recalled:

> *When I was in graduate school, one of my best friends was from India. After we had spent many months studying together and learning to trust each other, she finally got up the courage to ask me, "Why are you Americans so cold to your children?" I couldn't figure out what she was talking about and asked her to explain. "Oh," she said, her voice filled with sorrow, "you make them sleep all by themselves in separate rooms! How can you do that to a tiny child?"*

Cecelia Alvarado, director of the Early Childhood Department at Santa Barbara City College and past president of the California Association for the Education of Young Children, commented:

Working with children over the years, I've been struck with the different ways that parents comfort their children. Some parents sit down next to a child and talk about what happened. Another might rub the hurt foot. The problem comes in when we start judging the different approaches. When I was at Migrant Head Start and a child was crying, the mom came rushing over and held the child and offered him food for comfort. It was easy to think, "Isn't she just reinforcing the child's dependence?" We were all from the same culture, but as ECE people we were trained to see independence as the key.

For children from families with different cultural foundations than the dominant society, it can be a struggle to maintain cultural roots. In the United States, the dominant society is rooted in an Anglo European, white, Christian experience. According to Lynch and Hanson, values which characterize the dominant culture of the U.S. are:

1. The importance of individualism and privacy
2. A belief in the equality of individuals
3. Informality in interactions with others
4. An emphasis on the future, change and progress
5. Belief in the general goodness of humanity
6. An emphasis on time and punctuality
7. High regard for achievement, action, work and materials
8. Pride in being direct and assertive.

Other values commonly acknowledged as characteristic of dominant U.S. culture include meritocracy—or the belief that those with ability will rise to the top—and the right to freedom of speech.

While some of these values are shared to varying degrees by other cultures, they are not universally accepted. Even when values may be basically harmonious, cultural groups may realize them through different behaviors and practices. For example, education may be prized by many groups, but some cultures believe children should question and develop their own thinking in order to become educated, and others believe that the teacher is never to be questioned, even by a parent.

Caregivers Can Make a Difference

The values and accompanying behaviors of the dominant culture are taught through schools, emphasized by institutional policies and practices, and promoted by the media. For children to learn about these values is not in itself a problem. But, unless adults are careful, the inundation of these values to the exclusion of others can result in some children feeling that their cultural ways are inferior. After all, children from the non-dominant culture have very limited opportunities beyond their homes to learn about their own family cultures in the first place. Meanwhile, white children, who are not taught to respect and appreciate other cultures, assume that theirs is the superior and only appropriate way.

Traditionally, it has depended greatly on the parents' capacity to help young children to develop a strong sense of cultural identity and to learn to interact respectfully with people of other cultures. Parents who desire this for their children have had to strongly emphasize it in their child rearing, in spite of societal messages working against them. But, given the amount of time children now spend in care—and the younger ages in which children are in care—parents no longer can do this job alone. Whether they realize it or not, child care providers tremendously impact the development of cultural identity and appreciation in young children.

Traditionally, it has depended greatly on the parents' capacity to help young children to develop a strong sense of cultural identity and to learn to interact respectfully with people of other cultures.

Providers are often unaware of the ways that their culture(s) conflict or harmonize with a child's family. Providers working in cross-cultural settings may not necessarily understand the cultures of all the families. Ron Lally, director of the Center for Child and Family Studies at Far West Laboratory for Educational Research and Development, believes that the risks are greatest for infants and toddlers who are at the beginning stages of identity development. In his article, "The Impact of Child Care Policies and Infant/Toddler Identity Formation," Lally says:

> *When infants are cared for by caregivers from a different cultural background, particularly by a caregiver from the dominant culture, very often the child has his background either subtly or blatantly challenged. This is done often from the best of intentions. Different ways of doing things are often seen as strange. A child may become torn between how he is expected to behave at home—not to make such a mess—and how he is expected to behave in care—to touch and feel most anything. Issues of feeding, sleeping, toileting and the like often become issues of conflict between home and care, with the young child caught between. Sending children mixed messages is not the greatest danger; early in their development, children begin to discern that certain behaviors are more appropriate in different settings. But without careful attention, over time, children from non-dominant culture families are likely to learn that what happens in one setting is considered not simply different, but bad.*

When providers are of the same culture(s) of a family, the transmission of culture may occur rather naturally—both consciously and subconsciously. However, great variations exist among families within cultural groups, and it is essential that providers not assume that because some people share a language, religion or ethnicity, they will necessarily agree on child rearing values. (For suggested strategies, please see our Principle on Parent-Provider Relations.)

Whether or not they share the background of families, providers can help to affirm children's identity and build upon the cultures of all the families in care.

Providers can use their position to broaden children's cultural horizons and increase acceptance of others. Providers can also model for children how to respectfully negotiate cultural differences, which is not always an easy process, particularly when strongly held points of view and values are involved.

Promising Strategies and Challenges

This chapter highlights innovative approaches used by early childhood providers and trainers that affirm the cultural identity of children and also promote cross-cultural understanding among children. Some of the challenges involved in this work are also described.

Strategy 1

Use program activities to validate the cultural backgrounds of children and to promote cross-cultural understanding and respect.

> *We have multicultural potlucks where we try to represent the nationalities of all the children in the center. Even though I am not a great cook, I try to make a cultural dish. The parents share dances, songs and photographs. It helps the children to see we are different and why we are different. Each group gets to do their own thing. Last year I made costumes for my daughters and three other African American children. A father from Kenya taught them a song. It was part of the entertainment for the African American family potluck which is held around Martin Luther King's Birthday as part of our Black History/Culture Week. The center also holds a culture week during Chinese New Year and Cinco de Mayo.*
>
> —Bernita Toney, African American parent at the Davis Child Development Center

California Tomorrow found many early childhood programs incorporating care activities that sought to: (1) validate the cultural backgrounds of children, and/or (2) promote cross-cultural respect and understanding. There was a range in exactly how programs addressed and balanced these objectives, which are both critical regardless of the demographics of a program.

Marilyn Allen runs a family child care program serving children of diverse ethnic backgrounds in Torrance. She built her program on the belief that it is important for children to feel proud of their own cultures and to learn to respect others as well. During circle time, she reads the youngsters stories about children in other countries as well as about the cultures of the children in her group. A few of the Japanese children in her care have moved back and forth a few times between the United States and Japan. Marilyn invites these children to tell stories and memo-

ries about their trips back to their ancestral country. This encourages the children to feel proud of their roots and exposes others in the program to information about different ways of life.

The most common approach to validating children's cultural identity among the programs we visited was the celebration of major cultural holidays such as Cinco de Mayo, Kwaanza, Chinese New Year, etc. This has become such a popular practice that major educational companies now supply kits with traditional materials to be used for the occasions. Providers should try to work with parents and other individuals of the related group when developing activities. This will demonstrate respect for authentically representing cultures. It should also be remembered that families within cultures celebrate holidays differently.

Great effort should be made to ensure that traditional holidays are not celebrated in an offensive manner. At Thanksgiving, for instance, a growing number of educators feel that the traditional classroom portrayals of pilgrims and Indians deny or obfuscate the detrimental impact of the settling of this country by Europeans upon Native American peoples. Some try to also use the time to learn about Native American tribes.

Many programs incorporate dancing, music, arts and crafts of different cultures on a regular basis, frequently inviting parents, relatives or community members to make presentations. Games and learning tools from different cultures are also sometimes used to help children gain academic skills. For example, some programs use the game Mancala, which is of African origin, to teach children both beginning math concepts and African culture. In the Fresno Native American program, buckwheat kernels, symbolic in tribal cultures, are used as counting manipulatives. In these cases, the learning tools not only honor the cultures but spark further dialogue about cultural issues among staff. In one culturally diverse program we visited, the Japanese tradition of Girls' Day was celebrated. This activity not only validated the culture of the Japanese children in care, but promoted understanding among the children who were not Japanese.

If a program serves only one ethnic group, other steps may be necessary to ensure that both goals—validating the cultural backgrounds of children and promoting cross-cultural respect and understanding—are met. At the Marin Learning Center, a predominantly African American program, special attention is given to marking occasions important to the African American community, such as African American History Month and Kwaanza. Once a week, an African American drummer arrives at the center with traditional instruments to teach the children music and dances from Africa. Staff at this center also take the children on trips to different ethnic neighborhoods in the community so they can be exposed early on to other cultural groups; staff members consider this important for the children to succeed in a diverse society. Ebony Ashby, a teaching assistant in the program, explained that this "gives kids a sense of the world outside of their home."

The Marin Center example demonstrates that even when a program serves a particular ethnic group, an emphasis on cross-cultural understanding is possible and appropriate. For instance, Hintil Kuu Ca, described at the beginning of this chapter, serves children and families of different Native American tribes in the Bay Area. Because it serves an urban community rather than a specific reservation, the center works with more than 60 different tribes. As part of the curriculum, children are taught to recognize and appreciate the differences between the beliefs, lifestyles, languages and traditions of the various tribes.

Challenges to Strategy 1

Challenge: Designing age-appropriate activities

Providers need to remember to shift from an adult orientation and develop cultural activities which are concrete, experiential and appropriate to children's level of cognitive development.

Cultural activities that adults might enjoy, such as listening to a lecture about the origin of a tradition or the history of an ethnic group, have limited value for young children. Young children cannot yet understand abstract concepts that they cannot touch, feel, see or create themselves, and they do not yet think in terms of timelines or geographic distances.

As with other learning activities, providers need to remember to shift from an adult orientation and develop cultural activities which are concrete, experiential and appropriate to children's level of cognitive development. A growing number of excellent resources, such as the *Anti-Bias Curriculum*, *Roots and Wings* and *Helping Children Love Themselves* (see bibliography), now offer ideas and suggestions for age appropriate cross-cultural activities. These resources tend to focus on older children, however. There is still a great need for research and development to support the cultures of the growing numbers of infants and toddlers entering care.

Challenge: Balancing validation of the cultures of children in the care setting with promotion of understanding of cultures not represented in care

Several programs we visited seemed to be struggling to find the appropriate balance between focusing on the cultures of the children in care and teaching about other cultures. For example, one program centered its entire curriculum around teaching the children about other countries. They spent up to six weeks studying about the plants, animals, foods and costumes of a particular country, starting with Europe. Even though the program served an ethnically diverse group of children, no conscious effort was made to match the curriculum focus with the children. The cultures of the children in care were only drawn upon if a certain child's country of origin happened to be the topic of study. In this case, the curriculum was designed out of the best of intents—to increase awareness of the different world cultures. The drawback was that it may have been too abstract for young children. Connecting children to their own cultures and the cultures of the children around them gives them a concrete experience of cultural difference. Then, by extension, they may be better able to understand that there are other people and cultural practices, even if there are not children or adults from those cultures in the program. The center also missed an opportunity to boost the cultural identity and self-worth of some children by not making sure to cover their countries of heritage while they were in care.

We also found ethnic specific programs which appeared to pay little attention to how they might equip children to understand and negotiate the cultural traditions and beliefs of other groups. This may be because some providers in ethnic specific programs feel that their role in preparing children for a diverse society is to first ensure that they have a solid understanding and sense of their own culture. Because children are unquestionably being exposed to the dominant culture outside the program and will be immersed in the dominant culture when they reach primary school, the limited resources of the center are spent on nurturing the child's home culture.

Clearly determining the appropriate balance between a focus on the cultures of children in care and teaching about other cultural groups is a program-by-program responsibility. The demographics of the population as well as the philosophy of the program will weigh in the decision. It is our sense, however, that all programs—whether they are ethnic specific or multiethnic—need to develop a strategy for addressing both goals of validation and cross-cultural understanding.

Challenge: Moving beyond the most obvious cultural attributes

While holiday celebrations and classroom cultural activities are important, they only represent the most obvious aspects of culture and tradition. Because they are the most quickly identified, providers can easily limit their focus to these types of activities and fail to pay attention to the much more subtle and sometimes even more important ways in which culture influences what is being taught to children through daily caregiving routines.

Strategy 2

Understand how culture influences your approach to caring for children.

Most of us cannot precisely explain why we do things a certain way—we just know that we do it and it seems to feel right. Usually these attributes have grown with us from childhood.

Rose Chou is a Taiwanese early childhood educator. She formerly provided a part-time preschool program for children in her neighborhood in Rohnert Park, a suburban community in Northern California. The racial background of the children in her care at the time we visited was white. During the snack of sliced apples and popcorn, the children sat around the table and patiently waited to be served. As Rose sat at the table observing the children's table manners, she asked them to bring their bowls closer to their mouths, as is customary in Chinese culture so that food can be scooped out with chopsticks. The children did so, although in this case they were eating with their fingers. Here, young white children were being taught

Excerpt from
CULTURE AND LEARNING IN INFANCY: IMPLICATIONS FOR CAREGIVING
by Jayanthi Mistry

TO RECOGNIZE THE MANNER in which you affect children's learning, try a self-observation exercise. When involved in an activity with an infant or toddler (for example, when building a block tower or working a jack-in-the-box together) try to note mentally the role you are playing. What is the purpose behind your various actions? Jot down notes later. Keep the following questions in mind as you take mental notes:

1. Note when and how the child indicates a desire for assistance from you. How do you respond to the request? For example, do you encourage the child to try to complete the activity without help, or do you immediately provide help? What kind of message does your response give the child?

2. When you help a child, do you tend to do so verbally or nonverbally? Do you demonstrate actions for the child? Do you give explicit instructions or directions to the child? Do you take over the activity or let the child remain in charge?

3. How do you expect the child to respond to your help? Is it appropriate for the child to sit quietly and watch or listen to you? Or is it appropriate for the child to try a new action right away and learn from trial and error? Do you expect the child to be a cooperative partner with you or to be as independent of you as possible? ❧

Chinese cultural eating behaviors. However, in U.S. culture, people leave their bowls on the table, and children may even be admonished for lifting their bowls to their mouths. When we noted to Rose that she was teaching children the table manners grounded in her culture, her response was one of surprise and interest:

> *I didn't realize that I was doing that. I was teaching the children to eat the way I was taught.*

As an early childhood education professional, Rose has given great thought and attention to diversity issues. Yet in this case she discovered a new angle of her own practice that she had not yet fully reflected upon, because, as she put it, her culture was so innate. There would be no harm in a provider teaching children to eat with bowls to their mouths, but the key would be to be aware that it may well be different from what the children are expected to do at home. Providers and parents should communicate together so children are not "blamed" for behavior about which they may be receiving mixed messages.

Rose's story contrasts to the experience of a provider at another center we visited. In this case, the provider, who was Filipina, started to correct a Chinese boy for eating "improperly" because he brought his bowl up to his mouth to eat. The boy said, "But this is how I eat at home." The boy's response helped her realize that she had incorrectly assumed that the way she was taught to eat also applied to the child.

Understanding the impact of culture is often most difficult for teachers who are members of the dominant culture. Because they are surrounded by a society that embraces their patterns of thought and behavior, they can easily assume what they do is simply "normal" as opposed to a manifestation of a particular cultural perspective. For example, a caregiver may think it is only acceptable to place a baby in a crib in another room to sleep, not realizing that the baby is much more accustomed to falling asleep with the sounds and noises of other people around her.

A similar lack of awareness can be found among teachers in programs that predominantly serve members of their same ethnic group. Because they are surrounded by adults who approach caregiving in a similar manner, they do not have the opportunity to reflect on how child rearing practices might differ by cultural groups. Even when providers are exposed to a person who operates differently, they may not recognize how those differences are related to culture, particularly if they have limited exposure to members of another cultural group. During one of our site visits, an African American operator of a family child care program talked about how her Vietnamese teaching assistant tended to be extremely overprotective. In this case, the provider attributed the difference to individual preference. A deeper analysis might suggest that the actions of the Vietnamese provider were rooted in a cultural perspective that places a far greater emphasis on adult-directed interaction than on promoting a child's sense of independence.

In the previous article, Jayanthi Mistry offers an exercise to help providers reflect upon and identify the subtle ways they may be influencing children's learning.

The process of reflection on the cultural embeddedness of care cannot stop with the individual. It must also be applied to what happens programmatically. For example, the decision to use a curriculum which stresses individual areas, individual activities and individual choice reflects a cultural emphasis on individualism. On the other hand, a program which pays much greater attention to collective experience and the importance of being a member of a community is more culturally focused on group values. Our Workforce chapter further explores the influence of culture on child development theory. It is critical for providers to understand how culture influences the approach to care or the overall philosophy of a program. This understanding can help prevent a provider from assuming that there is only one way of interacting with a child, and to recognize situations where a parent or family member may use a different approach.

Challenges to Strategy 2

Challenge: Limited opportunities for providers to reflect upon how their approach to caregiving is embedded in culture

Our research suggests that providers rarely have opportunities to think about the impact of culture on caregiving approaches on the individual level, and even less often on the program and curriculum level. While most recognize that child

Anthropology for Four-Year-Olds

by Julie Olsen Edwards

MY EXPERIENCE WITH very young children has taught me that they have great difficulty with abstract concepts, such as culture, ethnicity, ancestors, history, even group identity (except their own). One approach to supporting their understanding of human diversity has been to work on the theme of "We are all the same, we are all different." This theme is carried out all year long. All people eat, but they eat different foods. All babies are carried, but they are carried in different ways. All people sleep, but they sleep on many different objects. All people move, but they move in different ways.

Sometimes these themes are built into ongoing curriculum—a baby curriculum (there are many different ways people take care of babies), a curriculum on human mobility (we move in many ways, sometimes use crutches, wheelchairs, braces), a bread curriculum (everyone eats some kind of bread, let's make corn bread, tortillas, bagels, pita). The playhouse dishes may include a wok and lacquerware, or a matate and tinware. After all, we all cook, we just do it differently.

Often the theme is repeated and deepened in "teachable moments" throughout the day. "All the children are painting, but you each made a different picture." "Everyone at the table wanted a snack, but some of you liked the orange juice, and some wanted water." Human sameness and difference become a major topic of conversation. In this atmosphere, it is natural that we also look at the differences that create such schisms and injury in our world. We all have skin, it has many colors—and most of the names for skin color don't make a lot of sense! We all have eyes.

care practices can differ across families and individuals, they generally were unaware that differences can be connected to group cultural norms. Few had spent time considering how their own caregiving strategies reflected their own upbringing and cultural values. Opportunities to focus on and talk about such issues were clearly needed.

Additionally, if programs focused on children of one cultural background, it required concerted effort for providers to notice and learn about differences, given the absence of a diversity of cultures among families and providers.

The providers most articulate about the cultural embeddedness of care tended to have worked in situations where they learned to adapt and respond to the cultural practices of another group, either because they lived in another country or were a cultural minority in their own community. Most staff we interviewed were unable to recognize or discuss the values and cultural foundations of the most commonly used curricula, such as High Scope, Montessori and NAEYC guidelines on developmentally appropriate practice.

There are many colors, shapes, and some have glasses. We all have words, but we have different words, different languages (still, we all say, Mama!).

Given young children's difficulties with abstract ideas about things they cannot touch, taste or experience, it is important to ground teaching about culture in everyday common issues. We focus on family as the basic unit. "In some families, grandma and grandpa live with the children and parents. In some families, they live in separate houses, or even very far away." "In some families, people speak Spanish at home, and in some families, people speak Cantonese." "In some families, big sister cooks dinner, and in some families, daddy cooks dinner, and in some families, everyone cooks dinner together." The tone of this approach is delight, interest and respect. We knew we were getting through when we heard Audra trying to become part of the fantasy play, saying, "Well, in some families, there is one Momma, but in this family, there can be two!"

The basic rule in our school is that we don't hurt each other's feelings or things. It's important to recognize that we all have feelings, but that we may feel differently about the same things. Hurtful comments, stereotypes and racial/cultural misinformation are challenged with the clear understanding that it's the results of an action that count. Monica didn't feel mad or hurtful when she said, "he's dirty" about a dark skinned child. But her words hurt anyhow, and her information was incorrect. So we correct the misinformation ("no, his skin is darker than yours, but it is not dirty"), help both children understand the hurtful behavior—and start another version of the "same and different" curriculum. Everyone has skin, but it comes in many colors.

Celebrating holidays is often seen as a way to broaden children's cultural perspective. There are, however, so many holidays in the year that the children's curriculum can become driven by one event after another until they lose all significance. Holiday curriculum out of context can lead to a "tourist" mentality. "Let's go visit those strange exotic people who put on costumes, eat strange foods and have parties. And then we come back to the everyday world of us ordinary folks." This approach leads to the misunderstanding that culture is about special events rather than about how people live.

If a program does Christmas and Chanukah and Kwaanza and Solstice, in most three-year-olds' minds, they become mixed up as "all those Christmas things." If a program celebrates only those holidays celebrated by families in the program, children can develop the sense that their way of celebrating is the "real" way and everything else is strange and "other." Ignoring holidays is to pretend that ritual and celebration are not significant, central parts of families' lives. One solution to this dilemma is to make holiday discussions specific and concrete. "When Eric's family celebrates Chanukah, they sing a prayer while lighting the Menorah. When Julie's family celebrates Chanukah, they dedicate each candle to a freedom fighter." "When Markeem's family celebrates Easter, they sing special songs at church. When Emily's family celebrates Easter, they color eggs and have a picnic." After all, we are all alike, everyone celebrates something. After all, we are all different, even when we celebrate the same holidays, there are many ways to do so. And it is so interesting how we are different. And so wonderful how we are all the same. ❧

Strategy 3

Use community resources to find out about the cultural practices and beliefs of families.

In addition to reflecting about oneself and one's program, cultural sensitivity requires learning about the different cultures and child rearing techniques of the families and communities of the children in care. Workshops, books and other types of information about the history and practices of groups can offer a good beginning. Providers can also learn about respectful practices by calling upon people in the community, for example, from neighborhood organizations, religious centers, health clinics and schools.

Learning from community members includes hearing them when they ask the program not to do something. In one center we visited which serves white families and members of a Native American tribe, the white director detected serious concerns on the part of the tribe's families about the center's role in reinforcing certain cultural traditions. This director had a history in the community and established relationships with the tribal leaders. She found that the tribal community felt that the center should not attempt to impart the complexities of certain traditions because of their experience of seeing their culture exploited by white society. The leaders preferred to keep responsibility within the tribe for imparting cultural traditions to the next generation. This information helped the director better understand the community she served and to work on developing a curriculum that respected tribal concerns.

Challenges to Strategy 3

Challenge: Be aware of the limitations of general cultural information

While community resources can offer useful insights, it is always important to keep in mind that the values, beliefs and practices of an individual are not necessarily those of his or her cultural group, and vice versa. The definition of culture offered at the beginning of this chapter suggests that the culture of a family is influenced by a number of factors, such as national origin, socioeconomic status, length of time in the United States, religious orientation, experience with racial discrimination, etc. The complexity of culture must be remembered, or it becomes too easy to assume that people or resource materials speak for all of a group— when they do not. Caregivers should be wary of over-reliance upon single individuals, or upon resource materials that provide information only about general behaviors.

Strategy 4

Hire and draw upon the knowledge of staff from the cultures of the children and families served.

The Live Oak Migrant Head Start Program, in a rural community in Northern California, serves Mexican and Punjabi migrant families. The staff at the center reflects both cultures. In their interviews with us, staff members talked about the value of sharing knowledge and using one another to answer questions about the children and families in their care. For example, when a Punjabi boy appeared at the center with his hair pulled up into a ball, the Mexican teachers learned that this hairstyle, called a ghuti, was common among boys of this East Indian culture. Balwinder Singh, the family service worker, observed:

> *Culture is talked about all the time. It is part of daily conversation. It is through cultural sharing and communication that we learn about our differences as well as our similarities.*

While a caregiver from a different cultural background can be caring and responsive with a child, a caregiver who shares a child's cultural background is more likely to naturally follow practices harmonious with those of the home. Even if a provider who shares the background of certain children does not directly care for them, she or he can suggest effective strategies for working with the children and preventing potential cultural misunderstandings. Providers should again, however, be wary of assuming that one staff person's beliefs necessarily hold true for all of the families perceived to be from the same general cultural background.

The presence of staff from various cultural groups does not assure others will benefit from their knowledge unless dialogue is encouraged in the center (see our Principal on Dialogue). Discussing issues of racial, cultural and linguistic differences is not easy. Child care facilities must build supportive, safe climates where staff feel comfortable sharing diverse perspectives and raising concerns. Rosa Paras, center director/teacher of the Live Oak Migrant Head Start Program, uses a specific technique to draw upon the knowledge of the Punjabi staff:

> *Talking about culture is a sensitive issue. I am very careful about how I seek information about cultural differences from the teachers. I don't ask the teachers, "Why do you do this or that"... rather I begin by saying, "In my culture we do... What do you do in yours?"*

Creating specific opportunities for staff to share their expertise can make it easier for them to talk about issues of race and culture. For example, staff from different cultural groups can be invited to make presentations, and time can be devoted regularly during staff meetings to discuss the cultural appropriateness of activities and policies. Such conversations help staff to recognize common values across cultures and to expand their appreciation and understanding of different perspectives and approaches.

Challenges to Strategy 4

Challenge: Hiring culturally reflective staff with limited numbers of staff positions

It is not always easy or possible to compose a staff that reflects all of the cultural backgrounds of the children in a program. Sometimes the demographic composition of children in a program rapidly shifts, but no positions are open that might be filled by someone from the incoming community. Also, typically the number of cultural groups represented among the children served is far greater than the number of staff positions. Clearly, there are no easy answers to either of these common situations. However, programs should keep in mind concerns about cultural composition when making hiring decisions, and if possible plan ahead for new populations of children that may be entering care.

Challenge: Addressing staff fears about discussing cultural issues

We found that work on diversity issues in programs often seemed to be stymied by people's fears of talking about their own culture or asking others about theirs because of fear of offending or making a mistake. But not talking about issues of culture can cause serious communication breakdowns among staff. For example, at one center which primarily served Jewish children, non-Jewish staff were uncertain about what types of celebrations were acceptable to the Jewish families and community. As Halloween approached, non-Jewish teachers were unsure whether it was appropriate to talk about Halloween, which is rooted in ancient European Christianity, the eve of All Saints Day.

Sometimes, when a provider is in the minority, it can seem easier to conform to the practices of the majority group rather than raise concerns or questions about what might be a more appropriate course of action. Ebony Ashby, an African American provider, shared the following experience:

> *There are very different expectations about the way Black children and adults interact. In my community, you can just look at a Black child and they will sit down. At the all-white center where I used to work, there was a child who was totally out of control. The white teacher let him scream and hit her. Her response was, "I'm not going to get angry, you will just get tired." The teacher felt she wanted to let the child vent his*

anger. I thought her response was shocking. But, at the time I was young, I just wanted to fit in. So I changed the way I interacted with the children.

In some cases, communication is hampered by a lack of strong facilitation skills and activities that help to break through people's fears. A fundamental barrier for many programs was the sheer lack of time for providers to meet about any subject, including cultural diversity. Staff meetings were impeded for many programs by a variety of factors, including lack of resources to compensate staff for meeting time, over-extended staff and scheduling differences. Many more strategies and challenges affecting dialogue in child care programs are discussed in our Principles on Parent-Provider Relations and Dialogue.

Strategy 5

Work with family members to ensure that the provider and the program take into account the cultural practices and beliefs of the families.

How do parents handle particular situations when they are at home? What are typical child rearing strategies in their community?

Families are usually the best and most accurate sources of information about individual children. Intake interviews, which will be covered in more depth in our Principle on Parent-Provider Relations, provide one opportunity to begin gathering such information.

In addition to these one-time opportunities, staff needs to find ways to incorporate talking to parents about their traditions into daily communications. How do parents handle particular situations when they are at home? What are typical child rearing strategies in their community? At the Marie Kaiser Center, for example, teaching assistant Jennifer Brown explained that she often asks parents for advice when her efforts to work with their baby don't seem to be effective. In one case, she was puzzled about how to comfort a fussy Afghani baby who often cried and always wanted to be held. She asked the mother, "What do you do at home to help her stay content and relaxed without being held?" The mother replied, "We wrap her up in a blanket, hold her for a bit and then put her down. It makes her feel secure and loved." Jennifer took the mother's suggestion and it worked immediately. She also learned that this was a typical practice among the family's ethnic group in Afghanistan.

Providers should pay close attention when parents seem uncertain or uncomfortable with a caregiving practice. This is often a sign that the parents would normally respond to their child in a different way at home. This is an important opportunity to ask the parents about their beliefs. On the flip side, it is also common for a provider to feel uncomfortable with the caregiving approach of the parent. In either of these cases, providers and parents need to find the time to talk about their respective beliefs.

While most will agree that providers and parents need to be aware of each other's caregiving approaches, there is little consensus about what steps should be taken if differences are detected. Is it the role of the provider to teach the child how to adapt to a different cultural setting? Is it appropriate to allow the child to continue behaving as s/he feels most comfortable, provided the behavior does not disrupt the other children in care? Is the role of the provider to encourage parents to change their practices to match those of the center? Should the provider change practice so that it mirrors what occurs at home? Should the goal be to encourage children to be able to behave differently in two different settings? How does a provider help a child feel okay about the differences?

Our visits with providers suggested they took a variety of approaches. University of Southern California Child Care Center teacher Aileen Valino, who is of Filipino descent, works with two- and three-year-olds and spends a lot of time potty training the children. One year, she was startled to discover that one Chinese child in her care did not wear underwear. When she asked the child about this, he didn't seem to know what she was talking about. The same question arose for her the next year with a second Chinese boy. At this point, Aileen made the connection that this was perhaps not the peculiar behavior of one child or family, but a cultural difference. A discussion with the parents confirmed her suspicion. Wearing underwear was not the norm in their home; in mainland China where they were from, children typically wear clothes with slit bottoms so that they can easily go to the bathroom. This information enabled Aileen to understand the situation as opposed to being critical of the parents for failing to appropriately dress their child. Ultimately, she came to the conclusion that it wasn't necessary for the child to wear underwear while at the center since that was what he was accustomed to in his home.

Should the provider change practice so that it mirrors what occurs at home? Should the goal be to encourage children to be able to behave differently in two different settings?

Other providers voiced the belief that it was important for them to help children make transitions. For example, when a child first starts in her program, Laurel Ross of the USC child care center encourages families to bring whatever they want to make the child feel comfortable and to do as much as they can with the child—sit, eat, clean up. The person who accompanied one young boy during his first few days at the center was his grandmother—who had played a major caregiving role with him up to that point, and who would soon be returning to her home in another country. In these initial days, the boy experienced a mix of both center routines and many of his usual interactions with his grandmother. By the time the grandmother was ready to leave the country, the child had adjusted to life in the center, and she had an opportunity to make some peace with the separation.

Food is one of the most recognized manifestations of culture, and many of the programs we visited sought to provide children with the types of food they were accustomed to at home. At the Live Oak Migrant Head Start, the cook makes a point to serve Mexican as well as Punjabi foods. Mexican herself, she already knew how to cook the foods of her own culture, but initially she had no experience in preparing Punjabi foods. So, she asked parents for recipes. Now, often parents from both cultures will come into the kitchen to help the cook prepare traditional foods. They even ask the cook for recipes to prepare at home.

Programs run by the Foundation Center for Phenomenological Research, which focused on affirming the cultures of children by training parents to become provid-

ers, made it a point to hire a cook from the community to prepare the food served at each center. The Foundation Center also took this a step further. Food is not necessarily healthy just because it is what a family traditionally eats in their home. So cooks who worked in these programs were given extensive training in preparing food with children's health in mind. The cooks were then encouraged to experiment with making traditional foods with more nutritional ingredients.

At some centers, these types of cultural food adaptations were much more difficult because they weren't equipped to prepare their own meals. Food was sent to the centers from other facilities—e.g., a central kitchen or the cafeteria of a nearby school—so staff had little control over what was cooked. Still, some staff were able to develop creative ways to get around the constraints. For example, when a Head Start teacher realized that many of her Vietnamese children weren't eating lunch because it was so different from their traditional foods, she asked to purchase a rice cooker for her room. This way, no matter what type of food was sent to the center by the main cafeteria, she could use the cooker to provide rice with every meal without placing a burden on the kitchen staff.

What these examples suggest is that the process of working with families is not simple—it is complex, depending upon many variables. For example, exchanges can take place between individuals, between groups of individuals, between a parent and provider, or between a program and a group of parents. The article by Janet Gonzalez-Mena at the end of this chapter helps caregivers look at ways to improve sensitivity to cultural and individual differences and increase communication across cultural barriers.

Challenges to Strategy 5

Challenge: Dealing with strongly held differences of opinion

Clearly, one of the most difficult and touchy scenarios is when a provider finds out about the cultural beliefs and practices of a family and ultimately realizes that she or he feels strongly opposed to them. Striking a balance between standing up for what you believe in and respecting a family's culture is not always easy. What should a provider do, for example, if she discovers that a child has been whipped with a belt by one of the parents? Is this part of the family's culture, child abuse, or both? What about when a parent allows a baby to "cry herself out," without comforting her? How do providers build upon the cultures of the families without compromising the values they strongly hold?

In these cases, it helps if providers have carefully thought about their bottom-line. While people may disagree about the appropriateness of spanking and other physical discipline, if a situation poses danger to a child, the provider must of course respond quickly and be able to clearly articulate the rationale for the action.

But in less obvious cases, providers should seek to gain a deeper understanding of why a family may behave a certain way. "Coining" is a healing tradition practiced by some Southeast Asian cultures in which a hot coin is pressed against the skin closest to the ailing body part. The purpleness on the skin that coining leaves has caused many a non-Asian practitioner to fear child abuse. Only by learning about the cultural foundations of the families can practitioners respond appropriately to such experiences.

Behaviors are usually responses to what people have experienced in their environment. Low income families may have relatives or friends whose children have contracted lead poisoning from eating chipping paint in unattended buildings; they therefore may be much stricter about not allowing the young children to place anything in their mouths. In another example, people of color often keep a very tight reign on their children when they are in malls and department stores. While some may view this as unnecessarily strict, it often reflects the reality that minority children, especially African Americans, are more likely to be accused of shoplifting if they are seen touching items on shelves; their families too often know this from personal experience in a racist society. On the other hand, a family may continue to enforce strict codes of behavior even when they are among friends, and this too is most likely based on lifelong experiences. Talking about cultural roots can help the provider and the parent understand why and whether a particular approach to child rearing is appropriate.

In a diverse society, differences of opinion about child rearing are bound to occur—whether they are about the role and value of girls, the appropriateness of physical discipline or less volatile issues. As long as the health of the child is not at stake (which is in most cases), parents and providers sometimes must agree to disagree. Providers may disagree with parents, but they must respect their positions as parents and not let the disagreement affect the children, making them "choose sides" or feel bad about what their parents do at home. All involved must learn how to not jump to the conclusion that if someone else does something differently, then it is wrong. Learning to appreciate, understand and build upon our diversity requires all of us to question the roots of our beliefs and to be open to the beliefs of others.

Excerpt from Young Children

Taking a Culturally Sensitive Approach in Infant/Toddler Programs

by Janet Gonzalez-Mena

FOR SEVERAL YEARS I've been examining areas of disagreement surrounding infant caregiving practices—routines such as diapering, feeding, toilet-training, holding, comforting and "educating" babies (Claudill & Weinstein, 1969; Clark, 1981; Hale-Benson, 1986; Hopson & Hopson, 1990; Hsu, 1970; Tobin, Wu & Davidson, 1989). I have discovered that people—caregivers and parents alike—hold very strong views about how babies are supposed to be taken care of. These deep seated ideas are embedded in each of us and remain mostly subconscious.

My aim is to help people find ways to manage and resolve conflicts related to caregiving practices so they can make a better match. The more the adults in babies' lives work at settling disagreements, the fewer inconsistencies in approach the babies will experience. My theory is that with adults working hard to manage their conflicts, the children will be exposed to fewer culturally assaultive experiences. Not all children in care outside the family are in culturally assaultive environments, even when they are cared for by people from a variety of cultures. With the crossing and mixing of many cultures in America, many positive outcomes result. Just because a caregiver isn't always of the same culture as the infants and toddlers in his or her care doesn't necessarily mean that care will be inconsistent or that conflicts will arise between caregiver and parents. It has been my experience, however, that conflicts do occur occasionally—conflicts that stem from both cultural and individual differences. It is to the conflict situation that this article is addressed.

So what do you do when you are a caregiver and you and a parent disagree about what's good for babies? I see four outcomes to cultural conflicts (or other kinds of conflicts, for that matter) in infant/toddler caregiving situations. The first three involve movement and result in change that resolves conflict. They are:

1. Resolution through understanding and negotiation. Both parties see the other's perspective; both parties compromise.
2. Resolution through caregiver education. The caregiver sees the parents' perspective; the caregiver changes.
3. Resolution through parent education. The parent sees the caregiver's perspective; the parent changes.

The fourth outcome is no resolution. I see two scenarios here:

1. The worst scenario is that neither side sees the other's perspective; neither changes. There is no respect, and conflict continues uncontained or escalates. Sneaking around may occur, or underhanded fighting. The caregiver and the parent may hide their actions from one another, or they may draw in other parents or caregivers, getting them to take their side.
2. The best scenario is that each has a view of the other's perspective; each is sensitive and respectful but unable, because of differing values and beliefs, to change his or

her stance. Here conflict management skills come into play as both learn to cope with differences. The conflict stays aboveboard—although perhaps not always out in the open.

The fourth outcome is fairly common as people deal with diversity while hanging on to their own cultures. Conflict management skills (as opposed to conflict resolution skills) are important for all of us to learn as we go through life bumping into conflicts that can't be resolved. Handled sensitively and with respect, learning to manage these conflicts in healthy ways provides challenges that make life interesting.

Following are examples of each of these outcomes.

Resolution through understanding and negotiation—both parties see the other's perspective; both parties compromise.

Here's the scene. We have on one hand a parent who hates to see her child messy. On the other hand we have a caregiver who provides messy sensory activities. At first these two expressed angry feelings toward each other, but they were developing a relationship at the same time they clashed over this issue. They talked about their feelings and their perspectives regularly. Gradually they began to understand each other.

The caregiver educated herself. She went to some trouble to find out why being clean was so important to this parent. It took lots of talking before she understood that clean meant "decent" to this family. She found out that this family had had an experience with Child Protective Services accusing a neighbor of neglect because her child often looked dirty. It wasn't just a defense stance this family took, however. They believed that clothes indicated the quality of the family. They believed they were sending their child to "school," and a child who goes to school clean and well dressed shows the parents' respect for education. So naturally it was upsetting to them when the child was picked up wearing clothes full of grass stains, food or fingerpaint. They couldn't accept the suggestion of sending their child to school in old clothes; it didn't fit their images of decency and "school."

While the caregiver was getting educated, she was also educating the parents about the importance of sensory experiences that involve messes. Finally, they came to an agreement that the caregiver would change the clothes of the child during messy play, or at least make very sure she was covered up, so that when the parents returned they would find their child as they left her. The parents were not completely convinced that messy experiences were important, but they said it would be okay as long as their daughter's clothes weren't involved. The teacher continued to think that they were overly concerned with appearances. Neither side completely gave up on reforming the other side, but both felt okay about the arrangement.

Resolution through caregiver education—the caregiver sees the parent's perspective; the caregiver changes.

Here's the situation. The caregiver believed that babies should sleep alone in a crib—tucked away in a relatively dark, quiet spot (the nap room) (Gerber, 1988; Gonzalez-Mena & Eyer, 1989; Leach, 1987). Licensing agreed. But along came a baby who couldn't sleep alone. He cried and got very upset when put into the crib by himself. At first the caregiver thought that the baby would get used to the center's approach, but he didn't. He became distraught and refused to sleep when he was put into a crib in the nap room. Upon talking to the parents, the caregiver discovered that the baby had never slept alone in his life, and the parents didn't even have a crib. He came from a large family and was used to sleeping in the midst of activity. Actually, the caregiver had already discovered that the baby went to sleep easily in the play area on a mattress with other children snuggling or playing around him. The caregiver had no objection to letting him nap in the play area, but that approach to napping was against regulations, so going along with what the parents wanted presented a problem.

Instead of trying to convince the parents (and baby) to change, the caregiver went to work to convince licensing. She was able to get a waiver once she convinced them that she was only able to fulfill the spirit of the regulation—that each child has a right to quiet undisturbed sleep—if she didn't isolate the child in a crib in the nap room. In this case the caregiver made the changes—accommodating the wishes of the parent and the needs of the child. You might not agree that the caregiver should have done what she did, but she felt quite comfortable about what she considered to be a culturally sensitive decision.

Resolution through parent education—the parent sees the caregiver's perspective; the parent changes.

Here is the story. The caregiver kept putting babies on the floor to play with objects and toys (Gerber, 1988; Gonzalez-Mena & Eyer, 1989; Leach, 1987). She found out that most of the parents in the program believed human relationships were much more important than playing with objects and being on the floor. They wanted their babies to be held all the time. Although they complained to the caregiver, instead of stopping the practice, she started a series of discussions—both individual and group. She educated the parents about the value of freedom of movement. She knew that safety issues were a big concern for them, as well as dirt, germs and drafts. She knew that in their own homes the floor wasn't a safe place for babies. The caregiver discussed this subject with the parents more than once. She didn't resolve the conflict with all the parents, but she continued to work at it.

Once the caregiver helped them clarify their goals for their children, the parents realized that freedom to move was vital to their children's development! Because this caregiver had a philosophy that babies should not be confined either by being held all the time or by being in infant swings, high chairs or infant seats, she didn't compromise. She showed parents how their children would be safe on the floor by having the immobile ones fenced off from the mobile ones. She practiced in the open what she believed was so important, and after she convinced a few parents, they began to convince others. This caregiver was of the same culture as the parents, so she wasn't an outsider coming in telling them what to do without understanding their culture. She was an insider who had a different perspective and was able to help them see that their goals and their practices were in conflict with each other. You may not agree with what she did, but she felt very strongly that she was right in changing the parents—in educating them to another view.

Conflict management when there is no resolution.

The caregiver in this example was uncomfortable when a new parent told her that her one year old was toilet-trained. She didn't believe it; she believed that the parent was trained, not the baby. She and the parent started a series of conversations about this subject. Even though the caregiver didn't change her approach to toilet-training, which was based on accepted practice (Brazelton, 1962), through the discussions the caregiver was able to stop feeling critical of this parent because she was eventually able to understand her point of view.

The caregiver came to understand that toilet-training means different things to different people. To the caregiver it meant teaching a child to go to the toilet by herself, wipe, wash hands and so forth. The child must be old enough to walk, or at least talk, hold on to urine or feces, let go after getting clothes off and wash hands. In other cultures, where interdependence (sometimes called mutual dependence) is important, adult and child are partners, and the adult reads the child's signals and trains the child to let go at a certain time or to a certain cue. This process occurs very young—when the child is only a year old, perhaps even younger (Clark, 1981; Hale-Benson, 1986). This approach works best without diapers or complicated clothing such as overalls.

Although this caregiver didn't change her own approach to toilet-training, she was respectful of someone who did something different from what she did. She was accepting of the difference and stopped feeling angry or superior to the parent. The parent came to understand the caregiver's perspective, too, although she still wanted the caregiver to give it a try. The very few times the caregiver did try, this method didn't work because she didn't have the time or the relationship, or the techniques, or an understanding of the interdependence point of view. This conflict was unresolved but was managed by both parties. The mother continued to "catch" her child at home, and put diapers on when she was in day care. Neither parent nor caregiver felt entirely satisfied, but both parties managed to cope and weather it through until the child was old enough to become independent with her toileting.

Some thoughts about working in a culturally sensitive manner with parents.

It's much easier to do parent education (when appropriate) if we are of the same culture as the parents (Fantini & Cardenas, 1980). We can see their perspective better. We can work from the inside. Working from the inside of the culture is very important. The story about the babies on the floor is the story of a caregiver who worked with migrant workers from Mexico and who was, herself, the granddaughter of a migrant worker. She felt confident about working to change what seemed to be a cultural approach because she was a cultural insider.

Is it ever all right to go along with something you don't feel good about? It depends on your bottom line and how flexible you are above that. It's not all right, from my point of view, to go along with sexism, oppression or abuse, even if you are told that it is cultural. What do you do about limited options for little girls who come from a culture where women are in a subservient role? The questions get tricky! ❧

Chapter 4
Principles of Quality Care in a Diverse Society

Principle Three: Preserve Children's Family Languages and Encourage All Children to Learn a Second Language

Walk into Hilltop Nursery during circle time and one is likely to hear sounds from around the world:

Uno, dos, tres (Spanish),

bir, iki, uch (Turkish),

isa, dalawa, tatlo (Tagalog),

yut, ngee, sahm (Cantonese),

echad, shteim, shalosh (Hebrew),

en, to, tre (Norwegian),

eins, zwei, drei (German),

ichi, ni, san (Japanese),

obu, abua, ato (Ibo),

um, dois, treis (Portugese),

and...one, two, three.

At Hilltop, in the Silverlake District of Los Angeles, counting in all of the languages spoken by the children, families and staff is one of the most popular circle time games. This activity not only validates the home languages of the children in care, it also promotes interest in learning other languages.

Michelle Harris, an African American mother at Centro VIDA, chose the program for its community groundedness and bilingual focus. She was very pleased that her daughter Tiffany was learning to understand and speak a great deal of Spanish. This was becoming more and more apparent in such situations as the check-out line at the grocery store; her daughter could often tell her what Spanish-speaking shoppers were talking about.

Why Are Language Issues Important?

California Tomorrow proposes as one of our Principles of Quality Care in a Diverse Society that child care programs foster bilingualism by: (1) helping to preserve the primary languages of children from families whose first language is not English, and (2) encouraging children whose first language is English to take an interest in learning a second language. This chapter is not an assessment of effective bilingual programs or a "how to" guide. More, it seeks to explain how and why fostering bilingualism can be incorporated as a positive goal when working with young children, and suggests strategies toward this goal. This first requires addressing many questions and myths about language development and bilingualism. Working through some of the misunderstandings about bilingualism and language development exposes far greater common ground than many people expect—which ultimately can benefit children.

While English is the dominant language of the United States, this nation is home to many families and communities whose members also speak other languages. Nationwide, one out of every 25 children comes from a home where a language other than English is spoken. In California, this figure is one out of three. In Los Angeles, the children speak some 100 different languages. In the United States, it is a tremendous asset socially and economically to speak English as well as another language. Yet, on the whole, we do not do a good job of fostering bilingualism in the United States.

The California early childhood education community is beginning to grapple with the challenges of serving multilingual communities. California Tomorrow's 1993 survey of child care centers found that more than 80 percent served children from two or more language groups, and 77 percent served at least one child who did not speak any English or spoke only a little English. Issues of bilingualism and second language acquisition are among the newest and most complex in the field. How should providers adapt their practice to ensure the positive development of children's primary language in an increasingly multilingual society? There is an emerging consensus that all programs and providers need to at least think about these issues and the linguistic needs of the children in their care. In a few cases, child care providers are offering bilingual curricula that seek to foster bilingualism. In many cases, providers recognize the importance of bilingualism and preserving family languages, but they are stymied by the dearth of information reaching the profession regarding language acquisition and how to provide appropriate language development instruction to young children. In still other cases, programs do not foster bilingualism, choosing to focus solely on English. All in all, the language needs and potential to become bilingual for many children are going unattended.

Differing Views, Not So Different Values

Some parents and teachers resist programs that promote bilingualism or the use of non-English languages in the mistaken belief that this will hinder children's ability to become fluent in English. English-speaking families may think that if staff is using, for example, Spanish or Mandarin or Tagalog, then instructional time in English is being lost. Research shows, however, that children living in an English-speaking society are literally immersed in the language, absorbing the structure, vocabulary, tone and gestures of English at all times. Rather than being at risk of losing English, exposure to another language enriches their language capacity and comprehension. In most of the world, bilingual instruction is seen as fundamental to education.

Families who speak languages other than English often feel that they are sending their children to school specifically to become fluent in the new language, and so may not feel comfortable about the use of their home language in the program. They often do not realize that if their child's first language is not nurtured and developed, chances are great that he or she will lose the ability to speak it. Such a loss can be devastating and far-reaching, depriving a person of not only potential future economic opportunities, but the ability to communicate with family and community. Because language is so core to culture, a child's cultural identity will be impacted by his or her connection and fluency in the family language. Many providers and parents are not aware that, in fact, the use of the home language also promotes the cognitive development, self esteem, second language (usually English) acquisition and academic preparation of children.

Working through some of the misunderstandings about bilingualism and language development exposes far greater common ground than many people expect.

Some individuals and organized groups adamantly oppose supporting children's home language out of fear that the use of non-English languages creates division among Americans. But we believe that division is, in fact, created by discrimination against people who speak other languages and by practices which prevent them from participating in the larger society. One such practice is denying children the use of their home language in the classroom and the beneficial academic preparation that it fosters. A truly multilingual society is stronger and better equipped to contribute to an international community and economy.

Some opponents of bilingual programs do not recognize that, in fact, learning English is a shared value among monolingual English speakers and speakers of other languages. Most people in the United States agree that children must eventually acquire English to succeed in this society, where English is the language of government, business, media, schooling and virtually all major arenas. Children must speak English to access higher education and well-paying jobs. Our interviews with parents and providers for this study paralleled the broader society: recently arrived immigrants placed just as high a value on speaking English as did citizens whose families have lived in the United States for generations.

And, studies of children who have immigrated to the United States indicate that virtually all eventually acquire English. The greater threat to these children is the very high likelihood that they will lose the ability to speak their home language, as has happened among many earlier immigrant groups, such as Italians and Poles. This happens for a complex set of reasons that includes the stigma this society places on speaking another language. Many English speakers express open disdain when they hear other languages used publicly. People who cannot express their ideas clearly in English are assumed to not understand issues, or to not have any useful contributions at all. This is one of the first lessons non-English-speaking children learn when put in an insensitive setting that does not validate their language. The immigrant children quickly learn that the English spoken by their peers is more highly valued than their home language, and many internalize this view themselves. Recent studies report that many eventually refuse to speak their home language out of embarrassment or shame, even with their family.

Preserving the Home Language and Fostering Bilingualism

Achieving bilingualism requires different strategies for different types of children. English-speaking parents who wish for their young children to learn other languages commonly encourage this interest in the home and seek out opportunities for the children to interact with speakers of other languages, including in the preschool setting. This is discussed further later in this chapter. For children whose families speak a language other than English, bilingualism is fostered through nurturing the continued development of their home language while creating the conditions for them to acquire English as well (Wong Fillmore, 1991). Steps must be taken to ensure that English is learned in addition to—as opposed to "instead of"—the language of the family.

There are differences of opinion among language acquisition scholars about how to best support a child's non-English home language, and when and how to introduce English. Some believe it is appropriate to introduce English at a young age—provided adequate attention is paid to the home language (Sandoval-Martinez, 1982), while others feel it is most effective to wait until after a child has developed basic literacy in the home language (Wong Fillmore, 1991; Cummins, 1989; Diaz Soto and Smeaker, 1992).

In any case, all of these scholars agree that providers and parents should encourage children to speak and develop their home language. Young children are in the process of developing cognitive skills that are not language specific—for example, learning that a word on paper is a symbol of something that is spoken. It is easier for most children to learn such complex concepts in the language in which they are most comfortable—their home language. Once basic literacy concepts have been developed, children can more easily transfer this knowledge to a second language, such as English (Cummins, 1989).

Children's ability to retain their home language is essential to maintaining strong social and emotional ties to their parents, grandparents and extended family members, particularly if the primary caretakers do not speak English. Language minority parents, unlike their children, are much less likely to have opportunities to learn English even when they are highly motivated to do so. Consequently, when language minority children lose their family language, their parents may lose their ability to provide verbal comfort and support, offer guidance and discipline, or transmit family values, hopes and traditions. Parents find themselves feeling more and more inadequate and ineffective, and children often grow alienated from their families (Wong Fillmore, 1989).

But through language, ethnic and cultural groups transmit customs and beliefs to the young. Values and traditions are embedded within words and expressions unique to the language. Children who cease to speak the language(s) of their community begin to miss the subtle, but often crucial, nuances of their heritage. In many languages, specific words are used to address relatives. For example in

Mandarin, there is no generic term for "aunt"; rather each relative is referred to by their exact connection to the child, as in "my mother's oldest sister." These words teach a child fundamentals about the importance of family and esteem for elders. In most languages, there are at least a few words which cannot be meaningfully translated into any other language—illustrating the unique interplay between language and culture. Knowing the home language helps children to build a strong cultural identity, which, as discussed in our Principle on Culture, can promote the development of a secure, confident individual who can function effectively in cross-ethnic and multilingual situations.

In recent years, Black English, or Ebonics, has become recognized as another legitimate language with a standard set of rules spoken by many families. In her book, *Testifying and Talking*, Geneva Smitherman (1986) defines Black English as "an Africanized form of English reflecting Black America's linguistic-cultural African heritage and the conditions of servitude, oppression and life in America." Black English traces its roots to both Africa and the U.S. South, developing among enslaved Africans who arrived speaking many diverse African languages and dialects. Smitherman estimates that 80 to 90 percent of African Americans use Black English at least some of the time. With a few notable differences, the challenges facing African American children who use Black English parallel those who speak entirely different languages. African American children are still able to understand "standard" English. On the other hand, like other languages, Black English is a critical vehicle for the transmission of culture and for retaining a strong sense of connection to family and community. Speakers of Black English also learn very early that the language of their home is not respected by the dominant society. If African American children are constantly corrected or humiliated for their speech, their self esteem can suffer and they may even refuse to speak.

Fostering Bilingualism By Nurturing the Interest and Ability of English-Speaking Children to Learn a Second Language

For children whose home language is the dominant language of society, fostering bilingualism begins with introducing them to languages other than English. Because their home language is dominant in society, these children are not at risk of losing English. The early care setting is, in this case, a very appropriate time to introduce a second language to children, with many important benefits. Although for children of higher socioeconomic levels, bilingualism has long been viewed as an asset for future careers in trade and international affairs, the United States is still the only industrialized nation in the world where children grow up monolingually unless they are motivated personally to learn another language. Learning another language offers children greater appreciation and insights into people from culturally diverse backgrounds. At the same time, learning words in different languages for the same concepts teaches children about commonalities across groups. Many believe that becoming bilingual has cognitive advantages because it promotes greater mental flexibility (Hakuta, 1986). The development of bilingual children is an opportunity which the United States can ill-afford to miss.

How Child Care Providers Can Help Facilitate Language Development and Foster Bilingualism

Acquiring language is one of the most important developmental tasks facing young children. Of course, for this age group this is not an academic process; young children naturally learn language and form attitudes about the languages spoken in their environment through their interactions with people. Language development for young children is embedded in all of the aspects of care, rather than tied to certain activities.

Early on, children pick up messages from their surroundings too about the value of the languages spoken. Providers are constantly conveying messages through verbal and nonverbal responses to the language spoken by children and their families. Children, who are careful observers, don't miss these messages. For example, if a child observes that when his mother greets the bilingual teacher in Spanish, the teacher always responds in English, the child gets the message that Spanish is unacceptable. In the video, *Essential Connections: Ten Keys to Culturally Sensitive Child Care*, Yolanda Torres makes the following observation:

> *If you shame a child because he is using his own language, or if you shame the parents of the child and say his mother shouldn't do that, and the child knows that this is very important to the mother, that is terrible. You are telling the child that his parents don't know how to raise him.*

When language minority children lose their family language, their parents may lose their ability to transmit family values, hopes and traditions.

In the worst cases, children may be openly put down by adults for using their family language. One teacher we interviewed shared the following story regarding a child whose language was Black English:

> *One of the kindergarten children in the afterschool program was sent to see a school psychologist because she wouldn't talk. It turned out that the problem was her teacher had been constantly ridiculing her for the way she spoke. Her response was to simply stop speaking.*

Standard English-speaking students who observe such negative exchanges can easily absorb the message that speaking another language or dialect is bad, and that their language is the only "good" or "right" one.

Whether providers actively support and validate the languages of families has a tremendous influence on how children feel about their home language—and whether they will lose or retain it. This may be particularly true for infants and

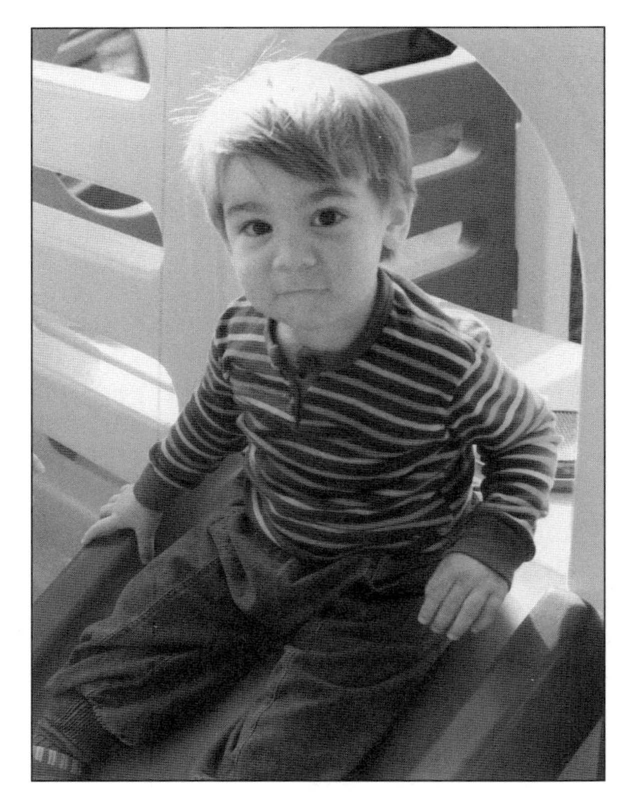

toddlers whose language needs should not be overlooked because they are still at a pre-verbal stage. Infants and toddlers are just beginning to develop sounds and form their first words. But traditionally, infants and toddlers have been primarily cared for by parents or family members who speak the home language. Unfortunately, very little research has been conducted on the impact of placing a language minority child for long periods of time with an outside caregiver who does not speak the home language. Caregivers could provide tremendous insight into such research. For example, Darlene Correia, director of the Marie Kaiser Center, observed:

> *In my experience working with infants, I observed that six- and seven-month-olds whose home language was Spanish responded when I spoke to them in Spanish. They would look at me very intently, or respond with their bodies differently than when I spoke in English. In cases when the language was not English or Spanish, I would make it a point to learn words or phrases in the family's language. Not only was it important for the child, it was important for the family. It was important that the family know and observe that the language—in some cases the languages—they spoke at home were valued, supported and viewed as an asset.*

What happens in care also influences whether English speakers develop an interest in learning other languages. Some early care and education programs can and do encourage children to interact and play with children or adults who speak other languages.

Promising Strategies and Challenges

What child care strategies can contribute to preserving children's home languages and/or fostering bilingualism among all children? The following approaches focus on one or both of these goals. Some of the strategies are obviously easier to implement when a provider is working with several children from the same language group. Most strategies also have some relevance for settings where one child speaks a language different from the rest of the children, or where the children represent many language groups. This chapter offers no definitive answers, but does glimpse at the variety of promising strategies we observed in the field.

Strategy 1

Validate languages in the care setting.

> *At Anita Surh's family child care program in Oakland, Mandarin, Cantonese and English are spoken throughout the day. For the last 14 years, Anita's program has been a place where Chinese families find reinforcement for their culture and non-Chinese families are exposed to another way of being and communicating. Many of the Chinese families who enroll their children in the program are first, second, third or fourth generation in the United States. Anita's goals are to preserve and validate the children's Chinese and begin to prepare them for the transition to English. "The children are exposed to Chinese through the verbal interactions and simply hearing it in the environment." For example, on the morning of our visit, two Chinese-speaking parents and one set of grandparents dropped off their children. Mandarin was the language used to transmit information about the children. Anita feels this exposure is important for non-Chinese-speaking children as well. "When these children hear someone out in the community speaking Chinese, it is not unfamiliar. They don't ridicule it."*

Children need to know what they say is important and valued. One of the most fundamental ways to demonstrate respect to children is to assure them that they are understood. Melinda Sprague, the director of the Reducing Exceptional Stress and Trauma Project (REST) in Los Angeles, recalled:

> *I saw a Spanish-speaking child who was trying to ask for something from somebody who didn't understand the language, and there wasn't any caring validation that the child had something important to say. I think it is extremely harmful to any child, but particularly harmful if it gives the message, "What you say isn't important and I don't understand you."*

The growing awareness about the importance of validating children's home languages has resulted in providers seeking to ensure that children can speak and hear their own languages, and that a multilingual assortment of materials is available in the environment, such as books, wall hangings, music and stories on tape. Some providers we visited had collected songs in written and taped form from families and co-workers. This can be an especially invaluable strategy when only one child speaks a certain language in the program; music in the child's home language shared with the other children and staff can be wonderfully validating and educational.

Some programs also made an effort to spark children's interest in languages not necessarily spoken by the children in care. For instance, Live Oak Migrant Head Start Program served Punjabi- and Spanish-speaking children together at some of its sites, but at the time we visited one of the satellite centers, it happened that there were no Punjabi children enrolled. Still, as the Mexican head teacher explained, the providers continued to sing Punjabi songs with the children to nurture appreciation for the Punjabi people who lived within the community.

Within the African American community, there is a broad range of opinion about the appropriate way to respond to the use of Black English in the classroom (Cazden, 1981). Some believe it is important to have teachers who speak Black English to the children. Others believe the most important role a teacher can play is to model standard English and help a child develop skills in code-switching—the ability to alternate between speaking Black English and standard English depending upon what is appropriate given the environment. Regardless of the specifics of the approach, however, providers must help children develop language skills in manners respectful of the children and their home language. It is important for providers to work closely with parents to determine their desires and expectations regarding the use of Black English and standard English in the program.

English-speaking children benefit from observing demonstrations of respect for speakers of other languages and nonstandard English. Validation of other languages in the care setting helps to spark the interest of English-speaking children in acquiring a second language. The children may even begin to learn a second language.

Challenges to Strategy 1

Challenge: Lack of opportunities or time to reflect upon and discuss strategies for effectively supporting home languages and dialects in the care setting

While the providers in most programs we visited agreed with the notion that languages other than English should be validated, they often underestimated the importance of taking the time to discuss and reflect upon how this principle should be carried out in practice. For example, we visited a program where most program staff spoke Spanish and used it throughout the day. While observing one teacher, however, we noticed that she used the home language primarily only to reprimand or discipline the children. In this situation, the provider did not seem to be aware of the negative message she was conveying to the children about the home language, nor the program's goal to foster home language.

In our site visits, we also found providers struggling with how to balance validating Black English spoken by children and helping children develop communication skills for succeeding in school and the future. A white teacher at a center that served several African American children said she believed it was most important to affirm children's way of speaking which was part of their family identity. Therefore, she never corrected children when they used Black English. While this provider was sensitive to validating children's home language, it was not clear if she had had any opportunity to discuss an appropriate approach with her colleagues at the center or the parents of children.

Strategy 2

Hire staff who speak the home language of children from language minority families.

> *Centers have a role in supporting the child's identity. This is accomplished by accepting and reinforcing the culture and language of the children. In our center we accomplish this by making sure that there are staff who speak the home languages of the children.*
>
> — Carmen Espinoza, head teacher at Plaza Child Development and Observation Center (a bilingual program) in East Los Angeles

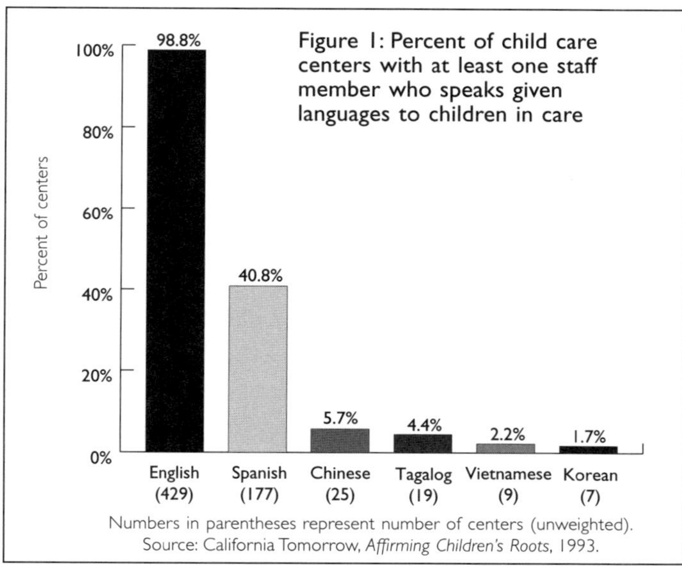

Numbers in parentheses represent number of centers (unweighted).
Source: California Tomorrow, *Affirming Children's Roots*, 1993.

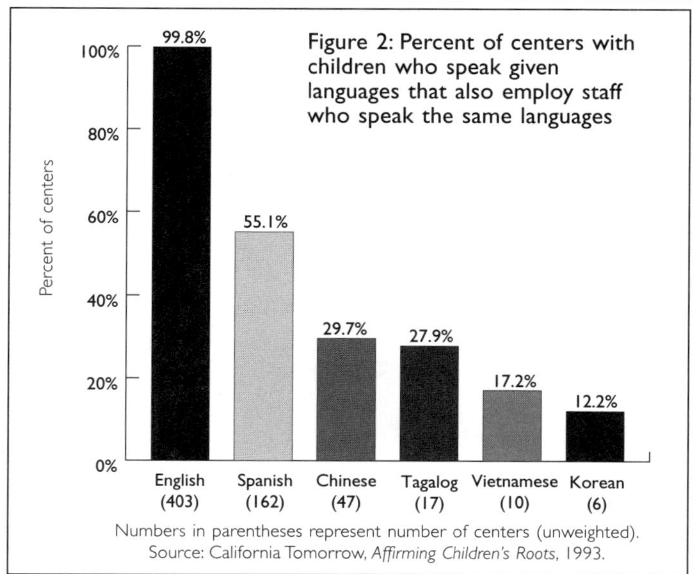

Numbers in parentheses represent number of centers (unweighted).
Source: California Tomorrow, *Affirming Children's Roots*, 1993.

In our first two principles, we discussed that hiring staff members who reflect the races and cultures of children in care is necessary to support and affirm their racial and cultural identity. For most programs, hiring English-speaking staff is a given. Nearly all of the 434 centers surveyed for California Tomorrow's *Affirming Children's Roots* reported the presence of English-speaking staff. But programs were much less likely to employ staff who spoke the home languages of children from language minority families.

For this study, almost all of the centers we visited had some children who spoke a language other than English. And most of the directors at the programs we visited placed a high priority on staff who spoke the primary languages of the children and families. They deemed this important because it strengthened communication with the families and promoted language development. They agreed that for children of this age, interaction with adults in their environment is perhaps the most important to acquire language.

These providers also stressed the desire to smooth the transition from home to child care for language minority families. Given that often children of all backgrounds are wary of their new caregiving environments and parents are anxious about leaving their children, the goal was to help reassure language minor-

How can providers prevent inadvertently sending negative messages about home language to children?

By first striving to answer "yes" to the following questions:

- Do I respond to children when they initiate contact with me in their home language?
- Do I take care not to use the home language only to reprimand children?
- Do I take care not to use home language only to give the children directions?
- Do I use the home language to give the children positive reinforcement?
- Do I encourage the use of the home language by both children and parents?
- Do I create opportunities for different languages to be used in day-to-day activities?
- Do I offer nurturing phrases and reassuring sounds to children in their home language and non-verbal repetitives?
- Do I let children giggle, cry or share confidences with me in their home language?
- Do I have materials in the classroom that reflect home language—and are these materials of equal quality to the English materials?
- Do I understand the concept of code-switching and do I work with parents to identify when to appropriately validate home language and dialects and when to emphasize standard English? ❧

ity families by having someone at the program who could understand and comfort their child with familiar words and gestures. Guadalupe Rodriquez, a bilingual teacher at Live Oak Migrant Head Start, said:

> *It is very important, especially in preschool education, to have people who speak the language spoken by the child. If you take a two-year-old who is beginning to develop his/her own language and speak to them in English, they aren't going to understand. If a child then attends a program where teachers don't speak his language, the teachers will attempt to comfort him at the time of separation, but won't know what to say to him. It is very important to have teachers that speak the child's language.*

At Live Oak, all of the teachers are bilingual in English and in either Punjabi or Spanish. Many of them also have some knowledge of the third language. Sakina Gorsi was an East Indian parent with a three-year-old daughter enrolled at the time of our visit. Sakina's three older children also had attended Live Oak. She said when the two oldest children, now eleven and nine, were in the program, there were no Punjabi-speaking teachers. She remembered worrying whether her chil-

dren would be understood when they spoke. She also worried that their learning would be affected:

> *When the children first came to the center they didn't have a Punjabi teacher or teaching assistant. The children didn't understand what the teachers were saying or doing. They could not learn very well.*

The two youngest children had a different experience because by the time they enrolled, the center employed teachers who spoke their language. This experience influenced Sakina's perspective about the importance of hiring teachers who speak the language of the children:

> *It is important for the center to speak Punjabi. The children don't understand Spanish or English. Punjabi children speak Punjabi at home and they need to be understood. I want my children to speak Punjabi. Keeping the language is the responsibility of the parents as well as the program.*

Staff who speak languages other than English are important role models for the children who speak those languages, as well as for the other children. At the Alpine Children's Center, the presence of a teaching assistant who could speak Spanish as well as English was beneficial to all the children. Located in rural Alpine County, the children in the center were primarily white and Washoe Indian, with a few Latino children. Parent Lucy Sprute, who originally immigrated from Colombia, felt that hiring Spanish-speaking staff was a symbol of acceptance of Latino culture. At the same time, Terry Peets, a white parent, appreciated that the teaching assistant Maria helped expose the children to a person from a different culture and language.

Finding staff who speak the languages of the children served can require creative hiring and placement of staff. For further information about steps that can be taken to recruit staff who reflect the linguistic as well as cultural background of children, please refer to our Workforce chapter. Programs with larger staffs or more than one site can implement more creative options. For example, Santa Clara Head Start, which is a network of centers, monitors demographic data in the communities of existing and potential new program sites. These data are used to develop new-hire criteria, including language capabilities. If necessary, the program also transfers staff members to different sites in order to ensure that the language needs of children are addressed.

Challenges to Strategy 2

Challenge: Finding bilingual staff

Programs can "grow their own" by creating career ladders for bilingual staff who begin as teacher assistants.

A number of directors expressed that finding staff who are bilingual and have an early childhood background can be difficult, particularly for positions requiring a certain level of education. Their dilemma reflects that training institutions are currently not providing adequate educational opportunities for adults whose primary language is not English. This issue is discussed in more depth in our Workforce chapter. Meanwhile, programs can take steps to remedy the situation. Programs can "grow their own" by creating career ladders for bilingual staff who begin as teacher assistants. This strategy, however, requires long-term investment and planning on the part of the program and the caregivers.

Staff positions are only one avenue for bringing in adult speakers of other languages to the program. While hiring staff is ideal, programs can also draw upon other resources in their communities: parents, grandparents, older siblings or sometimes community residents. Programs can encourage these people to spend time in the classroom singing songs, reading or engaging in other language-based activities. Programs on high school or college campuses may well have access to students who speak a variety of languages. Often, students can receive course credit for spending time working with children in the center. Over time, these students or family members might even become the valuable bilingual staff programs are looking for.

Challenge: Recognizing the importance of staff's fluency in the home languages

We saw a number of cases where it was clear programs valued the importance of ensuring parents could participate in their home languages, but they relied on staff members who were not really fluent enough in the home languages of parents to meet this goal. In one center we visited, for example, we observed a parent meeting where the head teacher conducted the business in English and Spanish, but she was not able to translate significant agenda items into Spanish or to maintain the flow of the meeting. Parents were not engaged in a meaningful exchange of information. While this may have been an outstanding caregiver in other dimensions, the situation illustrated the unfairness—to her and the parents—of using her to communicate important information.

In some situations such as this, it appeared providers were trying hard to learn a new language in order to communicate with parents, but had not yet achieved fluency. In other cases, it seemed very possible that practitioners had lost the ability to fully communicate in the language of their culture—perhaps due to the societal forces against bilingualism that we have described in this chapter. Directors should not assume that a staff member of a cultural group is fluent in the language of the culture—nor expect that person to be responsible for communicating to parents in a language in which they are not comfortable. Nor should they assume staff members who have studied a language to some degree are yet bilingual.

Programs need to seek out the best translation possible, perhaps by working closely with some parents to ensure accuracy and continuity. Leaders of programs also need to realize that if they speak a little but are not fluent in the languages of families, their efforts to try to communicate in more informal matters will be greatly appreciated, just as they appreciate families' English efforts. However, when it comes to the exchange of critical information, leaders will do everyone the best service by ensuring that fluent bilingual translators are utilized.

Challenge: Lack of exposure to concepts of second language acquisition, bilingualism and dialect

Most of the programs we visited had some children who spoke a language other than English. But with a few exceptions, most staff reported receiving minimal or no information and/or training about second language acquisition and bilingualism. Although directors typically possessed some knowledge, among the staff who interacted most directly with the children, such knowledge was not prevalent. At times, programs seemed to be operating under the assumption that the ability to speak a language translated into knowing how to appropriately promote bilingual language development among young children. But, our observations suggested that, unfortunately, this is not necessarily the case. For example, in one bilingual program, we observed a teacher simultaneously translating, naming an object in one language and then repeating it in the other language. This approach was not in keeping with the prevalent belief that young children need to learn language naturally, and that mixing two languages together in the same sentence can create confusion. The lack of exposure to strategies was perhaps even more common among English-speaking staff. A teaching assistant offered a common refrain:

> *I would like to know more about working with children who can't speak English. I really don't know what to do.*

STRATEGY 3

Use flexible grouping approaches with children to fully expose them to their home language and possibly help them begin to learn a second language.

Programs can encourage the retention of home language through the way they conceptualize and structure the care setting as a whole. California Tomorrow identified three approaches among the programs we visited: (1) speaking only children's home languages in the care setting, (2) grouping children by classroom based on language, and (3) grouping children by language groups within a classroom. While all three sought to ensure preservation of the home language, the latter two also provided opportunities for children to learn about other languages. While these examples are not the only ways to effectively group children to support language development, they offer readers insights into what is possible. There are many other approaches to bilingual language development that we did not observe in our research.

GROUPING APPROACH 1: SPEAKING ONLY THE CHILDREN'S HOME LANGUAGES IN THE CARE SETTING

An exclusive emphasis on Spanish was the approach of the Delta Child Development Center run by the Foundation Center for Phenomenological Research. The program offered a child care and education program entirely in Spanish, the home language of all of the children in the center. This center served Mexican migrant families that worked in nearby agricultural fields and canneries. The teachers and 24 children—two months to five years of age—interacted in Spanish. Spanish was the primary language and, in some cases, the only language of the center staff; the program philosophy called for training community members to become child care providers. Like the other programs that were run by the Foundation Center, Delta used a Montessori curriculum to promote child-directed learning.

The home language policy was instituted at Delta out of the belief that children learn best if they are grounded in their first language. Children developed complex concepts such as counting and reading in Spanish—skills that would be the foundation of their future academic success. This approach sought to prevent the children from having to struggle to learn an entirely new language while taking on these other challenges.

As part of the research for our first book on the early childhood field, *Affirming Children's Roots*, California Tomorrow visited a similar Foundation Center program located in a public housing project in Winters. At the time, director Antonia Lopez told us that the success of the program in academically preparing children had begun to transform the views of the staff at the area's local elementary school. At first, the elementary teachers complained that the children at the center needed to be taught English. Then, as they began to see the skill levels of the students who transferred from the center and their quickness to learn English, they began to

understand the benefits of the Foundation Center program. The head of curriculum for the school district later came to visit the program. The center even "graduated" children with a record of their skills to carry on to the elementary school.

Grouping Approach 2: Grouping children by classroom based on language

Discoveryland, a church-based bilingual program serving members of the Chinese community in San Francisco, designed a program to slowly introduce Chinese-speaking children to English while introducing Chinese to English speakers. The program had three components: preschool, kindergarten and after-school care. In the preschool, there were four classrooms, including two for the two-and-a-half-year-olds. One of the two-year-old classrooms emphasized Chinese and the other emphasized English. Because Dr. Wong, the director of the program, believed it was important for children to be grounded in their home language before they were introduced to a second language, she recommended that incoming parents of the youngest group select the classroom that would support their child's home language.

Children from each language background were then mixed together in the class for four-year-olds. Chinese was used the first few months with the children who were transitioning from the Chinese-only two-year-old class, though the emphasis was on English in the four-year-old class. By the time children reached kindergarten, English was used exclusively in the regular classroom. But the emphasis on Chinese was not lost; kindergartners also attended Chinese classes everyday for an hour and a half during the afternoon. Outside of the classroom the children could speak whatever language they wished. Shirley Tang, a parent whose children went through the program, felt that it had played an important part in supporting her children's two languages:

> *My husband and I want to raise our children to be bilingual. When they first started in the program they were in the Chinese class. Later on they picked up English. Our children are bilingual. It is important that they have both mother tongues.*

Children from different language backgrounds who spend time together can also, in fact, help each other learn a second language through their interactions. Also, when children see that no language dominates another in the classroom, this fosters both self esteem and respect for other languages.

The director of Discoveryland was very clear with parents at the time of enrollment about the language goals of the program and how they were implemented. All of the providers were also clear about this goal, and all of the parents interviewed enrolled their children in the program because of its emphasis on supporting the two languages.

Grouping Approach 3: Grouping children by language groups within the classroom

Some programs group children by home language during certain parts of the day. Las Casitas Head Start Program is centered in a low income housing complex in San Jose. The families in the program are primarily Vietnamese and Mexican, as are the staff members. Head teacher Lorrie Guerrero is Mexican American and bilingual English/Spanish, and the assistant teacher at the time of our visit, Lyly Vu, was Vietnamese and bilingual Vietnamese/English. Las Casitas has the dual goal of supporting the home language of the children in care while exposing them to English. This goal is in accordance with the Multicultural Principles for Head Start Programs, which states that "effective programs for children with limited English-speaking ability requires continued development of the primary language while the acquisition of English is facilitated." Vietnamese, Spanish and English are all used in the program.

At Las Casitas, the home languages were supported by placing children into three small same-language groups during certain parts of the day. During this time, the children all did the same activity, but in their respective languages, led by a teacher or assistant for each group. For example, when we visited, the groups listened to the story *The Very Hungry Caterpillar*, each in their own language, and sang a variety of songs. After the small group work, the children convened as a large group and the story was read once again in one of the languages. Since the children had already just heard the story in the language they knew best, when they regrouped in the large circle, regardless of the language the activity was conducted in, they could understand the gist of the presentation. Similarly, numbers and shapes were reviewed daily in groups and then all together.

At the time of our visit, dividing the class into the language groups was still a new strategy—Lorrie and Lyly had been trying it for a month and a half, after Lorrie learned the idea at a Bilingual Institute sponsored by Santa Clara Head Start. She explained what they formerly did at the center:

> *We thought we were doing things right by exposing the children to concepts in all three languages at every circle. For example, I would review the Personal Safety Lesson in English and Spanish, and then Lyly would do it in Vietnamese. Circle times always took longer. The children were often fidgety and restless with only a few responding verbally. We wondered just how much were they actually comprehending.*

Lorrie attributed the decreased wiggling and disruptive behavior during circle time to the fact that children now understood what was going on. She also shared an incident which led her to believe that she needed to place the children into separate groups:

> *Every day we did colors in English, Spanish and Vietnamese last. All the time we would say, "What color is this?" in all three languages and then respond in all three. The last language was always Vietnamese. So then when the time came to assess Henry, one of the Spanish-speaking children, I asked him in Spanish, "What color is this?" and he gave me all the correct answers—but in Vietnamese, because that was the concept he had retained. It wasn't until I had attended the Bilingual Institute training seminar that I started grouping the children by language. It was then I had almost 100 percent participation and the realization that they were actually comprehending the subject matter.*

How much English and how much home language should be used with young linguistic minority children is a source of considerable debate.

Challenges to Strategy 3

Challenge: Little consensus among programs that identified themselves as bilingual about how and when to introduce English

How much English and how much home language should be used with young linguistic minority children is a source of considerable debate. This is clearly demonstrated in the earlier discussion of grouping strategies. Some programs built their curriculum on the notion that children are better prepared academically and socially if English is not introduced until after they develop basic literacy in the home language. Other programs gradually introduce English. Some use both English and the home language for children of all ages. In some situations, there is little consensus even within a site about the appropriate approach.

This lack of consensus reflects several issues. Because of the minimal access to training on bilingual language development, many providers do not base their approaches upon academic research, and instead draw conclusions from personal or anecdotal evidence. In addition, the field continues to suffer from a lack of research exploring bilingual language development among children under the age of five. Most of the current bilingual research involves school age children. Some studies of young children have been conducted by researchers such as Jim Campos and Lily Wong Fillmore. But, clearly much more research is needed. Finally, it is important not to underestimate the influence of the larger political debate in U.S. society over bilingualism and efforts to instill in people the unfounded fear that support for other languages will lead to national division. After all, this is an era when a judge in Amarillo, Texas told a mother she was abusing her young child by speaking Spanish, which he called the "language of maids."

Challenge: Difficulty in grouping children when they represent many language groups

Flexible grouping approaches are, of course, more challenging when there are more languages spoken by children than it is possible to match with adults. In these cases, it is especially important to encourage parents to speak their home language with children, and to use strategies to validate the children's languages. More research would greatly benefit the field to find answers to this challenge.

Challenge: Lack of connection to elementary education

Even the best efforts of a child care program to foster bilingualism can be dismantled if the work is not supported when the children move into their next educational setting. Unfortunately, many schools do not have solid bilingual programs or classrooms in place. As a result, earlier efforts to support home language development may be negated. As mentioned earlier, some researchers believe that home language support should continue until a child has achieved basic literacy, which does not typically occur until second or third grade. This problem is compounded by the absence of communication mechanisms between early childhood programs and kindergarten. As a result, schools that are unskilled in assessing children who speak languages other than English may have a tendency to place a child in a remedial classroom even if she or he has developed strong academic skills in the home language. The most commonly expressed concern by parents is that their children will have trouble in school unless they learn English from their child care provider. Clearly much more work is needed to bridge the world of early childhood and K-12 education, including building stronger alliances for change across both sectors.

Strategy 4

Encourage parents to support the development of the primary language.

Although children are spending more time in care, providers need to appreciate the core role that parents do and can play in supporting the language development of their children. What parents say, for example, also has an impact on how a child feels about his or her home language and can help to encourage a child to continue to speak it. Lillian Ikeme, a Nigerian teacher working at Hilltop Nursery in Los Angeles, observed:

> *Children are sometimes ashamed to speak the language of the home. To them it's something they shouldn't do in public. They reject their native language. The family can prepare children by telling them that the language that we speak in our home does not make us different. We need to learn English but that does not make us forget or reject our own language.*

Providers can help foster home language development by creating greater awareness among parents of the importance of continuing to speak the home language, as well as offering strategies parents can use. David Longaker, education coordinator at the Center for Education and Manpower Resources for Migrant Head Start, said:

> *We try to make parents aware of the language acquisition process and the techniques that they can use to help. We utilize the parents' strength. If parents are monolingual Spanish-speaking, we do not see their role as trying to teach English. We see their role as helping to provide that very rich language background in their native tongue which research indicates is an excellent springboard into a second language. They can, for example, demonstrate an interest in literacy by reading to their kids in whatever language they speak. Parents who have marginal literacy skills are encouraged to continue their oral traditions of sharing family history and stories. If children have a good linguistic foundation in their native languages, it is easier for them to bridge to the second.*

Lorrie Guerrero developed resources aimed at helping parents to join her in the classroom to reinforce home language:

> *We have many books now in English, Spanish and Vietnamese. I've been able to buy some. I've also had parents, or my teacher's aide, write Spanish, English or Vietnamese into the book itself. We provide a lending library. Sometimes the parent feels uncomfortable reading the story that their children love in English. So we offer it in Spanish or Vietnamese. It's wonderful for the parent to be able to take the time to read to their child and share something that they love so much. And, when they come here, they're comfortable taking a small group and doing it in the native language. They feel good about themselves as a result.*

Challenges to Strategy 4

Challenge: Conflicting parent/ provider perspectives about language

Clearly, one of the most difficult challenges about language comes in negotiating situations where parents and providers do not share the same perspective about the importance of supporting the home language. Working through this requires that parents and providers take the time to understand each other's fears and hopes for the child, and to share their respective knowledge about language development—whether it is from academic research or life experience. Further possible strategies are covered in the next chapter on our Principle on Parent-Provider Relations and in the article by Janet Gonzalez-Mena, which appears in our Principle on Culture.

Chapter 5 Principles of Quality Care in a Diverse Society

Principle Four: Work in Partnership with Parents to Respond to Issues of Race, Language and Culture

We all need to learn how children learn and what they need in order to understand the world. For parents in my program, an important issue is understanding their children's bicultural experience and the duality they are living. We are always going to come into contact with worlds that are like us or very different from us. We are going to be seeking those pieces with which we identify, and when we don't, what do we do with that information? Reject it? Assimilate it? Parents have to understand what children constantly have to go through in their learning environment.

—Beatriz Leyva-Cutler, director of Centro VIDA

Every month the center puts up something I call "sound bites," provocative notices, questions, etc., asking parents to pay attention to certain issues. For instance, to look at how many examples in the classroom there are of brown and black colors. Or a notice might suggest that parents talk to their child this week about Santa Claus with brown skin. That kind of thing on an ongoing basis is really useful.

—MARGIE CARTER, AUTHOR AND TRAINER

WHY IS THIS PRINCIPLE IMPORTANT?

Both the home and the care setting greatly impact whether a child grows up with a strong sense of self, the ability to resist racism, and the knowledge and language to remain rooted in family and community. The success of any effort to instill these ideals in children depends upon caregivers and family members working together. The impact of caregivers or parents can be limited if there are contradictions between the two in what they model to children—whether to respect people who look different, to be proud of speaking their home language, to combat racism, and beyond. Both family members and caregivers hold critical pieces of information about how to support a child's sense of identity and ability to connect to others. Their respective knowledge and effectiveness are deepened when they have a chance to share their insights and strategies.

Clearly, families have a very important role to play in the quality of a child care program, as partners with the caregivers and as advocates for their children. They play a critical role in ensuring that the Principles of Quality Care in a Diverse Society are reinforced throughout the various dimensions of a child's life. In this book, our references to parents encompass the adults who have primary responsibility for children, including parents, foster parents, grandparents, aunts, uncles or other family members. Many communities have a strong culture of extended family, and caregiving is shared among adults close to a child, sometimes including older siblings. All of the people who care for children are in a position to shape how children view themselves and others.

Families will most powerfully influence the development of young children's identity, attitudes and skills for living in a diverse society. Even though there may be periods when young children spend more of their waking hours with a paid caregiver, over the course of their lives children will spend many more hours in the fold of their families. Most parents wish to spend more time with their children than their circumstances allow, and child care providers can play a role in supporting parents in their maintenance of family bonds and authority. Child care, as the first experience most parents have of sharing responsibility for their child's development with non-family members, can also lay the foundation for parents to recognize their role in ensuring issues of diversity are addressed by schools and other educational institutions which will shape their children's views and beliefs. The foundation laid may be particularly critical for racial, cultural and linguistic minority families who are often the most likely to feel alienated and isolated from the people and institutions which care for their children.

What Does this Principle Involve?

Just like providers and others in the field, parents and other family members often have not had the chance to explore the concepts or research related to the development of children's racial identity, bilingualism, attitudes toward others, etc. Without access to such knowledge, it is difficult for parents and providers to work in partnership to equip children to thrive in a multiracial, multicultural, multilingual society. Providers and parents need opportunities to exchange information about their respective backgrounds, beliefs and approaches, and they need forums for negotiating their differences.

Once providers have developed an understanding of the Principles of Quality Care in a Diverse Society, they can help to introduce them to parents and other family members in a number of ways. They can share written materials, clearly explain the philosophy and approaches used in the care setting, and invite parents to observe their interactions with children in the program. Sharing this information can build parent support for the program and help parents determine whether the approaches are appropriate for their children.

Parents and other family members also need opportunities to let providers know specific information about their cultures, languages and racial experiences. Providers can learn basic information, such as a child's home language and ethnic heritage, by asking parents. However, time needs to be dedicated for deeper discussions. For example, as addressed in our Principle on Culture, we often do not realize that our actions are a cultural expression until we see a person behave differently from ourselves and take the time to analyze why. Parents and providers need to talk to each other when they notice that they do not approach an issue with the children in the same manner.

Both family members and caregivers hold critical pieces of information about how to support a child's sense of identity and ability to connect to others.

This principle promotes the development of strong working relationships between parents and providers so that they can identify and understand their differences, as well as better appreciate their common goals to serve the best interests of children. As with any relationship, this requires creating an environment where people feel comfortable raising issues and discussing divergences of opinion. What happens at the outset just as children enter a program lays a strong foundation for whether a productive relationship will grow between providers and parents. An ongoing commitment by providers to working with parents on all issues related to their children, including those specific to diversity, is of great importance.

Promising Strategies and Challenges

This chapter describes a variety of strategies for building strong working relationships between providers and families, specifically to exchange insights about how race, language and culture play out in the lives of children. Each strategy is followed by common challenges—many of which apply to more than one strategy.

Strategy 1

Clearly articulate and orient parents to the focus and intent of the program around issues of diversity.

This book opened with the perspectives of different parents, child care professionals and others about the role of care in a diverse society. These perspectives illustrated that not all families need or want exactly the same type of program. One family, for example, may want their son to be exposed to children from different racial or linguistic backgrounds, while another family may want their daughter to gain strength for the future through contact at a young age with children from her same racial or cultural background. Programs need to be able to clearly articulate their focus and intent so that families can identify whether what they offer meets their needs.

Ideally, providers should try to make it as easy as possible for families to understand their overall focus on diversity from the moment they come in contact with the program. Is the program recruiting children of diverse backgrounds in order to promote a multicultural, anti-bias approach? Is the program primarily focused on preserving the language and culture of an ethnic group? Is the program incorporating diversity issues into the overall curriculum to better serve its given target population, such as teen parents, parents of an employer, low income families or residents of a geographic neighborhood?

The point of providing clear information is not to exclude families from any programs. Rather, it is to make sure that families fully understand and desire what the program is trying to offer. For example, California Tomorrow visited a number of programs where the curriculum focused on a specific ethnic group, but children of other backgrounds were enrolled as well. Such an arrangement can be appropriate and enriching as long as parents have been made aware of the overall thrust. Parents may wish to know, for example, how the center is teaching children to appreciate people of all backgrounds within the curriculum. One center addressing this challenge was Centro VIDA, a Spanish/English bilingual program focused on the Latino culture. Director Beatriz Leyva-Cutler explained:

> *We are doing something few other people do. We are immersing ourselves and others into a cultural experience, and that is rare indeed. We are inclusive and we are diverse, to an extent, but everybody is here to experience the dominant culture of being Latino.*

Information about a program's intent and focus can be conveyed through brochures, parent handbooks, and through verbal orientations provided to parents by staff. Following are several examples.

• • • • •

The **MARIN LEARNING CENTER** in Marin City primarily serves African American children. Its program guidelines and parent handbook include the following description of the multicultural programming:

Multicultural Programming

The Center recognizes the importance of positive cultural and community traditions and values as an integral part of the development of the children's self-esteem. Celebrations such as Kwaanza, Martin Luther King's Birthday, Black History Month, African drumming, dancing and storytelling, etc. are a regular part of the program. It is the staff's goal to share this richness, the values and the pride of these celebrations and activities to symbolize to African Americans with all of the children. With a multicultural staff, celebrations from other cultures are also presented to give the children a sense of the joy and beauty that exists within other cultures as well.

• • • • •

SIMCHA is a Jewish preschool located in Santa Cruz. Included in the first page of its parent handbook, which also provides information about its overall philosophy, goals, staffing and expectations for parent participation, is the following Jewish Philosophy Statement:

Philosophy

Simcha is a Jewish preschool. We want children to feel good about their Jewish heritage and traditions. Warm memories of Jewish life and rituals come through a child's early experiences. Being in a community with other Jewish children helps each child to feel part of a larger Jewish community.

Curriculum

We hope to build early Jewish identity through a variety of experiences.

1. On a daily basis the classroom environment will include Jewish pictures, objects, books and music. The appropriate blessing over food will be said before snack and lunch.
2. Given that we are at the Temple, the children will visit the sanctuary, when appropriate, to learn about synagogue life.
3. Learning about the celebration of the Jewish holidays is important. We celebrate the Jewish holidays through art, science and cooking projects, stories, songs, dramatic play and the special ritual objects that are used at that time.
4. Learning about how we celebrate Shabbat is an important part of the week. On Thursdays and Fridays we make challah, light candles and sing blessings and songs.

Family Participation

All Simcha families are encouraged to celebrate Jewish holidays at home and at the Temple's family programs. Simcha will provide information about Jewish holidays and rituals through parent meeting in-services and monthly newsletter articles. Sharing families and Judaic knowledge with your child's class is another way of integrating home and school.

• • • • •

STEP ONE SCHOOL, another program we visited, included the following statement in its introductory information package for parents:

The Anti-Bias Commitment at Step One

At Step One, families have a unique opportunity to help their children develop awareness of and respect for the diversity of human experience. The Step One staff works to examine the nature of bias and its effects on young children, on them-

selves and on our community as a whole and to respond to bias in their daily work with children. Throughout the year, parents are encouraged to learn more about the evolving anti-bias perspective at Step One and share their own views through our anti-bias newsletters and parent-staff meetings. Here are our goals as we currently see them.

- Expand our understanding of how young children develop a sense of personal identity and positive attitudes towards others different from themselves.
- Increase staff and parent awareness of our own attitudes about groups which are targets of bias in our culture on the basis of the following: race and cultural background, gender, sexual orientation, diverse family structures, physical differences and disabilities, social class and religion.
- Learn to identity (1) ways that bias affects children's self-image, and (2) ways that institutional forms of targeting and stereotyping various groups impact children, their families and school community.
- Continue developing thoughtful anti-bias curriculum for Step One classrooms, including the following: gathering materials that reflect the diversity of the world (e.g., books, visual images, dolls); identifying appropriate language for discussing various aspects of diversity with young children; providing models for children of resolving conflict that may be rooted in bias.

Step One is actively engaged in efforts to increase the diversity of our families and teachers. This includes people of diverse ethnic and cultural heritage, male and female teachers, lesbians and gay men, people with different family structures and religious practices, and people with physical differences and/or disabilities.

Anti-bias work is challenging, and it requires a willingness on the part of parents and teachers alike to examine and work toward confronting biases in ourselves and in our work with children. We at Step One are committed to meeting this challenge and we invite you to join us in this work on behalf of your children.

Challenges to Strategy 1

Challenge: Clearly articulating a program's philosophy and approach to diversity

Not all programs we visited seemed to have developed a way to clearly articulate their approach to diversity. Only a few included information about diversity approaches in parent handbooks and their general program literature. Some conveyed the focus primarily through their verbal descriptions of program activities to parents. Many programs offered little or no clear information.

To some extent, the clearness of program articulation depended upon whether the setting had access to the human and financial resources to produce written materials. Consequently, family child care programs appeared to be least likely to provide information in a written form. Whether a program clearly articulated its philosophy also seemed to reflect whether or not the staff felt it was important to do this. Among those we visited, programs seemed more articulate when they had been established out of a specific concern to help children and families address some issues of diversity. Clear descriptions were also more often available from programs which served a particular ethnic community or those which consciously sought to recruit ethnically diverse families in order to create a multiracial environment.

We often do not realize that our actions are a cultural expression.

The challenge for all programs—regardless of whether they are driven by a particular mission related to diversity—is to recognize the importance of devoting some time to developing a clear philosophy and description of their approach to diversity.

Challenge: Working with families who may not realize that child care can and should play a role in helping children understand issues of race, language and culture

As program staff plan ways to articulate their diversity approaches, they should be aware that this may be the first chance for some families to think about child care in the light of diversity. Some parents did not seem to have much considered the role of child care in preparing children for a diverse society until we interviewed them. Sometimes, this apparently stemmed from their newness to child care in general. Donald Yee and Joyce Carlson, parents at a Chinese family day care program in Oakland, explained:

> *Many parents don't really know what they want in a day care program. Often parents are unfamiliar with child care. As you evolve, you realize what you want for your children.*

In other cases, parents strongly wanted their cultural and linguistic heritage transmitted to their children, but did not believe that a program could contribute to this goal. One Ethiopian parent said:

> *The program doesn't have a role. Children learn about culture at home. How can the center reinforce the child's culture when they don't know it? A parent can't expect it.*

Program staff need to be ready to spend time explaining and answering questions upfront, including why they believe their approaches are important. Some parents, for example, may not believe that a program should play any role in teaching children to resist racism and bias. For some parents, an upfront understanding of the strategies used to promote diversity are necessary before they would ever be willing to put their child in a program.

Challenge: Working with parents to determine whether the center will meet the most important current needs of their children

Providers also need to be prepared to help family members assess what type of program fits with the specific needs of the child. While addressing issues of race, language and culture for children is vital, a child's additional priorities must also be weighed, and if a center cannot currently fulfill all needs, it must be determined which are most critical at the time. Yolanda Torres, director of the Pacific Oaks Children's School, recalled:

> *I worked with a child whose Armenian grandmother wanted her daughter to pull out her grandson at the age of two-and-a-half and put him in an Armenian-speaking school. The daughter was reluctant. I said, "I hate to see him pulled out right now, but I think he should eventually because I believe he needs to keep his language and culture. Your mom's right. But the reason I don't believe in it right now is that developmentally, he's just beginning toilet-training, weaning and developing social skills. You stop that and send him to another school and you've got to start all over again." I then offered to speak with her mom. I reiterated my words with the daughter translating. The grandmother said that she would think about it. The baby stayed until he was three.*

STRATEGY 2

Use intake and orientation procedures to exchange information about race, language and culture.

Most programs already conduct some form of intake and orientation procedures when families first enroll their children. These are often the first-time meetings between parents and providers and can set the tone for the ongoing relationship.

Therefore, intake and orientation sessions are critical opportunities to begin an exchange of information with parents on issues of diversity, and to lay the foundation for open communication on potentially sensitive issues.

In the orientation process, providers give parents an overview of their program and policies. Usually the director and sometimes a teacher talk to the parents and encourage appropriate family members to spend some time observing the program. In family child care homes, orientation may be a straightforward meeting during which the provider explains the daily routines to the parent. Orientation can be an ideal time for programs to explain and provide written materials about their overall program philosophy and approaches to fostering bilingualism, anti-racist attitudes and cultural exchanges. It can also be the best chance for providers to let parents know their hopes for developing a strong partnership, to encourage parents to feel comfortable raising concerns, and to invite family members to bring their cultural heritage and home language into the program.

Intake is the process by which programs collect basic background information about children enrolling. Typically, centers collect this information through a face-to-face interview as well as through a written form filled out by parents. In family child care homes, the intake process may be a less formal meeting between parent and provider. In addition to being a time to collect basic data (often required for funding), intake procedures can be opportunities to gain a much fuller understanding of the families. Insights into the cultural embeddedness of child rearing beliefs can be revealed through a provider asking basic questions about the family's practices around sleeping, eating, napping, toilet-training and discipline.

During intake or orientation, providers should make an effort to ask families at minimum the following:

- How would you like your child to be recognized ethnically? (This question is particularly important for the growing number of biracial/bicultural children and families about whom incorrect assumptions are often made.)
- What family traditions would you like the program to recognize?
- What can we learn about your culture to help us be as respectful as possible?
- What languages are spoken in your family?
- What other people are involved in caring for your child?
- Can you play a role in helping us to support your child's racial, linguistic and cultural heritage?

Challenges to Strategy 2

Challenge: Recognizing the importance of race, language and culture issues as part of a comprehensive approach to intake

Most programs have some form of intake procedures. The most comprehensive intakes appeared to be conducted in the programs working with infants and toddlers, probably because providers in these settings must rely upon parents for critical information about what a child is accustomed to for feeding, napping, toilet-training, etc. Often, however, providers seemed to place less emphasis on much data collection when children were older. Moreover, most providers do not currently think about using intake as an opportunity to obtain information which will help them support a child's cultural, linguistic or racial identity. There is little recognition that a full picture of families would require asking about these issues.

Challenge: Feeling comfortable about asking questions related to race, language and culture

Our interviews suggest that some providers may be afraid to use intake interviews to ask families about race, language or culture issues because they are unsure how to appropriately raise these sensitive topics. Broaching these issues can feel particularly daunting during intake because providers and parents have not yet developed a relationship. For example, at one program we visited, a provider indicated that she never asked parents about the language spoken at home because she was afraid of offending them. Some providers are worried that it is illegal to raise such issues. Being able to ask questions in an appropriate manner helps to establish a foundation for easily discussing issues of race, language and culture throughout the relationship. This includes clearly explaining why you are asking the questions and asking if parents feel comfortable discussing these issues.

Our Principle on Dialogue offers a variety of approaches programs can explore in order to create a culture where providers have the skills to talk sensitively about issues of race, language and culture.

Orientation can be the best chance for providers to let parents know their hopes for developing a strong partnership and to invite family members to bring their cultural heritage and home language into the program.

Challenge: Understanding that soliciting information from families is necessary even when the providers and parents are from a similar racial or broad ethnic group

Asking questions and exchanging information should not be overlooked in ethnic-specific or homogenous contexts. Providers certainly often have cultural and linguistic knowledge about parents from backgrounds similar to their own. Still, providers should not assume necessarily that their viewpoints and practices are shared by these parents. In any racial group, ethnic group or community, there is a tremendous diversity of opinion and practice. A family's customs may differ due to religious background, class background, length of time in the United States and many other circumstances.

Challenge: Making sure the caregiver responsible for the child receives the information exchanged through intake and orientation

In center-based settings, intake and orientation are often conducted by the director or some other administrator. Unfortunately, programs sometimes do not have

a mechanism in place to transmit information collected from the family to the person(s) directly responsible for caring for the child. We visited one program, for example, which collected information on home language from families in order to meet state data requirements, but did not convey this information to the teachers. Teaching assistants are even more likely than teachers to be left out of the information loop, even though they may play a primary role in caring for a child or communicating with certain parents in their family languages.

Some programs have begun addressing these information gaps by restructuring the intake and orientation procedures to include the person(s) who will directly care for a child. The benefits of this approach are several-fold. Information is less likely to fall through the cracks. It also allows teachers to explain to parents their approaches to working with children; even when a program has a strong overall philosophy, some variation will always exist in teachers' styles. Programs need to consider further steps to ensure information flows to all concerned staff members, including assistants.

Strategy 3

Encourage forms of daily contact which allow for information exchange.

One of the strengths of child care is the opportunity to build relationships with parents through daily contact as they pick up and drop off their children. Different programs have found ways to make the most of those precious moments. Many establish a system of primary caregivers where each provider is responsible for the care of a small group of children along with the communication with their parents.

One center we visited scheduled each staff person to stay late one or two evenings a week to be available to talk to parents. Many programs encouraged parents and teachers to write each other notes. Some use folders. One program simply placed the sign-in log at the far end of the room, so parents would spend a few seconds longer in the center walking to and from the log. A few programs actively encouraged parents to "hang out" in the facility and simply talk to staff.

Used resourcefully, these forms of daily contact can help to build trusting relationships between providers and parents. The key is to build the comfort of parents and providers alike to use these ad hoc encounters for asking questions about why a child is behaving in a certain fashion, why the other adult is taking a particular approach to child rearing, and whether there are racial, cultural or linguistic implications involved.

Challenges to Strategy 3

Challenge: Finding time for daily contact

Child care professionals have hectic schedules. Providers are typically not in a position where, at any time during the day, they can drop what they are doing to meet with a parent. For a productive meeting with parents, providers need time to focus their attention on the specific child. This type of concentration is difficult if a provider is in the middle of looking after the well-being of an entire group of children. Moreover, given the low wages typically paid to child care providers, they should not be asked to donate their own time to meet with parents —even though many already do. Programs need to develop specific plans and strategies for making sure that staff have time for developing relationships with parents.

Challenge: Overcoming attitudinal barriers of providers and parents

Parents and providers can become discouraged from communicating their concerns or ideas because of attitudinal barriers. In one center we visited, a Chinese mother expressed her frustration with the care setting because it encouraged children to "crawl around on the floor." Now her son was crawling around at home as well, even when adults were in the room. From her perspective, this was highly disrespectful behavior. When she tried to talk to her son, he replied, "But this is what I was taught by my teacher." Asked whether she had communicated this concern to a teacher, the mother replied that she had trouble expressing her concerns in English and she was worried that the providers wouldn't react positively. She said she had mentioned the issue to some Chinese teachers, but their response was, "This is America."

In this case, the center had not created an atmosphere where the Chinese mother felt comfortable talking to the English-speaking teachers about her concerns. And, while the Chinese teachers probably felt they were helping the parent to adjust to a new country, in reality they discouraged her from finding ways to work with the center to find a solution. If dialogue had not been silenced all around, the teachers and the parent might have found ways to communicate to the child that some behaviors learned in the classroom may not be appropriate at home, and that he also needed to respect the judgement of his elders.

Lisa Lee, the associate director of the Parent Services Project, observed:

> *We [child care workers] wear professional hats that are hard to broach. We have a lot of biases ourselves toward parents and their social or economic situations and class and language.*

Biased attitudes can prevent providers from seeing the strengths of family members and treating them as equal partners in a child's development. Parents sense these attitudes, even when the providers themselves may not be aware that they are projecting bias or condescension.

Providers need to examine their beliefs and assess whether they hold attitudes which may hurt their ability to engage a child's parents. Many groups share the cultural belief that parents should never question a teacher because it is a sign of disrespect for their position. This appeared to be at work for both the Chinese mother and the caregivers in the interaction described above. At other times, providers do not respect the wisdom or judgement of parents because they come from different backgrounds. Ironically, many biases against parents can be a reflection of the same societal attitudes and "isms" related to race, language, gender, class, etc. which programs are seeking to change among children.

Parents also need to examine their attitudes that may present barriers to developing partnerships with providers. We found that parental attitudes were particularly troubling to providers serving middle/upper class parents; here some teachers expressed frustration with the tendency of parents to treat them condescendingly or take them for granted. In these cases, providers may be inhibited from sharing information about anything, including race, language and culture issues. Unfortunately, the field of early care and education does not currently enjoy the public respect it deserves, even though our society now relies upon child care providers to fulfill a tremendously consequential role.

Strategy 4

Increase understanding by encouraging parents to spend time in the care setting.

Encouraging parent participation in the care setting is an excellent strategy for increasing understanding and building relationships. Programs do this in a variety of ways. Many programs invite parents to participate in events such as holiday celebrations or children's birthday parties. Often, parents are utilized as resources of cultural information and invited to make presentations to their children's class. These presentations not only teach children but give providers important information about the traditions and beliefs of the families. And, having parents assume such roles conveys a message to children that their families and heritage are held in high esteem.

A number of programs also encourage parents to drop in at any time, for any length of time, to observe and/or assist. Sometimes programs ask parents to participate a certain number of hours throughout the year, perhaps assisting staff in the classroom or on the playground. A few programs, typically parent cooperatives, formally require parents to spend a specified amount of time helping out in the classroom. Because in some of these cases parents operate as classroom assistants, such programs typically must invest time in ensuring parents are properly oriented to policies and the practices of the program before they work directly with children.

Parents spending time in the classroom is an effective orientation to the caregiving philosophy and approach because it allows them to learn through observation. For example, if parents do not speak the same language as the provider, they can observe the provider in action to gain a better sense of what their child will learn under their care. Even if parents and providers speak the same language, observation can be critical because conversations out of context can be misunderstood.

Parents spending time in the classroom is an effective orientation to the caregiving philosophy and approach because it allows them to learn through observation.

Challenges to Strategy 4

Challenge: Parents don't always have time to participate

While parent participation in the care setting is extremely valuable, providers should be aware that it is not an option for all parents. This is particularly true for low income, working class parents who must devote every spare minute to working so that their family can survive economically. Unfortunately, many workplaces don't allow parents flexibility in their hours that would make it possible for them to spend time with their children in care.

Thought needs to be given to how to inform parents about what happens in care even if they can't participate. Some programs maintain resource libraries where parents can check out the same materials and books used by staff. Here, interested parents can read about the approaches to care and diversity issues on their own time. However, this would not be as useful to parents of a lower literacy level. Providers can also show parents relevant materials. At a family child care home in Los Angeles, a provider participated in a Sesame Street class that dealt with issues of bias. She then sent copies of a tape about bigotry and prejudice home with some parents, and asked them to write about their own experiences with bigotry. This process made a deep impression on a number of the parents.

Strategy 5

Use parent conferences and goal setting for individual children to ensure that issues of language, race and culture are being effectively addressed for each child.

Many programs have a policy of holding meetings where parents and providers can—without distraction—discuss the welfare of a child. Some programs conduct parent conferences by visiting the families' homes rather than asking parents to come to the center. During home visits, providers can see the child and the family in their own environment, and gain a better understanding of their culture and practices. Live Oak Migrant Head Start, which serves Mexican and Punjabi children, pays home visits twice during the year, before the child begins attending the program and several months later. During the first visit, they ask parents a variety of questions including what the child is like, whether the child can feed him or herself, whether the child is toilet-trained, what the child's favorite activities and interests are, and what the parents' goals for the child are. During the second home visit, the parent and the teacher discuss the child's progress.

During conferences, providers and parents often establish goals for a child. Such goals can include those specifically related to cultural understanding, language development and anti-racist attitudes. The process of goal setting can also reveal cultural differences between the home and care setting, even if the goals themselves are not explicitly about race, language or culture. A common goal can create opportunities for providers and parents to examine what each can do to help realize it. For example, providers and parents may agree that a child should be grounded in his or her cultural traditions. But, it may not be realistic to expect a provider from a different background to learn and then teach those traditions, especially if there are children from a number of different cultures in the classroom. In this case, parents may assume responsibility for teaching traditions to their child while the provider finds ways to demonstrate that they are valued in the classroom. If both the providers and the parents share the same traditions, both may play a role in explaining and deepening the child's understanding of the family heritage.

If a child comes from a family that is bilingual or speaks a language other than English, parents and providers can set a goal together to help a child retain the home language and eventually acquire English. It is often critical to discuss the goals for both languages simultaneously. As one Head Start administrator once said:

> *We always ask parents, do you want your child to learn English? But, we rarely ask parents, do you want your child to lose his or her home language?*

Once bilingualism is established as a shared goal, a provider and parents can talk about the steps which both can take to promote the acquisition of both languages. If the approach of a program is to only use the home language, this is an opportunity for the providers to explain why they believe this will help a child to eventually learn English. Providers can also emphasize the critical role of parents in encouraging a child to value and speak the home language. This message is particularly crucial if the program is bilingual or predominantly English-speaking.

A clear definition of goals gives parents and providers a basis for assessing—as time passes—whether a child is progressing as hoped. It can also offer an opportunity for knowledgeable providers to allay parent fears. For example, parents of bi-

lingual children may not realize that children who are exposed to two languages often experience a delay in speaking; then when they first start speaking, they may mix languages. Over time, however, with the appropriate support, children can easily negotiate the two languages and learn with whom they should use which language.

Finally, discussing goals can help to uncover more subtle forms of cross-cultural differences which might otherwise pass unnoticed. Consider the experience of one infant/toddler caregiver who, despite her own bilingual (English/Spanish) and bicultural background (Mexican American), found she was unable to anticipate a cross-cultural issue which arose for a Korean toddler under her care. Employed at a university child care center, this caregiver often cared for babies of international students. One year she found herself responsible for an 18-month-old Korean girl who always allowed the other toddlers to take her toys away from her. Wanting the child to be able to stand up for herself, the provider patiently worked to teach the girl to be more assertive and to hold on to her toys. During the course of a regular parent conference, the provider mentioned to the parents, who would soon be moving back to Korea, that helping the child to stand up for herself was one of her goals. Although the parents appreciated her efforts, they wondered, "What will we do when we return to Korea? Her grandparents will think we have raised a selfish child!"

Challenges to Strategy 5

Challenge: Recognizing the importance of hiring staff who can work effectively with parents

Building strong relationships with parents is easier when a program has staff with the backgrounds and skills to facilitate communication and bonding. For example, when parents and providers do not share a language, it is of course extremely difficult to exchange ideas and information. Discussions about culture, language and race can be extremely sensitive and involve very important nuances that are easily lost if two adults are not fluent in the same language. One provider we interviewed worked at a center run by the Foundation Center for Phenomenological Research, which placed a high priority on hiring staff from the community who spoke the languages of families. She shared the following insight:

I used to work in another program where the head teachers couldn't speak Spanish and, as a result, could not communicate with the parents. Only the teaching assistants could talk with them. At this program, any teacher can talk to the parents. As a result, parents are more likely to believe the child can do something. They want to see what their children are doing here.

Parents also appreciate seeing that the staff includes people from their racial background. If, for example, the staff of a center serving a predominantly African American community is entirely white, African American parents may wonder whether people of their racial background are valued by the center. Having someone on staff who looks like them helps to establish trust and a visible comfort zone for parents, especially if such individuals can be found at various levels in the hierarchy.

Staff members must have the patience and the skills to communicate respectfully with parents who are different from themselves even when they do not speak a common language.

Providers have an easier time establishing a bond when they have overcome some of the same challenges confronting the parents in care. Janet Gonzalez-Mena observed:

Someone who has been through a similar experience often has greater insight into what is happening and as a result is better equipped to talk to parents about what they want...For example, if you are a monolingual, non-English-speaking parent, it is very hard to tell a provider that it may be more important for them to speak their home language to their child than English.

Common experiences—whether related to race or other types of life experiences—can be integral to credibility. At the same time, at some point most staff will work across differences in race, language and culture. Regardless of their personal background, staff members must have the patience and the skills to communicate respectfully with parents who are different from themselves even when they do not speak a common language. Strong interpersonal skills, flexibility, and a real appreciation and respect for parents are necessary qualities of providers under any circumstances. These qualities should be prioritized during hiring and professional development activities.

Challenge: Balancing the knowledge and beliefs of parents and staff

Clearly, one of the greatest challenges to the parent-provider relationship is balancing the knowledge and beliefs of parents and staff, especially when there is serious disagreement. Parents know the personalities and behaviors of their children intimately and hold strong beliefs about what will be the best care for them. Providers are professionals grounded in child development concepts. The article by Janet Gonzalez-Mena in our Principle on Culture chapter offers many useful real-life examples about parents and providers negotiating their differences regarding child care.

Strategy 6

Involve parents in decision-making to ensure the program as a whole recognizes and addresses issues of diversity.

Many providers create mechanisms for parents to impact what happens programmatically. These can range from parent advisory committees, to including parents on the board of directors, to creating opportunities for parents to work with staff to develop policies and guidelines. If parents are invited to become involved in this way, however, providers still must facilitate opportunities for issues of race, language and culture to be addressed.

David Longaker, education coordinator at the Center for Education and Manpower Resources for Migrant Head Start, described Head Start's approach to this:

> *Having parents in policymaking positions is one way cultural issues are addressed through the Head Start design. Parents from the different centers are elected by other parents to represent the family interest at the local level and also at the broader program level. They are not just in an advisory capacity; they have to approve of all major decisions made by the program. So, when issues come up, there is a forum within our program for addressing them. For example, a couple of years ago, the issue of using food in learning activities—such as sorting beans, making macaroni necklaces, etc.—came up. Some of this may be socioeconomic rather than cultural, but parents found themselves uncomfortable with the notion of food being used that way. They felt children were being taught a value they really didn't share: food is something to play with. The policy council made it a policy that food would no longer be used in that context, except for playdough, and we have found ways to adapt activities.*

Challenges to Strategy 6

Challenge: Creating opportunities for parents to work on collective strategies

If parents are to be included in decision-making or governance, they need opportunities to understand the experiences of children overall in the program in order to best represent as many families as possible. Otherwise, a parent may only be able to promote the welfare of their own child based on their own experience with the center. Program staff may then find themselves negotiating complaints that they are catering only to the most vocal parents. Allowing all parents to air their viewpoints is essential to the development of program-wide policies which reflect the interests of the group and not just individuals. Even if parents do not reach consensus and the program cannot accommodate all of their wishes, understanding the differences of opinions helps providers and parent representatives to develop more appropriate policies.

California Tomorrow heard about just such an effort when we visited Centro

VIDA. Prior to our visit, the parent committee had been exploring at length what the balance should be between English and Spanish spoken in the center. A survey had revealed very different beliefs among parents about the topic. Some of the parents, particularly those who were monolingual Spanish speakers, wanted their children to be exposed to more English in preparation for school. Other parents wanted more Spanish, on the grounds that the children were already picking up English but not always retaining their Spanish. Some parents had no position. The director arranged for experts to come to the center to present information on bilingualism and second language acquisition to parents.

Programs can help build a sense of collective group understanding by providing parents with informal opportunities to meet and socialize. Events involving food and the sharing of different cultural traditions are a feature of many programs. The Davis Child Development Center holds a variety of functions for parents from multicultural potlucks to craft nights where parents make crafts together to be sold to support the center. According to parent Bernita Toney:

> *These functions offer times when parents can get together and talk about problems they are having with kids and school. It's like family here. These little functions make it easier to have someone to talk to. When there is a new parent, everybody is open and offers both advice and support.*

Challenge: Providers are often unaware of how their attitudes and behaviors might inhibit parent involvement in decision-making

According to the Parent Services Project, as a bottom-line, providers must understand that nurturing parent leadership is a two-way process. In order for parents to become leaders, staff must find ways to truly share authority. They must be prepared to work with parents to address their concerns. Lack of follow-through by staff can all too quickly result in parents feeling disempowered, even when providers express the best of intentions. At one program we visited, a parent shared with us the following observation:

> *The center holds parent meetings but parents aren't involved in making decisions. The meetings are mostly about fundraising, and the parameters of the meetings are clearly established. The program needs to allow parents to voice their opinions, but control is too tight. For example, parents suggested holding a benefit dinner, but the center staff decided they should sell candy. Parents no longer voice their opinions because they think it's useless.*

Beatriz Leyva-Cutler commented:

> *A lot of programs are afraid of utilizing parents. They worry that parents will take over. We have found that not being afraid is one of the greatest things you can do. Parents are what will move a program. When parents*

walk in, they know what is going on and what is not. They know what needs to be done. They are an invaluable resource. Parents at VIDA contribute to the curriculum, they shape the program, and they help to maintain the environment.

Challenge: Ensuring that all parents have the opportunity to participate in meetings

Ensuring that parents are not excluded from participation in the program requires careful thought and consideration. Otherwise, the parents who do participate will not reflect the community as a whole. Often, exclusion is unintentional, as providers do not recognize the barriers for parents. For example, if parent meetings do not provide child care, parents will be excluded who can not pay for a babysitter or utilize relatives or friends to care for their children.

Some programs overestimate the ability of parents who speak another language to communicate in English. For example, at one program we visited, a Chinese mother recalled attending a meeting along with the grandmother of another Chinese child in the class. Neither of the women spoke English, but the entire meeting was conducted in English. The center staff included a bilingual instructional assistant, but the assistant was assigned to take care of the children while the parents attended the meeting.

When programs use home language in meetings, it makes a noticeable difference. A teacher described the change that took place when her new director shifted the language of discourse. The previous director had held all of the meetings in English and parents were very quiet. Now under the leadership of the new director, all of the meetings were bilingual in Spanish and English. Meetings are now well attended and lively, parents express themselves more, and there is a greater sense of community. This is true even among parents who do not speak Spanish.

Working with Non-English-Speaking Families

by Lisa Lee, Associate Director, Parent Services Project

MOST CHILD CARE PROGRAMS, like all human service delivery systems in the United States, make English their primary language. The use of English makes perfect sense. Communication between parent and family, though sometimes challenging, generally works. However, when parents are new to this country and the second language they are learning is English, communication is another story, one that doesn't always work.

In fact, a child care center can be a strange and uncertain environment to parents whose primary language is other than English. Though unable to bridge language barriers, parents feel the need to be part of a system which socializes their children. For many, education is viewed as their family's path to success. Like parents everywhere, they want their children to do well, yet many feel uncertain about a language and culture that is different than their own.

Difficulties in communicating, while also creating challenges for providers, are felt more intimately by parents. Parents who can speak English have much to hear about their child's day and experiences. Non-English-speaking parents hunger for information about their child. When parents attend meetings, they often endure long stretches of English before the translation comes...if it comes.

Power and knowledge go hand-in-hand with the ability to communicate. When language barriers exist, it is common to feel frustrated, powerless or alienated. Some parents equate lack of recognition for their language as a lack of respect for their culture. Although unintended by providers, parents may feel rejected and may isolate themselves further. Parents who don't speak English often feel bad about not being able to understand. Out of respect for the teacher, they may nod affirmatively to comments without truly understanding what is being said. Others may apologize that their English is "not good" and decline to participate in school functions or to take leadership roles.

For the child care provider, crossing language and cultural barriers has much to do with recognizing one's own biases and attitudes toward people. One must consistently evaluate feelings and levels of trust and power in day-to-day interactions. It requires shifting from the expert role to one of collaborator and facilitator. It means understanding how communication, or the lack of it, affects feelings of power and the ability of individuals to be involved.

Parents and providers are more alike than different in our need to communicate. When a parent speaks another language, it is important to establish a relationship which is one of equality and respect from the start, setting the tone for the future. If parents feel embarrassed about their English skills, it is sometimes helpful for providers to share how frustrated they feel at not being able to communicate in the parents' language. This helps to break down any tinge of superior/inferior perceptions from the relationship, and keeps both on the same level as human beings.

Providers can also link parents who speak the same language with one another, encouraging informal support networks. Having someone who has shared similar experiences of being outside of the mainstream helps to create a sense of belonging. Parents count on one another, translating and problem-solving, or just commiserating about how difficult maneuvering through the system is.

Providers and parents can share a special bond. Both want to communicate and have to work very hard to do so. Unfortunately, many programs see communication as a one-way street. They place the responsibility on the parent to understand, to bring in the translator and to be the ones who lose out when the barrier is too formidable. It's an attitude that exists on an institutional level which is difficult to detect at times.

For providers who build true partnerships with parents, communication is a two-way street. Agencies work hard to reflect diversity of culture and language in staffing their centers. They translate notices in pertinent languages, finding resources to do so from staff, community agencies, colleagues and the parents themselves. Programs recognize the importance of the parents' presence and that ultimately both have a need and responsibility to keep the lines of communication open. ❧

Child Care Programs as Community Resources

FOR MANY FAMILIES, the care setting attended by their children is a source of community—a place to connect to new friends as well as to other resources in the area. California Tomorrow found that many programs, in spite of their own limited budgets and staffing, try hard to help families access a variety of services beyond child care. This comes out of a strong caring for the parents as well as an understanding that the well-being of children is intertwined with that of their families. We learned that the community resource role played by many programs was invaluable to the parents.

Many of the programs we visited connect families to the services of other agencies on an informal basis. For example, at Centro de Niños, executive director Nati Fuentes has spent her life working on behalf of her community. An active member of many local groups and committees, Nati is extremely knowledgeable about the types of resources available. During our site visit to the center, we ate lunch at a local restaurant run by Oscar Medina, whose granddaughter had attended Nati's programs. Oscar noted:

> *If you ever want to know what is happening in the county, just go to Nati. She is one of the most well-versed people in the entire community.*

Some child care programs are able to link families to other services because they are part of larger organizations that comprehensively serve families. Plaza Preschool, for example, is part of Plaza Community Center in East Los Angeles. Plaza Community Center offers community members —including the families enrolled in the preschool—a broad array of social services ranging from health care to employment and training.

Some caregivers work collaboratively with other agencies serving the same families. The Marin Learning Center operates under the auspices of Marin Community Action, which in turn is part of the Marin City Project. The latter is a community effort focused on housing redevelopment, social services and job training. As part of this project, the Marin Learning Center will be relocated to a space shared by a variety of other social services.

In some cases, child development programs obtain funding so that they themselves can provide additional services to families. For example, health fairs were frequently sponsored by the child development programs run by the Foundation Center, which served many migrant farmworker families in rural areas and low income families in urban areas. At these health fairs, all family members could receive information about health and illnesses, see a doctor and obtain immunizations. These services were important for families who did not have insurance and may not have had access to any preventive information or care. According to many parents and teachers, the health fairs made a tremendous difference for the children and their families.

Head Start programs are also well known for their efforts to support family well-being. Standard features include dental and health exams for all enrolled children and mental health services for children if needed. Every family that enrolls a child in a program is assigned a community social services worker. This worker initially conducts a family assessment and then assists the family on an ongoing basis to obtain services when needed.

The families who felt that their child care provider was a source of resources and support were very enthusiastic about this benefit. For many families, the fragmented bureaucracies of formal services are not pleasant—and sometimes very difficult—to negotiate. This can be even harder for families who do not speak English or whose past experiences have alienated them from public bureaucracies. Most programs for children and families only address specific issues such as poor grades, absenteeism, child abuse, mental health and health. Also, more often than not, programs focus on a problem facing a particular family member without fully addressing those of the others.

But what happens to one family member inevitably affects the rest. While providers are very aware of this in their work with children, they are rarely supported to offer the kinds of community resource services for which they have the potential. As we have talked about elsewhere in this book, as it is, providers are grossly under-resourced to offer the kinds of innovative child care and education they envision.

Therefore, more often than not, providers act as community resources informally on top of the multitude of tasks for which they are responsible in their caregiving. The mother of a child at Olivia Thompson Green's "Families Working Together" family child care home in Los Angeles described how important this was to her. She said that Olivia drew her attention to a free word processing class at the African American Unity Center. The mother, in turn, told her friends about the class:

> *Ms. Olivia is a major part of my life. She asks the parents, "Are you in school? Do you know about the services here or there?" She helps me with my parenting too. I think it is her way of giving back to the community.* ❧

What Kinds of Information Do Parents Need for Choosing Child Care in a Diverse Society?

PARENTS MUST BALANCE many hopes and needs for their children when choosing child care. Location, cost, program philosophy and curriculum, the reputation of the caregivers, etc., all come into play. While all programs would ideally expose children to the five Principles of Quality Care in a Diverse Society, different types of care settings may be more effective at imparting different principles, and many programs do not yet come close to touching on them. Making this decision is complex, requiring thought about a child's individual personality and what is happening in his or her environment. For parents who are not fluent in English, bilingual or home language child care may be a higher priority. Other families may choose an ethnically diverse care setting because their children would otherwise have no opportunities to be exposed to different kinds of people. And as we have discussed elsewhere, many parents do not feel that attention to their child's racial, linguistic or cultural needs can be expected from the child care setting.

Typically a family must weigh decisions about appropriate child care more than once during their children's young years. Many families use more than one type of care. Families also need to change care because of changes in their economic situation or residence. What a child needs in terms of a care setting may also change over time as he or she develops. As of now, we found that families are basically on their own to figure out the appropriate fit between their children's needs, their family circumstances and values, and the child care setting.

Although the group of parents we interviewed was relatively small and not a representative sample, we do know generally about the sources of information these parents used to find out about child care options. Although most parents use several sources of information—the Yellow Pages, employers, social service agencies, resource and referral agencies, pediatricians—the majority of the parents we interviewed based their final decisions on the recommendations of friends or family. Interestingly, it was not uncommon that the friend or family member recommending care was a child care teacher herself. We can not know the content of the information exchange among friends and family about child care, but it appeared from our interviews that information about quality care with regards to race, language and culture is lacking in the exchange.

Families need more information, both before choosing a program as well as while attending a program, in order to make the best choices for care in a diverse society.

What Do Parents Need to Know?

1. Child development relating to race, language and culture:

- How is caregiving influenced by culture—their own and that of the caregiver?
- How do children learn second languages and become bilingual?
- How do children develop racial and cultural identity?
- How do children develop prejudice and bias?

2. Child care options in their area:

– What is the philosophy and approach of the program in terms of race, language and culture?

– What languages are spoken by the provider or teachers in the program?

3. Supporting their child in the program and working with the caregiver(s):

– What can parents do to bring up issues of race, language, culture or bias with the program staff?

– How can parents bring their own culture and language into the program?

How can parents be informed?

Information to parents about the role care can play in helping children develop an understanding of race, language and culture is critical for them to make a solid decision about where their child should be enrolled. Child care facilities as well as other institutions are important sources of this type of information. It may seem like an overwhelming challenge to get this information to the millions of parents who have one or more children with a child under six years old (there are over 10 million in California), when they speak dozens of languages, and are very busy with work, school and family. Individual programs are important sources of information about all aspects of child care and child development, but they cannot be wholly responsible for informing parents, for several reasons. First, many programs do not have the information themselves about the implications of race, culture and language in early care and education. Second, parents need information before they get into a program, so that they can make an informed choice. Currently, however, there are few mechanisms for ensuring that all parents have the information they need to make the choices that are best for them and their children.

There are two aspects to the challenge of informing parents. First, what are the best methods for conveying the information—brochures, videos, classes, radio, hotlines? What languages are needed? What is the most crucial information that will assist parents in making the best choices for their families? Second, what agencies or individuals are best suited to deliver the information? There are a variety of agencies and individuals who have regular contact with parents—resource and referral agencies, hospitals/pediatricians, prenatal classes, parenting classes, libraries and school districts, to name a few. What kind of preparation do these service providers need to competently discuss child care and diversity issues with the parents?

Further research is needed to answer these questions. Organizations or individuals may currently produce some information about language, race and culture in early childhood education aimed at parents, but it is not being disseminated widely. Coordination of this information is needed, as well as increased research into the issues themselves. ❧

Chapter 6 Principles of Quality Care in a Diverse Society

Principle Five: Engage in Dialogue and Reflection About Race, Language and Culture on an Ongoing Basis

You don't ever "finish" with culture and diversity issues. They continue to surface in human relationships. It's forever. Part of the problem is that we don't have good ways in child care programs to sustain ongoing exploration of any issues.

—Marcy Whitebook, founder of the National Center for the Early Childhood Workforce

There has to be some way of looking at what it means to say that diversity is a high priority. What does that really mean? Is it a question about human value? Are you thinking about setting up a situation in the classroom where you believe every person in the classroom is trying to be as good as they can possibly be or achieve whatever is available for them in terms of their own human potential? As a first step you would have to do a lot of talking about what you mean.

—Mary Cardenas, Cabrillo Community College

Trust and communication develop over time, so there has to be a commitment made in terms of time and money to offering ongoing opportunities to build that trust and communication...I don't know that people can successfully jump over a horrendous value conflict or cultural conflict if they haven't invested any energy prior to that in communication and trust. People need to have time to learn about each other, as well as to go over what the program is going to be.

—Melinda Sprague, Reducing Exceptional Stress and Trauma Project

Why is this Principle Important?

The four Principles of Quality Care in a Diverse Society we have suggested thus far are all reliant on the fifth. Open and ongoing dialogue about race, language and culture—as they relate to the children in care, their families and the practices of caregivers—is crucial for programs to effectively and positively address diversity issues.

In preceding chapters, we have highlighted the need for caregivers to reflect on their views, beliefs and biases regarding race, culture, language, relationships with parents and the role of the program in preparing children for a diverse society. We have also discussed the need for programs to analyze their philosophy, policies and practices (e.g., regarding enrollment, hiring, grouping of children, parent involvement, language use, cultural activities, racial representation in the environment, etc.) and to strategize about how to improve the way the program addresses diversity issues.

Implicit in all of this work is the need for continual, thoughtful dialogue and personal reflection. California Tomorrow, in its own experience as an organization committed to equity, as well as in its work with other educational and community institutions, has learned that a habit of open communication about race, culture and language is the foundation for any successful effort to address diversity. No strategy or policy can be fully effective without this foundation.

Becoming aware of our own identity as individuals, our own beliefs, values and philosophy is key to addressing issues when they arise with children in the care setting. So, too, is understanding that the views and values of other providers or families may be different based on their life experiences. Examining and discussing our own biases is critical in a program—each person's own biases, where they came from, how to become more aware of them and how to prevent perpetuating bias in the classroom. Eleanor Clement Glass of the San Francisco Foundation said:

> *What are the harmful things you bring and how does the harm manifest itself? It is also important for people to understand that they have been hurt themselves by biases and to share, on the emotional level, how it plays out in human interaction. I think people need to get back to their own feelings of hurt in order to start understanding others' hurt. Everybody has experienced that.*

The most important and accessible resources for discussions on issues of diversity are the adults connected to a program. There is a wealth of knowledge and experience among the teachers and parents waiting to be tapped into. Sometimes we don't even realize that we have a particular opinion or viewpoint until we come into contact with someone who sees the world differently. We may have a gut reaction but aren't able to explain it until we have had the practice of telling it to someone else. People who recognize how their beliefs are grounded in their background are less inclined to judge others negatively. Rather, they will weigh the information to see if their own approach may be enhanced, or consider whether they may be doing something wrong. Fully exploring different cultural styles of caregiving can also help people understand that not all practices can or should be universally applied.

Dialogue about diversity is important in any setting, whether or not the children and staff are very diverse. A homogenous or ethnic-specific center has just as much need to examine and clarify program philosophies, practices and policies regarding race, language and culture, and how bias and prejudice are to be addressed with children and among staff. Such dialogue may not be considered as pressing when most staff and families are from the same racial, cultural or linguistic group, and everyone seems to be alike. People may have a more difficult time, for example, articulating how culture influences their lives and how they care for children when there is no apparent contrasting culture in the environment. However, through sharing and discussion, a staff which appears to be all of the same background will learn that there are variations within the group. National origin, religious beliefs, economic class, gender, sexual orientation, as well as race, culture and language will vary even among people who appear to be the same.

It is also just as important to create vehicles for dialogue whether the child care setting is large or small. For example, family child care providers, who typically work alone or with one or two staff members, can greatly benefit from utilizing networks and associations to engage with other providers in discussions about diversity issues.

Programs should strive to create an atmosphere where diversity is discussed routinely, and where ongoing learning by all of the adults—caregivers and parents—is fostered. In the ideal atmosphere, people are encouraged to learn, to trust and support one another, to feel that it is safe to make mistakes while working to understand diversity issues, and to make it a habit to notice and discuss matters as they arise. A few of the programs visited by California Tomorrow had achieved atmospheres of open communication, and many other programs were working toward this goal. Providers and trainers offered a variety of thoughts on the value of dialogue and how to sustain it.

The Benefits of Creating an Atmosphere of Open and Ongoing Dialogue

Several teachers at Live Oak Migrant Head Start, a program of primarily Mexican and Punjabi staff and families, talked about their efforts to create openness among their staff to sharing experiences and learning about one another. Teacher Carmen Arredondo described how one of the Punjabi teachers brought her wedding sari to share with her colleagues. The dress inspired a conversation among staff about wedding traditions in their countries and the symbolism of the colors used in different rituals. At Live Oak, this type of dialogue took place informally during staff meetings and also more extensively during the planning of curriculum themes around culture. Carmen talked about the conditions necessary for this type of comfortable exchange:

> *Most importantly, we respect each other, so we are able to exchange information. We see a lot of similarities among the two cultures, despite the differences. We feel comfortable asking each other questions. We really appreciate one another. We are also role modeling for the children and parents.*

Another teacher, Balwinder Singh, continued to describe the open and supportive atmosphere among the teachers at Live Oak:

> *One person will say, "This is what we do in our culture. Do you do the same thing?" Then we share it with other staff or parents. It is easy.*

Opening up to co-workers is not always an easy thing to do. But it can be made less difficult if trust is created so that each person in the group will genuinely try to learn from others, forgive mistakes, and not misuse what others say. One trainer said that too often fear prevents innovation:

> *People are so afraid of making mistakes...because of not wanting to hurt someone or offend someone or appear to be racist, or appear to not know or not to do it right. When you get to application, you have to be willing to make some mistakes. You have to be willing to try it.*

Eric Peterson, one of the co-directors at Step One School, a center committed to an anti-bias philosophy, talked about how important it has been to foster an atmosphere where people realize that it is acceptable to take risks when talking to each other and asking questions:

> *Through our mistakes—that's where the learning is happening.*

Dialogue about diversity is important in any setting, whether or not the children and staff are very diverse.

Janis Keyser, an instructor at Cabrillo College, noted that in the most fruitful dialogue, people listen carefully and trust that they will also be heard:

> *Listening is not just a tool we can use to get information which can help us come up with common solutions. It is also a statement to the speakers that who they are as people is important to us. It is a way of bonding. It is a way of valuing people's experiences.*

One of the primary benefits of dialogue in a program is the development of deeper understandings of the complexities of race, culture, ethnicity, bias, home language and other concepts. Through this kind of dialogue, we can also sometimes best learn more about ourselves. For example, Eleanor Clement Glass talked about how difficult it can be to identify and articulate how culture affects our own lives. We are "swimming around" in our cultures, she said, so that it is sometimes hard to see what is cultural about the way we behave and what we believe. To help sort through this, she said:

It's best to juxtapose your culture with other cultures, and to discuss the various points of view and then where those points of view came from.

Eleanor stressed the importance of talking about the nuances and variety of experiences within a racial, cultural or linguistic group as well:

All African Americans are not alike and all are not going to have the same experience. Culture is not monolithic. When people have the opportunity to talk about it, that helps to break up the monolithic perceptions they have about other cultures, and to begin to understand it when they do have a monolithic perception about a culture and where it came from.

Carmen Arredondo at Live Oak told us that reflecting on the individual experiences of the teachers in the program has heightened her understanding of the cultural differences in child care:

We have children whose parents were born and raised in the States and children whose parents were raised in Mexico. Even though we are all Latinos we understand that we care for our children differently.

Ardella Dailey, adjunct faculty with Pacific Oaks College and an administrator with the Alameda Unified School District, said that personal reflection and dialogue have helped her sort through her questions about different child rearing values:

There are parenting styles which are authoritarian, versus permissive, versus empowering. How I really accept and respect a culture that doesn't have my values and approach it is difficult. I know I impose more than I should—but then, I don't know, because there are things I can't go along with. And it is possible that they are about a cultural difference and not about right or wrong. I've found that to be my most difficult personal struggle. I find that if you are not dialoguing it internally, let alone externally with other people, then you don't address it at all or you reactively address it without careful thought.

If people feel included and respected, open communication and dialogue about diversity will enhance the sense of community and trust within a program. Building this sense of a team has wide-reaching benefits. Specifically regarding diversity issues, providers can not only grow to rely upon others within the program, but become open to reaching out to extended networks for information and support. Mary Cardenas at Cabrillo Community College addressed this issue:

If we don't have the answer, especially if it is not something particular to our own background and experiences, there are ways to call on the expertise of one another and not to sit and stew in isolation.

In a program that incorporates vehicles for communication about diversity, problems have a better chance of being prevented or defused before becoming destructive. Melinda Sprague talked about the need to have this foundation in place:

If a crisis occurs, you already have the tools to handle it. If you don't do that stuff on an ongoing basis and you have a big problem come up, that's when people go underground and you have parking lot conversations where nothing gets resolved.

Finally, the most fundamental reason to engage in ongoing communication is the benefit it can bring to the children in care. Teachers who are comfortable talking about these issues will be more prepared to proactively respond to incidents in the classroom and to answer questions from children about race, culture, language, bias and differences. Teachers will be better able to use such incidents as teaching moments, rather than be silent or silence the children. Julie Olsen Edwards of Cabrillo Community College said she "tries to get people to move through the walls of silence."

The key is breaking the silence. What is ineffective with children is whatever people won't talk about. If the grown-ups are so immobilized, there is no way children will work their way through it. The worst things children carry are secrets. Nothing is more damaging, putting up huge blocks to their thinking and rigidity to their souls. The key thing is an atmosphere where the issues of bias, fear and differences are part of the conversation.

Building Personal Foundations for Dialogue

Among individuals California Tomorrow interviewed who have closely focused on diversity in their work, several attributed their ability to think and talk critically about diversity to their own strong sense of cultural and racial identity. The process of understanding cultural and racial identity is different for every individual. Programs striving for effective communication can encourage individuals to think about and share what the process has been like for them. This can contribute to a sense of community, and help individuals think about the sources of their beliefs and values.

Janet Gonzalez-Mena, who teaches at Napa Valley College and has written extensively about cross-cultural issues in child rearing, shared how important it was for her to come to terms with her identity as a white European American woman:

> *I realized early on who I had to focus on. One of the steps I had to take was to accept myself and my culture, to discover I had a culture. About the time I discovered that, I didn't like it very much. I thought maybe I could be somebody else. I do remember the day it hit me that I am who I am, and it is really okay. That was an exciting time for me and I've been working on learning more about my culture and its roots since then.*

If people feel included and respected, open communication and dialogue about diversity will enhance the sense of community and trust within a program.

Intisar Shareef, an instructor at Contra Costa Community College, found that being involved in the Nation of Islam contributed to her pride in and connection to others of her race and culture:

> *I spent seven years of my life in the Nation of Islam, in a Black separatist organization. So I was very steeped in an experience that elevated the Black experience. I saw Black people in positions of authority—uncompromisingly...People from communities that have been historically targeted, marginalized or oppressed need to be strengthened in their minority status. They have to connect in that marginal status to see their own strength and then to emerge from it. I don't think it has to last forever. As a matter of fact, from my own experience, I don't think it does.*

Individuals will have experiences throughout their lives which contribute to their understandings and emotions about race, language and culture. Child care programs alone can not be responsible for ensuring that teachers understand these issues, but they can provide a valuable service to adults and children as a safe and supportive place to begin the exploration.

There are several specific strategies we identified that programs can use to ensure ongoing and productive dialogue. Above all, adults in the program need to be encouraged to engage in discussion and exploration about race, culture and language, and to work from a framework that diversity in our society is a valuable asset. What follows is a description of strategies for helping to create ongoing dialogue and reflection:

- Create activities to engage people in discussions.
- Develop facilitation skills.
- Create the time and opportunity for dialogue.
- Include diverse perspectives in discussions.

The challenges associated with dialogue are often daunting, including the fear of saying something that will make things worse, and the lack of quality time, facilitation and other resources for child care providers to discuss many important topics. Because the challenges are interrelated and apply to most strategies, we discuss them together at the end of this chapter, in a small departure from the format of previous principles.

Promising Strategies

Strategy 1

Create activities to engage people in discussions.

> *"What is your earliest memory of noticing someone was different than you?" "What childhood messages did you get about differences and how you should view people who are different than you?" Sharing stories at an adult level or reviewing differences that exist among the staff in an open climate does a lot to alert people to how they need to think about these issues for kids. People get a heightened awareness of how young they were and how sharp the images still are for them.*
>
> —Margie Carter, author and trainer

There are a variety of strategies groups can use to spark self reflection and discussions about diversity. A structured activity can help take the awkwardness out of broaching these subjects, open up new ways of thinking, or provide avenues for sharing information or lessons. Here are a few tools to direct and enhance the discussion, whether in a single program or across programs.

Sharing Life Stories

Sharing life stories, values and beliefs is important for many reasons. It can help to create a safe and trusting environment. It can help in identifying ways in which the program can use the resources and expertise represented among the staff. And it can help individuals to clarify how race, language and culture are interrelated in their own lives and caregiving styles.

The *Anti-Bias Curriculum* strategies described in our Principle on Race give an example of how dialogue can be inspired through the sharing of life experiences. California Tomorrow has used "journey maps" to encourage personal sharing. Participants draw a map, or some representation using pictures and words, of their personal journey that shaped their views on race, language and culture. They then share their map with others, describing why they took certain roads. We used this technique at a retreat with a group of teachers and directors of centers whom we had visited for this research. Participants were asked to share their maps with someone they thought would have an interesting point of view or who they wanted to know more. One of the pairs was two African American women, one the director of a program with a multicultural philosophy, and the other the director of a program with an African American focus. Earlier in the day, the two had a debate about the merits of their respective approaches. After they had a chance to talk about their journey maps with each other, they shared their conclusion with the larger group: "We are much more alike than we are different." The process led them to appreciate how their individual strategies were leading toward the same ultimate goal.

Trainer Margie Carter, who directed a program with a diverse staff, told us some of the ways she tried to encourage and facilitate dialogue about differences, bias and practice:

> *We devoted time in every weekly staff meeting to try to recognize and hear and listen to the different life experiences and the reasons we approach things differently. Some of these discussions are described in the "Honoring Diversity" chapter in the book* Alike and Different. *We started with simple, concrete things like, "What did you do in your family when someone had a cold?" which built up trust, interest and curiosity in each other. When we got to the more heated issues of race, and of lesbian and gay staff members, people had already developed a sense of trust and respect and were willing to look at things in new ways, to look at their own racism and homophobia. But it took this very strong commitment to look at this, talk about this, also to learn to get the conflict on the table and not be afraid. Then we looked at the implications of what we were discussing. Things would come up and we would recognize the inconsistency between what we said we believed in and what our actual policy or practice was. It was center-wide heightened awareness and focus of growth for all of us. Seeing each other as really valuable resources, we rarely brought in an outside person. We created the climate internally to recognize the expertise among each other. It was not without its anchor in tears, but we felt okay about that.*

Videos

There are a variety of videos on the market which address diversity in the early childhood care setting. One is *Essential Connections: Ten Keys to Culturally Sensitive Child Care* by the Program for Infant/Toddler Caregivers at Far West Laboratory for Educational Research and Development. *Ten Keys*, said Eleanor Clement Glass, "is the very first thing I've seen that illustrates how to begin those negotiations, to identify areas and raise them" among a group of providers. Dialogue can be sparked regarding how the issues raised in the video are impacting a program. In the Early Childhood Training Diversity Video Series coordinated by Janet Gonzalez-Mena for Magna Systems, Inc., a group of providers and professional development trainers of diverse backgrounds explores diverse child rearing practices through role play and discussion. According to Laura Mason Zeisler, a multicultural and anti-bias trainer:

The videos give viewers a lens through which to view their own practices and to consider other ways of addressing the many issues related to an anti-bias approach.

There are also videos available which focus on issues of race, language and culture, not specifically in early childhood education, but still very useful for program staff who wish to begin to identify their own biases. The video *The Color of Fear*, produced by Stir Fry Productions, can also inspire thought-provoking dialogue. Both of these videos are used in structured workshops where skilled facilitators lead the groups in discussions about the issues raised.

Reading Materials

Julie Olsen Edwards assigns her students at Cabrillo College to read novels about the experiences of people of color growing up in America. Novels are a wonderful way to gain insights into cultures other than one's own, and raise questions in readers' minds which can lead to a rich discussion. Manuel Garcia, the director at Plaza Community Center in East Los Angeles, regularly asks staff to read interesting and provocative articles which they discuss at staff meetings. Staff members also bring in articles they think would be of interest to their peers, and they take turns presenting and facilitating the discussion. Case studies, research, children's stories, magazine articles and other types of reading materials can also stimulate rich dialogue.

Anecdotes from the Classroom

Every day, providers "live" stories and observe examples of ways in which culture, race, language and bias emerge in the early care setting. If time is taken to focus on some of those anecdotes and to analyze their implications for the program, everyone can learn.

Role Play

Step One School sometimes uses role playing to help teachers gain the skills to address bias in the classroom. Sue Britson, the co-director at Step One School, talked about how role play can increase teachers' willingness to implement the curriculum, while strengthening their skills. For example, when a child or adult says something inappropriate or prejudiced, Britson says, "It is easy to pretend it did not happen, to ignore it, to [fail to] deal with it—or even see it." Teachers are asked to bring examples of any incidents like this from their classrooms to the staff meetings. Staff may first get into small groups to discuss the incident, and the ways in which the teacher might have responded. Then some of the teachers role play the incident, acting out some of the suggested strategies generated by the small group discussions.

Question of the Week

An innovation for bringing awareness of diversity issues to the forefront on an everyday basis is to post a question of the week, or a short scenario in the staff room

or somewhere staff can read it. Margie Carter uses this strategy to provoke discussion and offer staff new resources, with the understanding that they will commit to doing the work of exploring the questions.

STRATEGY 2

Provide appropriate facilitation.

Activities such as those listed above are helpful for creating opportunities to share, learn, reflect and analyze race, language and culture in people's lives and work. Often, however, it is also important for groups to pay attention to how to facilitate the discussions that can be sparked through these types of activities. Dialogue about equity and diversity can be intense and raise conflict. If participants have a bad experience participating in a discussion around diversity, they may not learn from the interaction and may resist future attempts to create a dialogue.

A variety of strategies can be used to ensure that a conversation is appropriately facilitated.

ADOPT GROUP PRACTICES WHICH FACILITATE DIALOGUE

Groups can adopt certain practices which increase the capacity of a group to engage in a productive dialogue with mutual respect. For example, it is often helpful if a group develops a set of ground rules by which everyone agrees to abide. Ground rules clearly state agreements between participants about how to conduct a meeting or event. Ground rules can be very helpful in creating an atmosphere where everyone's voice can be heard and positive dialogue can occur. Confidentiality, for example, is an important condition for dialogue about sensitive issues. When written down for everyone to see, ground rules become a record of the group's values about how to discuss issues. Such a record is a useful reminder for staff or parents who have been with a program for a while and a helpful orientation for new people.

At Step One School, staff have developed ground rules for meetings which include: "Use respectful terms," "No one speaks twice on a topic until everyone has had input," and "Try to keep your statements reflecting personal respect and sensitivity." Co-director Eric Peterson explains that the ground rules were developed through "trial and error." As the program grew more experienced in talking about anti-bias and diversity issues, they began to develop the ground rules. They periodically revisit the list to see whether the group is abiding by the ground rules and whether there is a need to add or make changes to the list.

Another approach is to create opportunities for the group to assess what works and how an event could be improved. Ardella Dailey observes:

We need to let people know it is a process [and that it won't always go right]. I have found teachers who even reflect with children. "How did the day go?" "What do you think we could have done differently?" and "Why did it work for you—or didn't it?" And, three-year-olds can tell you very clearly. Reflection is essential whether it is with children or adults because it opens you up for a diversity of style.

Time for debriefing and reflection is important because it allows a group to hear and draw upon the diverse perspectives of participants. It also creates a forum for people to express and address concerns and misunderstandings so that issues do not fester in the background. Groups can create these opportunities in a variety of ways. They can, for example, leave five minutes at the end of the meeting to review how it went. Evaluation forms can also be used as a mechanism for feedback, especially if there is an opportunity for the group to hear about the results and how concerns will be addressed.

Identify and Designate a Facilitator

Groups should identify people who are willing and able to take on the responsibility of facilitating a conversation or meeting to ensure that the discussion is productive. Typical facilitator tasks include making sure that everyone has an opportunity to express their opinion, creating and following an agenda, making sure the ground rules are understood and honored, helping the group to identify areas of consensus and recognize disagreements, and defusing tense situations. Sometimes, responsibility for facilitation is designated to one person. It can also be shared, provided the designated facilitators have time to plan how they work together.

Clearly designating to the group which person will facilitate is important. Individuals who take on this role often need time to plan how they will manage a meeting. Clarity of the facilitator's role is also important for group dynamics, to help ensure he or she has the authority to guide the process. Otherwise, participants may misinterpret attempts to facilitate as dominating or controlling. People also appreciate having someone to whom it is acceptable to direct comments about the process or the agenda. Facilitators need to let the group know whether and how they themselves will partake in the dialogue.

Facilitating can be difficult. Several directors we interviewed said that they wanted to have more staff discussions around issues about diversity, but they were not confident about their facilitation skills, particularly for when situations became emotionally loaded. While facilitation is usually easier for people with strong intuitive and interpersonal skills, the ability to facilitate can be developed through both observation and practice. Groups should think about ways to develop the facilitation and inter-group skills of staff and directors. People can:

- Attend workshops about facilitation and running effective meetings.

- Learn by observing and discussing the techniques and strategies used by facilitators running meetings and conferences.
- Team new staff with experienced facilitators and encourage the experienced staff to share their techniques and thinking.

As a start, it is a good idea to practice facilitating conversations in low-pressure situations. Some organizations, for example, encourage staff to practice facilitation by rotating responsibility for running their staff meetings.

There are times when the director or a staff person should not be the facilitator. It is important for everyone to participate in sensitive conversations, but this is difficult if you are also responsible for guiding the discussion. In some cases, staff or directors should not facilitate because they have a vested interest in the outcome of a conversation. Neutrality of the facilitator helps ensure that all participants feel comfortable expressing their views.

For such cases, programs should identify an appropriate outside facilitator. Paid consultants can be useful. If a program has limited resources, a trusted colleague at another program may be able to facilitate for a low fee, free or trade of services. However, outside facilitators should always be selected carefully. Programs should observe prospective facilitators in action or at least obtain references from other groups. Programs should also take some time to reflect on the characteristics they most value in a facilitator. Sometimes the top priority is effectiveness at negotiating issues, other times it is matching interpersonal styles with the staff and director. Particularly if the topic for dialogue is loaded, programs should spend time identifying a consultant with whom everyone feels comfortable.

One of the techniques used in diversity training is to break adults into discussion groups by racial or cultural groups, or by people of color and whites. These exercises can be very fulfilling and thought-provoking, allowing participants the chance to reflect on common strengths, personal and professional experiences as members of the group, and individual issues. But experienced facilitation should definitely be sought for exercises such as these. A skilled facilitator needs to be able to both explain to groups the purpose of the exercise, as well as be cognizant that some people may feel uncomfortable in the process. A facilitator should also be prepared to guide participants through difficult emotions or points of disagreement that may arise.

Strategy 3

Create the time and opportunities for reflection and discussion to take place.

> *Everything we are talking about requires time and training. Both these things require money. What we are asking child care workers to do is the*

hardest work that can be done. To ask them on the kind of pay they get, without the training, and with the time pressures they are up against is utterly unrealistic. We have to change these things. Things take time and time has to be made available. Child care workers are in the primary place to make a difference in family life.

—Julie Olsen Edwards

Talking and learning take time. There are two kinds of opportunities programs need to maximize for talking and learning about diversity, both of which involve time: "everyday" opportunities and "dedicated time." Both are critical; dialogue about race, language and culture must become second nature to the routines of the center.

"Everyday" opportunities are those times during which staff already get together to discuss work-related issues. In most programs, communication takes place daily about the activities and accomplishments of the children. However, this routine exchange does not necessarily delve into individual cultural expectations and assumptions about child rearing, or program policies about second language acquisition or bilingualism, among other questions. Each of the following can be an "everyday" opportunity to discuss some aspect of diversity:

Dialogue about race, language and culture must become second nature to the routines of the center.

- A standing item in staff meetings focusing on some aspect of diversity.
- Team/classroom planning meetings.
- Staff retreats.
- Staff development workshops/in-service trainings.
- Intake and orientation.
- Everyday in the classroom.
- Staff evaluations.

Once programs develop a supportive environment and a habit of discussing diversity, staff awareness will grow about the interrelatedness of race, language, culture and bias—in hiring, enrollment, parent relationships, curriculum, environment and practice. Thus, opportunities to address diversity issues will arise regularly in meetings and less formal conversations, lessening the need for staff to wait for "separate" or "special" meetings to get to important diversity issues.

Nonetheless, "dedicated time" to focus on diversity issues is still also important—time away from the children, during a professional development session or retreat. Both everyday and dedicated opportunities for dialogue require a work culture that prizes time for adults to spend together for co-professional development and learning. Child care workers have not often been afforded this kind of work culture.

Strategy 4

Include diverse perspectives in process.

> *Once a program opens itself up to dialogue with the parents, there is almost like a loop that develops between the school and the home. The school environment becomes sort of a laboratory for teachers to work on ideas they can share with parents. The parents also become resources that the teachers utilize. There isn't this sort of estranged relationship between the two. That cooperation seems to be the greatest asset toward children developing healthily. That would be the case anyway, but it's especially true when you have parents and teachers who are from different cultural backgrounds.*
>
> — Intisar Shareef, Contra Costa College

All dialogue, planning and learning about race, language and culture are enhanced by the inclusion of diverse perspectives. While it may be the ultimate responsibility of the administration of a program to make final decisions regarding policy and philosophy, it is still important for staff and often parents to be a part of the process. Assistant teachers, teachers, head teachers and directors all have important perspectives to offer. If the program has a board of directors, they, too, should be included in these discussions. The staff who work directly with the children, and who actually implement the philosophy and guidelines on a daily basis, must understand and feel committed to the approach of the program.

Step One School is committed to including parents in the process of learning about and implementing the *Anti-Bias Curriculum.* The program organized parents into caucuses which met periodically, separate from the staff and administration. During those caucus meetings, parents were able to freely express themselves, and to come to a common understanding of the issues facing parents in that group. They were also able to strategize about possible solutions. When they participated in a whole group discussion, the caucus leaders were able to clearly articulate the needs and concerns of those parents in a constructive way.

It may be a challenge to include the voices of parents with different language backgrounds who do not speak English, even if there are staff who speak their languages. Running a meaningful discussion in two or more languages is not easy, but it can be done well if the participants decide it is important and develop strategies to make it work. This means using effective translators, and making sure to fully translate not only what is said by providers, but what is said by parents for all to hear.

The more people included in any discussion around race, language and culture, the more perspectives, fears, hopes, expectations and experiences will be revealed for incorporation in the work of the program. Tension may arise regarding who to include in discussions about diversity, in analysis of current practices, or in decision making processes. Each program will have to decide the extent to which parents will be included. It is important to allow for some process by which, at a minimum, parents can give input, because of the important perspectives they can bring.

True, this will open more potential for disagreements and sometimes for misunderstandings and conflict. But this should not deter programs from trying to include the voices of many different stakeholders. The benefits to the quality of care to children outweigh the inconveniences and challenges. There are ways to work through conflict and misunderstandings, such as the use of facilitation techniques and tools.

Challenges to Dialogue

Dialogue about race, language and culture is usually missing in early childhood education settings—among child care providers, between providers and parents, and among faculty in college early childhood education departments. Yet, our interviews revealed that people in the field are hungry for dialogue. Caregivers want to give the best care possible to children, but at times they are at a loss as to what cultural, racial and linguistic differences really mean in terms of caregiving, and what to do regarding differences once they are understood. They want to feel that they can ask co-workers, parents or community members for advice on how to work with children or families from a particular racial, cultural or linguistic background. They yearn for opportunities to compare strategies and approaches with colleagues. They value the moments when they can engage in reflection about themselves and their programs. But, we heard repeated again and again that people rarely have the time or opportunity for these exchanges.

Challenge: Overcoming fear and hesitation about talking about race, language and culture

Talking about diversity means treading into difficult terrain, causing many to hesitate or remain silent. Carol Brunson Phillips offered the following observation:

> *We need to help caregivers be at ease in talking cross-culturally about things that they do not know or understand. The dialogue that could help teachers to be better teachers never happens because the teachers are afraid or don't know how to get the dialogue going. It is the questions we don't ask because we don't want to feel stupid or incompetent or be perceived as racist or ethnocentric...People could learn a lot from each other if they know how to talk to each other. Instead they talk about how to make playdough or what songs to sing.*

People's fears of being misunderstood or of inadvertently offending another person are not unfounded. The field of early care and education is not isolated from the larger social and political dynamics of society. Issues of race, language and cul-

ture have always been loaded, and this is a time of backlash. The current moves to abolish affirmative action, to deny immigrants access to education and social services, and to prevent people from speaking their non-English family languages are polarizing communities. The public debate is far from friendly. People find themselves in situations where even well-intentioned comments, observations or even questions about race, language or culture may be perceived by another person as offensive or attacking.

People hesitate to talk about race, culture and language also because the issues are so very personal; some simply do not feel comfortable discussing them in the workplace. Sue Britson, one of the co-directors at Step One School, realized this when her staff first started working to implement anti-bias principles in their program. There were people who did not want to come to work and be required to share their "childhood stories," and who did not see the direct connection between reflecting on one's background and one's work in the classroom:

> *We realized we had to be careful. There is always this tension between personal and professional...because we work so much with the heart and the head when working with kids. It takes conscious communication about what is our role as educators, what is going beyond our role, how far do we take things and how much do we have to delve into ourselves?*

The discussions can be hard and emotional. Sometimes confrontation will arise. Confrontation does not always fit into some people's vision of a professional culture where, "If you can't say something nice, then you shouldn't say anything at all." Louise Derman-Sparks observed:

> *People want to believe in the structure in which they participate. But, if you are going to face racism, you have to come up against the fact that*

our society does a lot of hurtful things to people. And that we perpetuate that, even if we don't want to... There are enormous resistance and defenses against facing it. It happens both to white people and people of color. Because what people of color also are facing is some of the internalized oppression that they've bought into. Here is where you get the explosions of emotions—great sadness, pain and anger. How can you think that the institutions you were raised to believe were benign and caring are, in fact, so screwed up without a strong emotional reaction?

Unless people are prepared with skills to face a certain amount of tension and emotion, dialogue is not likely to occur. People who feel uncomfortable or unskilled with dealing with conflict shut down, and those who may want to express a contrary viewpoint feel silenced. De Anza Community College instructor Christina Lopez-Morgan believes:

The real way to change is in the context of relationships that you care about, because those relationships provide the incentives for change. It involves taking the time to understand another person's perspective. Blowing up is part of the process. You need to be able to hang out with your discomfort. It is an essential part of change. If you don't, diversity will only be dealt with at a superficial level.

Coming to an understanding and agreement across cultures—or just between individuals—can be time and energy consuming. Carol Brunson Phillips encourages people to trust in each other's ability to communicate:

I think that if the group is committed to using the conflict situation as an arena to resolve, grow and transform everybody, they can do it. I have a lot of faith in people, even without an expert there to shepherd them through the process. Although expertise in that area is very helpful, I think the answer is among the people at work. The answer is not in any book that I know about. That is why I concentrate on the process, encouraging people to develop an atmosphere at the work site where these issues can be discussed when they come up—naturally—and where there is a commitment to work through them to some resolution, if not solution.

There are some techniques that can reduce people's fears of speaking out. Lorrie Guerrero, a teacher at a Head Start Program in Santa Clara, said that one of her most powerful professional experiences was a week-long session devoted exclusively to African American culture, history and experience. The consultants emphasized that participants should feel free to ask questions. To reduce fears that people may have been feeling, they placed a box in the room in which participants could drop in any questions they had but were always afraid to ask. They committed to trying to answer them as best they could by the end of the week. This session was then followed later in the year by a week on Latino families and culture.

Challenge: Avoiding tokenism

Multicultural Issues in Child Care by Janet Gonzalez-Mena speaks to some of the toughest issues around staff diversity and how it is easy for the one person representing a culture to become the "token opinion." This should be avoided by reaching out to find multiple perspectives by people of the same background. A program can draw upon parents, staff at other programs, and even friends and family to add additional points of view to the discussion.

Mary Cardenas suggested a strategy of interviewing parents to diversify the perspectives offered:

> *You could do parent interviews so the folks from the staff could find out what parents believe about how children develop and what values parents have for their children—what their goals and wishes are—so there is not just one person who is supposed to represent what every Hispanic believes about children. Each teacher might have an assignment to gather information to bring back to a staff meeting.*

Challenge: Extremely limited resources

The early childhood field is severely underfunded. All licensed child care programs have a battery of trainings they must provide to their staff within these limited resources. In many programs, a major reason dialogue does not occur is that resources are not available to set aside additional time for groups to engage in these discussions. Providers receive low wages and many are paid on an hourly basis. Often, meeting time is not compensated, and so the amount of time teachers are able to dedicate to meetings is very limited. Often, centers try to squeeze in meetings during children's nap times, but this is usually not sufficient, particularly if a group intends to address a difficult subject or one that requires the attention of all. Some programs rely heavily upon part-time staff, and schedules are such that there is no time during the day when all of the staff can be present for a meeting.

Given these constraints, very few programs can take advantage of the other types of opportunities for dialogue, such as holding staff retreats or hiring outside trainers or facilitators. Several directors said that even if they could hire a facilitator, they would not know how to find one who would have expertise in these issues.

However, as described above, several programs also found ways to foster an ongoing dialogue using time in staff meetings, encouraging teams to discuss issues in their planning meetings or posting a question of the week.

Challenge: Staff turnover

A symptom of the low funding of the child care field is very high turnover as a whole among teachers. When there is high turnover in a program, even if the program is committed to issues of diversity, there is a need to repeatedly establish a level of trust as the composition of the group changes. Also, when the members of the staff change frequently, people are at different levels of familiarity with the issues. As new teachers arrive into a group which has been discussing diversity in some depth for a time, there is a need to bring that person "up to speed," while at the same time continuing to address difficult issues of diversity.

Louise Derman-Sparks believes that the key to overcoming the challenge turnover creates is to have in place an atmosphere which encourages communication:

> *I think that if you've created a culture that allows, encourages and supports this kind of cross-cultural communication, it shouldn't be from scratch [when new staff are hired]. But that is theoretical. You'd have some of the old people still there; when new people come in you have to start again but at least you are in an environment that allows it to happen. It ought to be easier than if you're in an environment that doesn't even have the structure for it to happen. When you have a program that has regular time for staff communication, at least you have the potential for bringing new people in.*

Learn to understand the power of dialogue and the potential for implementing the Principles of Quality Care in a Diverse Society.

Challenge: Overcoming culture where adult time is not valued

On top of feeling underpaid and overworked, child care workers rarely enjoy a professional culture that supports adult time together away from the children. The first step to overcoming this is learning to understand the power of dialogue and the potential for implementing the principles. Author Janet Gonzalez-Mena talked about this phenomenon:

> *Everything about the way we work with children says, "This is a sacred place for children." Not for adults. Adults save their conversation for after work, maybe break (if you ever get one). You put aside your needs. But in full day care you can't do that; it makes people crazy. Yet the whole thing is set up and people are trained to keep themselves out of the program; to not show children any kind of relationships with other people (except maybe nice, happy ones). I think this is a huge issue and a big problem in the field. Children don't see adults behave normally. They don't see adults problem-solving with each other. This is all working against the idea of using each other as resources, because theoretically you can't do it while the kids are around.*

Challenge: The importance of leadership

Where California Tomorrow did find programs incorporating dialogue about diversity issues on a regular basis, the leadership of the directors was crucial. Directors play a key role in creating the time, opportunities, an open and supportive atmosphere, and commitment that allows productive dialogue to occur.

Directors, along with the whole staff, may feel that they do not have the skills or the information themselves and so do not feel prepared to take on a leadership role in focusing a dialogue on diversity in their program. However, the type of leadership which is needed does not necessarily require that the director know more than the staff about these issues, but that they place a high priority on diversity issues and be willing to learn. Ardella Dailey gave a picture of what leadership means in this context:

> *Many times we are all in the same boat and there is no captain because everyone is struggling at the same level. I think it is more that the person who is in leadership—in terms of focusing on diversity and addressing the needs of the different cultural groups in the program—has to have a commitment to always push at the door. That is almost more important than having more knowledge than another person.*

As Dan Bellm, writer and editor on early childhood education issues, put it, directors can make an incredible contribution by saying, "I may not know much about this, but I declare that this is important and we will explore it together."

Moving Forward

If I waited until I knew everything about how to address diversity issues, I would never get started. The learning really begins once you get going.

—Julie Olsen Edwards, Cabrillo Community College

IN THE PRECEDING FIVE CHAPTERS, we proposed five Principles of Quality Care in a Diverse Society, their importance, how they fit together, promising strategies for implementing them and challenges raised by the issues. Now what? Getting started is where many people get stuck, especially if they feel overwhelmed or unsupported. Keeping in mind the following four activities will help move a program forward. Every program is different—the individual staff involved, the demographics of the population, the history of the program, and the philosophy and goals of the program. Each program must decide how to proceed based on its own situation. The important thing is that the adults involved start a process of thinking, talking to one another and learning about race, culture and language and how they relate to quality child care.

The actions are:

- LEARN about the implications of racial, cultural and linguistic diversity in early childhood education.
- ARTICULATE the philosophy and goals of the program regarding diversity issues.
- ANALYZE current program policies and practices in relation to your philosophy and goals around diversity.
- COMMIT to addressing diversity in your program.

LEARN about the implications of racial, cultural and linguistic diversity in early childhood education.

Learn, reflect and talk about the concepts and implications of race, culture and language in early childhood education. Through talking with one another, individuals can learn about the backgrounds and experiences of others in the program, as well as reflect on their own experiences. Also, providers in a program may decide that they are lacking certain information or perspectives about diversity that they will seek out during the process.

This process of learning and gaining a better understanding of diversity issues is ongoing and will require dedicated time from the adults involved in the program. In a child care center, staff and administration should set aside staff development time, or time in regular staff meetings to focus on diversity issues. Opportunities for parents to be involved in discussions should be created. In a family child care home, the provider may want to reach out to other providers through a professional association, or perhaps engage parents in thinking about diversity issues related to the program. Both personal reflection and dialogue with others are important. A program may try to answer questions such as the following:

- What are things we want to learn more about? What kinds of training do we need?
- What kinds of discussions do we need to have? Who needs to be included?
- Do we need an outside facilitator for some of those discussions?
- How can we create the time and opportunity to revisit these issues on a regular basis?

ARTICULATE the philosophy and goals of the program regarding diversity issues.

Most programs have more or less a clearly articulated philosophy regarding child development and caregiving. But few programs have clearly thought out a philosophy around issues regarding race, language and culture. A clearly articulated philosophy is important for several reasons. It is invaluable for communication with parents. It helps in providing consistency across staff in a single program and with new staff who join the program. It also helps administrators and caregivers to make consistent decisions about policies and practices.

Family child care providers may be accustomed to transmitting information much more informally since they are smaller and more intimate than a center. Since homes tend to be run by a single provider, perhaps with an assistant, ensuring consistency across staff is not a major issue, so a formal philosophy and guidelines may not be necessary. However, even in family child care programs, it is important to develop and articulate a philosophy for the provider(s) and parents of children in their care.

A program may try to answer questions such as the following:

- Is the program seeking to enroll a multiracial and multicultural group of children? Is the program focused on a single ethnic group? Is the program responding to the demographics of the children in care and are these demographics likely to change over time?
- What are the program goals, values and practices aimed at reducing bias in young children?
- What are the program goals, values and practices aimed at supporting the culture of the children in care?
- What are the program goals, values and practices regarding promoting cross-cultural understanding among children?
- What are the program goals, values and practices regarding second language acquisition or the development of bilingualism?

- What are the program goals, values and practices regarding how providers interact with parents around issues of race, language and culture?

ANALYZE current program policies and practices in relation to your philosophy and goals around diversity.

Analyze current policies and practices through the "lens" of their goals and philosophy regarding race, language and culture. Look at hiring, enrollment, environment, relationships with parents and the community, and relationships with other agencies. Through analysis and discussion, think about what is needed—information, training, policies, discussions, changes?

Reviewing current status is important because as programs develop, it can be easy to lose track of why a particular approach or strategy was initially taken. A program may find that the original conditions which led to a strategy have changed, and the approach needs to be adapted or dropped. For example, a policy of using English in parent committee meetings may be based on a previous era when most of the parents spoke English, but now a shift is needed to communicate with Spanish-speaking parents.

A program may try to answer questions such as the following:

- How do policies impact and intersect with the cultures, races, languages, needs, experiences and awareness of the families and staff?
- How do the demographics of the children in the program—whether it is multicultural or ethnic-specific—influence the way the goals or practices are carried out?
- How does the environment support the development of children's positive racial identity?
- How can an open, supportive, learning environment among the adults in the program be created?
- How do the curriculum and activities support or obstruct program goals and values regarding race, language, culture and bias?
- How do program policies reflect the program goals and values regarding race, language, culture and bias?
- How can the values and philosophy of the program be turned into practice?
- Are teachers prepared to respond effectively to a young child who asks a question about the way someone looks or talks?
- Do staff feel that they have the skills to address prejudicial remarks made by children or parents?
- Is the program fully drawing upon the knowledge and skills of its providers and families?

COMMIT to addressing diversity in your program.

Finally, providers must decide what exactly will be changed or modified in a program and how. There are no "cookie cutter" solutions. After agreeing what to do and how to do it, the program should commit to a process of implementation, and to reviewing the ways in which the program responds to issues of race, culture and language on a regular basis.

The frequency of review and the inclusiveness of the process will change from program to program. For example, in a large center this requires thought and planning about how to bring together the appropriate stakeholders and create an environment where parents and providers feel comfortable expressing their opinions. In a family child care home where a single provider works with children from five or six families, the process can probably be simpler. It may merely involve the provider orienting parents to the principles upon which her program is based, and then reviewing these when discussing the progress of children with parents. Each program, with its unique population, history and philosophy, will come to a different conclusion about how to make the program more supportive and responsive to diversity. ❧

Chapter 7
Equipping the Early Childhood Workforce to Implement the Five Principles of Quality Care in a Diverse Society

To implement the five Principles of Quality Care in a Diverse Society that we have proposed, child care providers must have the skills and expertise to help children become successful and productive in a diverse society. This requires an investment of resources and attention to the preparation of child care professionals, as well as to who becomes and remains a child care worker.

A workforce which reflects the racial, cultural and linguistic diversity of children and families is essential to each one of the five Principles of Quality Care in a Diverse Society. When staff speak the languages of families, they are better able to establish strong communication with children and their parents and to support the continued development of children's home languages. Staff who share families' cultural backgrounds are invaluable because of their knowledge of the values and practices of families and their communities. This can help programs develop activities that build upon the cultures of the home and alert their colleagues to situations where they might offend a member of a cultural group. Racial diversity of staff is also critical. Although the larger society does not always give child care workers the respect they are due, in the eyes of children they are important and influential figures. When children see providers from their same racial group, it helps validate their identity. When providers are from a different racial group than the children, it can help to break down stereotypes. And diverse perspectives are essential to fostering meaningful dialogue among providers.

While the extent to which a program employs staff from a diversity of backgrounds will vary, the field as a whole should strive to reflect the overall demographics of families with young children. The racial composition of the staff of a specific program will depend upon its focus and intent as well as families served. While some programs will primarily employ staff from one linguistic, cultural or racial group, others will seek staff from a diversity of backgrounds. The demographic composition of the workforce as a whole, however, strongly determines whether a program even has access to the types of workers desired.

Diversity of staffing is important at all professional levels. Young children and parents notice when adults of color never hold positions as directors or head teachers, or only work as teaching assistants. While they may not have a precise understanding of the dynamics, children are quick to recognize who has authority and who is always being told what to do. Adults also feel the impact of power relations. Claire Chang, a participant in the Program for Infant/Toddler Caregivers, notes, "Just as children like seeing teachers who represent themselves in the room, I like seeing instructors who look like me."

The early childhood field must build upon the strengths and insights of people from a broad range of racial, cultural and linguistic backgrounds. But a diverse workforce in itself is not enough. While the life experiences of a provider are a critical asset, they can't alone ensure the most appropriate care. Practitioners from every cultural, linguistic and racial background need opportunities for gaining a deeper understanding of how to provide quality care in a diverse society. Professional development is needed for all levels, from the women and men who directly care for children to the individuals who conduct pre-service and in-service professional development. The theory and practice of the Principles of Quality Care in a Diverse Society need to become a consistent component of all professional development, not optional "add-on" learning. These concepts can help all workers, whether they are working with children from the same or different backgrounds, to provide care that nurtures children's skills for interacting in a diverse society.

This chapter of ***Looking In, Looking Out*** examines how to develop a diverse workforce with the skills and knowledge to implement the five principles. We begin with a description of the ways child care providers are recruited or otherwise enter the field and the vehicles for professional development. We then discuss issues of retention and advancement. We attempt to assess the extent to which the current workforce reflects the children and families served, highlight promising efforts to recruit a diverse workforce and describe challenges to attaining this goal. Recognizing that recruitment and retention are only a beginning, we then explore in-depth how professional development can be used to equip providers to provide quality care in a diverse society. We will offer readers suggestions about how professional development can more effectively address issues of race, language and culture as well as describe challenges which must be overcome in order to move forward.

What is the Current System of Recruitment and Professional Development?

The vast majority of child care providers have already started caring for children before they begin any formal education about child development theory or child care practice (Cohen and Stevenson, 1992). At the present time, most providers enter the child care field at the point of taking a job where they are paid to care for children. They may care for the children of other families in their own home or obtain a job as a classroom assistant in a center. In some cases, people receive some formal preparation through a vocational education program or a community college course before they actually start working with children. Occasionally teachers will move from teaching older children in the K-12 system to working with younger children. In these cases, the teachers have a background in education but may not have specific training related to the development of young children.

While credentialing requirements vary for different types of providers and from state to state, they are relatively limited, especially compared to related professions such as K-12 teaching. Most states, including California, do not require pre-service preparation for family child care providers beyond minimum health and safety training. In California, licensing requirements for family child care providers include 15 hours of pre-service training in communicable diseases, first aid and CPR. Credentialing requirements are typically stricter for teachers working in centers, particularly facilities receiving government funding. For example, teachers working in state-funded programs in California must have a minimum of six college semester units to be eligible for hire and a combination of 6 months and 12 units in Early Childhood Education to be considered a fully qualified teacher. These regulations are somewhat more stringent than in other states. According to Marcy Whitebook, Senior Research Policy Advisor and founding executive director of the National Center for the Early Childhood Workforce, current Congressional proposals aimed at reforming welfare are likely to lead to even fewer requirements for child care providers. To increase the availability of child care for welfare recipients who will be required to work, these proposals emphasize using unregulated care, as well as employing former welfare recipients as providers, without necessarily providing them with the appropriate training to ensure they can succeed in the work.

The current system of professional development is plagued by fragmentation and lack of coordination.

Professional development for child care providers is currently offered through a number of different systems and organizations, including four-year public and private colleges, community colleges, vocational education programs, resource and referral agencies, state education departments, Head Start centers, nonprofit organizations, school districts, and others. Community colleges are by far the largest training ground. California, for example, has 106 community colleges throughout the state in urban and rural areas, 97 with child development instructional programs. Eighty-nine community colleges in California, including five which do not have a child development instructional focus, operate child care centers where students can directly observe and interact with young children. California community colleges are open-enrollment institutions which currently charge low tuition ($13 per unit). Most courses are offered both days and evenings, and frequently weekends. To reach working students, classes are often offered off-campus in the communities targeted. In California community colleges serving rural areas, it is not unusual for early childhood departments to offer classes throughout a hundred-mile radius region. Community colleges currently access a wide cross-section of students in terms of language, gender, age and economics.

The current system of professional development, on the other hand, is plagued by fragmentation and lack of coordination. Professional development offered by one arm is often not recognized by another. For example, a provider is not likely to receive any units for participating in an in-house staff training. Some organizations and professional associations arrange for participants to receive units when they attend workshops at conferences, but not always. Community college units do not always transfer easily to four-year colleges. Frustration with this inconsistency and fragmentation led Pacific Oaks College in Pasadena to spearhead the "Advancing Careers" initiative. This is a project designed to increase professionalization in child development and provide a well-trained, stable workforce which better matches California's diverse families. The project's goal has been to create a coordinated system that: (1) welcomes people into the field from a variety of points; (2) offers clear career pathways with articulated training and credentialing systems; and (3) provides a variety of incentives to stay in the field. Over the past five years, beginning with a Scholar's Seminar in June 1991, Pacific Oaks College has led and collaborated with over 130 policymakers to develop strategies and combat structural barriers to recruiting, training and retaining child development providers.

Most recently, "Advancing Careers" has worked with the California Commission on Teacher Credentialing, the State Department of Education Child Development Division and the State Department of Social Services to develop a new process for certification of child care teachers and directors. This is resulting in new program standards, to be released in 1996, which all early childhood certification programs throughout the state will be encouraged to use.

Currently, financial aid for the continuing education of child care professionals is minimal. Often they must attend classes or workshops during their off-work hours at their own expense. Family child care providers typically have the fewest resources for training. Family child care homes are often run by a single individual who cannot easily take time off to attend a workshop or class because it could mean a loss of income. And, additional education does not always translate into higher wages for child care workers. Compared to other fields, the wages of even the most highly trained child care workers are extremely low. As a result, many people leave the profession once they achieve higher levels of education. For example, a number of four-year colleges report that many students in their child development programs do not become child care workers after graduation. The main reason cited is that the jobs do not pay enough, particularly for graduates who need to repay student loans (Cohen and Stevenson, 1992).

To What Extent is the Current Workforce Reflective of the Children and Families Served?

Answering this question requires analyzing who is being hired, as well as the extent to which people from diverse backgrounds have equal opportunities to advance into leadership positions.

The Diversity of People Entering the Field

Compared to some other professions, the early childhood workforce is much more representative of California's population at large. For example, the racial/ethnic composition of public school children in the state is approximately 46 percent white, 35 percent Latino, 8 percent African American and 10 percent Asian/Pacific Islander. One out of three public school students comes from a home where English is not the primary language. The population of California public school teachers, on the other hand, is more than 80 percent white and monolingual English-speaking.

While no statewide statistics exist for family child care or center-based providers, the most recently available county information suggests a much more racially and linguistically representative child care workforce. The Cost, Quality and Outcomes Study (Cost, Quality and Outcomes Study Team, 1995) found that providers in centers in Los Angeles County were 49 percent white, 9 percent Asian/Pacific Islander, 15 percent African American, 22 percent Latino and 5 percent other; U.S. Census data indicate that families with children under age six in Los Angeles County are 30 percent white, 9 percent Asian American, 12 percent African American and 48 percent Latino. A 1994 report prepared by the National Center for the Early Childhood Workforce found that in San Francisco, child care teaching assistants were 37 percent Asian/Pacific Islander, 30 percent white, 19 percent African American and 10 percent Latino. Teachers were 45 percent white, 33 percent Asian/Pacific Islander, 9 percent African American and 8 percent Latino. The child population of San Francisco is approximately 33 percent Asian/Pacific Islander, 29 percent white, 20 percent Latino, and 15 percent African American.

In assessing all of these statistics, several caveats must be remembered. First, while race is one of the few categories for which statistics are available, it is only one dimension reflecting the backgrounds of families. Second, general racial categories mask significant differences within groups. So, for example, while the percent of Asian providers in Los Angeles is roughly comparable to that of Asian families in the population, some groups such as Vietnamese or Korean may have access to very few providers of their background.

The fact that the early care and education workforce is more diverse than comparable fields is not surprising. Child care has traditionally been one of the few job opportunities open to women of color. Women of color have long played a role in caring for the children of the dominant race and culture, as well as for children within their own communities. Second, one of the positive benefits of the limited credentialing requirements in child care is that it makes the work more accessible. No formal training is required to qualify for a job as an aide at many centers or to open a family child care home. In many other fields, formal training requirements have had an exclusionary impact on low income minority groups who have had less access to higher education.

While the racial diversity of the child care workforce is impressive, the persisting major gaps cannot be overlooked. The survey of center-based care conducted by California Tomorrow for the report *Affirming Children's Roots* suggests that the field is much less likely to be reflective of families served in terms of language. We found that while nearly all of the centers employed staff who spoke the home language of their English-speaking children, little more than half (55 percent) employed staff who could speak Spanish to the Spanish-speaking children. This relates to the earlier finding that the percentage of Latino providers was significantly lower than the proportion of Latino children. Less than a third of centers employed staff who could speak the home languages of their Tagalog-, Chinese-, Vietnamese- or Korean-speaking children.

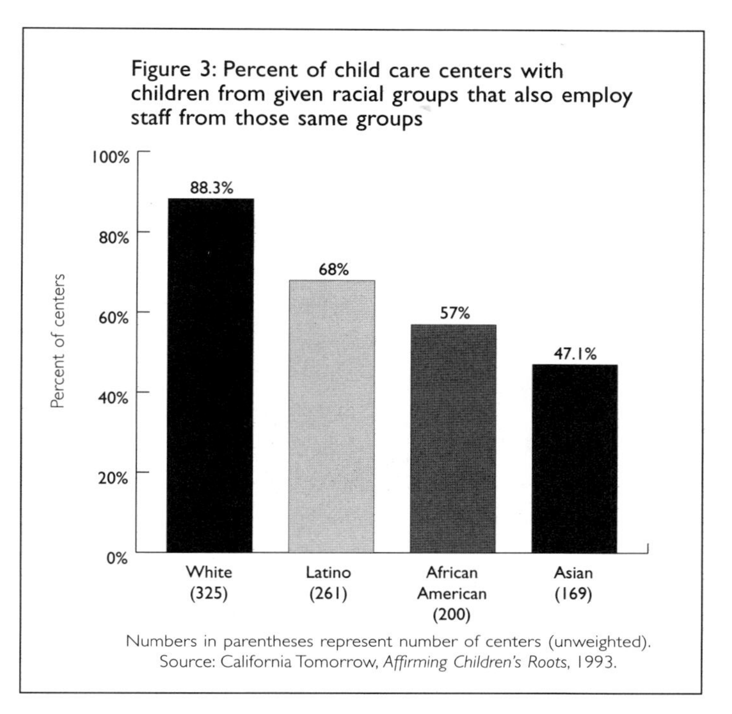

Perhaps the most striking gap in the child care workforce is in gender diversity. According to the Child Care Staffing Study, men comprise less than 3 percent of all center-based providers and less than 1 percent of family child care providers (Gallinsky, Howes and Kontos, 1995). The absence of men can be attributed to a number of factors. Traditional societal attitudes categorize the job of raising children as women's work, whether paid or unpaid. The extremely low compensation also makes it difficult to recruit men, who are still more likely to be considered the primary breadwinners in households. In addition, in recent years, highly publicized cases alleging the abuse of young children by male teachers have put men under much higher levels of scrutiny in child care. Unfortunately, this climate of fear has caused male providers to leave the profession and fewer men to enter child care training programs. And Marcy Whitebook of the National Center for the Early Childhood Workforce observes:

> *The few men who do enter the field tend to move out of the direct care setting into the administrative structure—often, much more quickly than their female counterparts.*

The Extent to Which Equal Opportunity for Advancement Exists

The limited information about the demographics of the early childhood workforce suggests that people of color are less likely to be found in leadership positions. For example, the racial breakdown of California community college faculty who taught child development-related courses in 1994 was 84.5 percent white, 2.4 percent Asian American, 7.3 percent African American, and 5.1 percent Latino (Whitebook and Sakai, 1995).

The National Black Child Development Institute (NBCDI) has conducted the most extensive exploration of this issue, focusing on the prospects for African American providers. According to their report *Paths to African American Leadership Positions in Early Childhood Education*:

> *Membership lists of several leading early education organizations reveal very little African American representation. For example, less than three percent of the 4,800 members of the Society for Research in Child Development in 1993 are African American (Kuhn, 1993). Of the 50 regular members of the National Association of Early Childhood Specialists in State Departments of Education in 1992-93, only six percent are African American (Mobley, 1993). Of over 400 local, state, and regional affiliate leaders of the National Association for the Education of Young Children, fewer than five percent are African American (Smith, 1993).*

According to NBCDI, African American providers tend to be more experienced in the field than their peers, but less educated. This represents a serious barrier to advancement, particularly for women seeking to move from assistant teacher to teacher or from teacher to teacher/director. NBCDI argues that the low levels of educational attainment reflect the fact that many African Americans do not have access to the finances needed for post-secondary education, particularly four-year college. In fact, nationwide the likelihood of attending college has been declining among Blacks compared to whites even though achievement levels have been rising. Unfortunately, over the past twenty years, the federal government has emphasized student loans rather than scholarship aid. Loans are not always a viable option for African American families, particularly when the compensation for the profession of choice makes repayment so difficult. Financing education is undoubtedly a barrier for any low income person, but it may be greater for people of color since they are more likely than whites to be poor. For adults who speak a language other than English, the problem is not only lack of finances, but lack of appropriate educational opportunities. Very few professional development opportunities, from conference workshops to community college courses, are offered in languages other than English. Performing academically in a second language—reading, writing and taking tests—is extremely challenging, even when a person may have acquired verbal fluency.

Unfortunately, similar data and analysis regarding paths to leadership positions are not available for other racial minority groups in the child care field. Nonetheless, these NBCDI statistics suggest that people of color face greater institutional barriers to advancement than their white peers.

Professional development is rarely offered in languages other than English. Furthermore, when it is, it is usually in Spanish; instruction in Asian languages is extremely rare. Texts and resource materials are often still only available in English. Meanwhile, in situations where students are of mixed English language proficiency, English-speaking instructors often don't know how to teach students with limited English proficiency. One community college faculty member expressed a typical frustration:

> *I need to be prepared to provide lessons that are comprehensible to the lower-skilled in English without losing the English proficient student.*

Consequently, people who speak a primary language other than English do not have equal opportunities for education needed to advance in the child care profession. Reflecting upon her experiences at Wu Yee Children's Services, Lisa Lee, now the Associate Director of Parent Support Services, noted:

> *We had many wonderful teachers who were excellent but were not proficient in English. They felt the institutional racism of not being recognized for their skills, not being recognized by the larger credentialing or certificate programs, not being able to move forward. They lacked access to quality caliber training at the college level and the workshop level. They don't even have access to research materials and articles translated into their own languages.*

While the racial diversity of the child care workforce is impressive, the persisting major gaps cannot be overlooked.

Promising Efforts to Recruit, Retain and Promote the Advancement of a Diverse Workforce

Through our research, we identified a number of promising efforts to recruit and improve opportunities for professional advancement for a diverse workforce. These examples demonstrate that many different types of organizations can and should be engaged in nurturing a skilled, reflective workforce. We found promising practices being employed by child care programs, colleges, and resource and referral agencies.

Center-Based Practices

Many of the child care programs we visited highly valued recruiting and hiring staff who reflected the backgrounds of the children and families served. Often during the hiring process, additional qualifications, such as language skills and residence in the community, were considered along with experience, personality and professional education. Several programs sought staff who would expose children to someone from a different racial or cultural background. Some programs rewarded staff with bilingual skills with higher salaries. A few programs recruited for other aspects of diversity. At Discoveryland, a bilingual Chinese program, the director paid particular attention to age diversity. Staff ranged from teenagers to Mrs. Ho, a 70-year-old teacher in charge of the Chinese-speaking toddler room. Mrs. Ho's presence in the center helped to maintain the Chinese tradition of high regard for grandparents and respect for the elderly. At Step One School, it was a top priority to include lesbian/gay staff to reflect the families of some of the children in the program.

Centers have devised a variety of strategies for recruiting diverse staff. Several created opportunities for youth to become interested in child care careers through summer work experience or regional occupational programs. After graduation from these programs, youths often found jobs in the child care facilities where they had been placed.

A number of programs facilitated the hiring of staff who spoke other languages by taking into consideration credentials earned in other countries. This approach also presented challenges, however. Most providers hired in this manner had backgrounds in primary and secondary education, as opposed to early childhood education. They still needed information about child development and working with younger children. Also, differences in educational philosophy sometimes led to the need to reconcile conflicting beliefs about how to care for young children.

A large percentage of centers encouraged staff to continue their education. A survey by the Cost, Quality and Outcomes Study (Cost, Quality and Outcomes Study Team, 1995) found that nationwide, 51 percent of centers supported staff through at least 15 hours of in-service training, 63 percent offered tuition reimbursement and 81 percent provided staff with release time. A sub-sample of centers operating in California revealed slightly lower percentages for these categories.

Directors often played a major role in motivating staff to continue with their education and careers. Encouragement ranged from serving as a role model to taking the time to talk to a staff person about his or her future. Staff at many different programs told stories similar to that of Cecelia Caruso, a teacher at Plaza Child Development and Observation Center in Los Angeles:

> *My director, Manuel Garcia, is very concerned about empowering staff and parents. He does not have a problem giving up responsibility—in fact, he wants staff to take on responsibility and to learn new skills. When Manuel first started, I thought it was strange because he would ask for volunteers to take on a task or to read an article and present it to the rest*

of the staff. Often, staff members are also asked to present a training that they received elsewhere. Frequently, if a staff person has an idea, Manuel will ask that person or another to take on that project and figure out how to test it out and report back to the rest of the staff. All of this practice with speaking, discussing and assuming responsibility has made me more confident. Before, I would never have thought about being a director. Now I believe I can do it.

Centers that are part of a larger infrastructure of support seem to have more opportunities for creative recruitment and staff development strategies. One promising effort we learned about was within the South Central Child Care Consortium, 17 agencies in South Central Los Angeles that pooled and shared their staff development resources.

Head Start programs and the Foundation Center for Phenomenological Research also practiced innovative staff development activities through their large network of facilities. Their strategies are highlighted below and on the following pages.

Live Oak Migrant Head Start

HEAD START PROGRAMS are funded federally and operated mostly locally. Although the quality and extensiveness of staff development depends somewhat on the capacity of the local administration, all Head Start programs clearly shared some important universals regarding staff development. First, Head Start national policy is for facilities to place a high priority on hiring staff from the community being served, often parents who formerly had their children in a center. Second, professional development opportunities are provided to staff as part of their employment. Trainings are free and constructed to allow staff from different centers to participate along with their colleagues from sister programs. Staff time for professional development is compensated.

The Live Oak Migrant Head Start program serves migrant farmworkers nine months out of the year. Staff receive a two-week training at the beginning of the season before the children arrive, in addition to monthly sessions held during the off-season. Staff work together to prioritize the kinds of trainings they desire each year. The two-week trainings include staff from the nine migrant centers located within the same geographic area. The exact nature of the training varies from year to year and topics covered range from child safety to bilingual language development. Some aspects are tailored to the needs of specific positions. For example, Balwinder Singh, the program's community social services worker, chose to spend one year learning about health and disability issues with her peers from other centers.

Migrant Head Start also conducts monthly staff in-service days during which centers are closed down. Staff surveys help determine the topics to be covered during these days each year. To encourage staff to use each other as resources, Migrant Head Start also encourages providers to visit and observe other centers. Resources are set aside to pay for teacher release time for these site visits. ❧

The Foundation Center for Phenomenological Research

THE FOUNDATION CENTER for Phenomenological Research is a nonprofit organization which, until recently, administered 23 centers in urban and rural areas through a contract with the Child Development Division of the California Department of Education. Its staff development approach offers critical insights into how to effectively recruit providers from communities of color and language minority communities.

A fundamental principle of the Foundation Center approach to providing care was the recruitment and training of teachers from the communities served because they felt that children would be best served by people who came from the same cultural and linguistic backgrounds. Families served by the program were low income and predominantly people of color, a large proportion being migrant laborers and recent immigrants. Unfortunately, usually when such community members have the desire and personal qualities essential for working with young children, they lack entree into the field because they do not have access to formal educational opportunities.

In order to create the workforce it needed, the Foundation Center developed its own internal professional development program. Members of the community started as entry-level teaching assistants and were trained on the job with the goal of eventually obtaining their California Children's Center permits and American Montessori credentials. The program was designed to be completed in five years but remained flexible enough to allow participants to graduate at their own pace. Some needed more time while others who had more educational background were able to finish in fewer years. The design included 15 days of paid training per year for which staff also received early childhood course credits.

Given that the focus of this staff development was on community members at different levels of English proficiency, education and background in child development, the Foundation Center found Montessori an ideal early childhood curriculum around which to focus the training. Montessori could also be imparted over the course of a number of years.

Designed to help children become independent, self-sufficient members of society, Montessori is also a useful concrete approach to teaching adults about the physical and cognitive development of young children. For instance, Montessori first studies practical life—concepts that adults already understand—using objects from the home to create manipulative activities for children. The Montessori program also offers opportunities for adults to acquire basic academic skills. Many of the Foundation Center participants learned math and arithmetic skills for the first time as they were introduced to the sensorial and math curriculum of Montessori. Many of the adults, thrilled at learning addition and subtraction themselves, clearly transferred their newly acquired love of discovery to the children.

Other aspects of the Foundation Center professional development program were also thoughtfully designed with the participants in mind. Teachers in training were offered on-site study time. Often, the trainers gave participants written questions so they could practice giving directly corresponding answers. Facilitated discussion groups encouraged each person to ask questions and learn from the comments of other teachers. This format drew upon the strengths of participants, many of whom had learned teamwork through their own life experiences. Instruction was offered in English and Spanish, the languages primarily spoken by participants. All participants—even those whose primary language was not English or Spanish—were allowed to turn in homework in the language in which they felt most comfortable. Finally, the program sought to operate at the pace of the teachers. While most took five years, some moved faster and others could also take longer.

California Tomorrow interviewed some Foundation Center teachers and parents at the time the administration for the centers was being transferred to other organizations. Staff were universally appreciative of the opportunities that the program had provided for staff development. Heidi Lozano, teacher/director of the Porter Way Program in Stockton, began working for the Foundation Center in Los Angeles in October 1993 as an assistant teacher. She remarked:

> *If it wasn't for the Foundation, I would never have been a teacher. I would have settled for being a teacher's aide. They gave me—and I took—this opportunity. I am a Montessori teacher. I am confident of the knowledge that I have. Even if the Foundation Center doesn't exist, it will always live with me.* ❧

Community Colleges

In California, the Community College system bears the greatest responsibility for credentialing and formal training opportunities for early childhood educators. In some of the rural parts of the state, community colleges may be the only local source for earning child development units. The practices of community colleges can make continuing education significantly more accessible to low income and minority providers. It makes a difference when classes are offered in community-based locations which reduce the transportation burden on students. It also makes a difference when classes are offered in other languages such as Spanish or Vietnamese. Community colleges also work with other organizations, such as resource and referral agencies, non-profits and professional associations, to arrange for providers to earn credits for professional development activities offered by those groups. The California Child Development Training Consortium is one innovative effort aimed at maximizing the potential of community colleges to increase access to education.

The California Child Development Training Consortium (CCDTC) currently consists of 71 community college Child Development/Early Childhood departments and is funded by the California Department of Education with federal Child Care and Development Block Grant monies. Dr. Sharon Hawley is the director of the program headquartered at Modesto Junior College. The program seeks to improve the quality of care for young children by increasing the number of staff who are eligible for the California Children's Center Instructional Permits. The program first began in 1983 using state carry-over funds focused on the migrant education staff. As the program expanded to include all child development staff, it has retained an emphasis on underserved populations. These include bilingual providers, migrant education providers, family child care providers, and other groups that have been less able to take advantage of college level courses.

Each of the participating departments has a local coordinator and a local advisory board. Within broad guidelines, the local coordinator can design the Consortium program according to regional needs. Funding is granted based on the number of students served. All students must be employed in a child development program in order to be eligible. Family child care home providers who are licensed or exempt from licensing are included. Qualified students are eligible for a tuition reimbursement for coursework that leads to the California Children's Center Instructional Permit. When they have completed the requirements, they are also eligible for a stipend that pays for the permit application fees. This direct economic support for students is imperative in a field where wages are so low and additional training may not make a significant difference in salary.

Economic support for students is imperative in a field where wages are so low and additional training may not make a significant difference in salary.

Beyond the tuition reimbursement for students, each campus uses the funds to support underserved groups of employed students to succeed in obtaining the permit. Consortium funds are used in a variety of ways, ranging from providing classes at the worksite to classroom support for students to increase their likelihood of success (e.g., Spanish language classroom aides and tutors, book loans or book purchase grants) or the purchase or development of otherwise unavailable materials (e.g., book translations).

Although relatively small amounts of money are made available to each campus (ranging from $2,000 to $12,000 per year), the funds have made a great impact. Over 5,000 child care staff are served a year by this program, and for the last two years, the participant profiles indicate that the students reflect the ethnic and language diversity of the state.

The program also provides a twice-yearly discussion forum for the child development faculty across community colleges. Because the costs of participating are covered, far more faculty than usual are able to attend the professional meetings. For many faculty, this has broken their isolation and provided a powerful ground for sharing effective teaching, recruitment and retention strategies. Sharon Hawley explained:

> *Through participation in the Consortium, instructors are empowered to think along new lines and to create new alliances in communities.*

Cabrillo College in Santa Cruz offers an illustration of what has been made possible with the support of the Training Consortium. Cabrillo used the CCDTC support to focus on outreach to family child care home providers and Spanish-speaking providers to offer information about the permit as well as training oppor-

tunities at the college and throughout the county. Cabrillo offered permit-required courses in Spanish within the neighborhood most accessible to these providers. All eligible students still in attendance by the twelfth week of the semester received a tuition rebate. Spanish language teaching assistants were hired where faculty had insufficient Spanish to teach bilingually or to help students transition to English language instruction. Consortium money paid for the translation of classroom materials, handouts, the development of culturally appropriate video tapes and book loans. As the number of Spanish-speaking providers increased, the college provided funding for opening up new courses. Currently over 125 students a semester are enrolled in the Spanish language ECE program and each semester a new group receives their Emergency Permit (12 units).

Working with the local Family Day Care Home Association, Cabrillo used Consortium money to hire experienced providers to reach out to newer providers. A special class on How to Operate a Successful Family Child Care Home was developed, and the faculty was assisted in instruction by members of the "mentor" providers. Providers were encouraged to move on through the major. Each semester the number of providers who continue on has doubled.

In Watsonville, many family child care homes were run by Spanish-speaking families who had no contact with the local family child care association. In this case, instructor Maria Castro used Consortium money in conjunction with a grant from the Small Business Development Center to develop a course in Spanish and to create a leadership team to develop a Spanish-Speaking Family Association. With the support of a Cabrillo College faculty member, the Association encouraged members to take advantage of professional development opportunities. In the three years that Cabrillo has participated, over 500 students have received Consortium support, of which, 400 are Spanish speakers.

Resource and Referral Agencies

Recruitment and Training

Resource and referral (R&R) agencies play a critical role in ensuring the availability and accessibility of quality child care. R&Rs have a mandate to serve all parents and providers in their service areas, which may incorporate whole counties or parts of counties. As the diversity of California's population increases, so do the communities served by the R&Rs. California Tomorrow interviewed staff at 33 R&Rs across the state for this report. We learned that, on the whole, R&Rs have successfully recruited staff with the language and cultural backgrounds that could enhance service to diverse populations. Additionally, despite limited resources, many R&Rs are working to advance professional development on issues of race, language and culture.

Multilingual and Multiethnic Staff

In order to effectively reach out to and provide information to diverse populations, many R&R interviewees felt it was important to hire staff from the local communities, particularly people of the same racial and linguistic backgrounds as the families in the area. R&R staff recognized that representatives from the communities could establish crucial trust and communication with families. Many felt that bilingual staff were essential to reaching out to communities and providing information to parents of all backgrounds.

The group of R&Rs interviewed had been very successful in hiring the diverse staff they sought. Approximately three-quarters of the R&Rs had at least one staff person from every "major" ethnic group in their service area (a "major" ethnic group is defined as 5 percent of families with children under 6 years old in the county or service area, according to the 1990 Census). We also found that R&Rs were generally very successful in hiring bilingual staff. Language skills of the staff tended to reflect most of the major language groups in the service area. All but one R&R we interviewed reported at least one Spanish-speaking staff person. A quarter of the R&Rs had at least one Chinese-speaking staff person (either Mandarin, Cantonese, or both). Slightly fewer than a quarter had a Vietnamese-speaking staff person. Other languages spoken by staff at various R&Rs included: Hindi, Punjabi, French, Tagalog, Urdu, Korean, Hebrew, Italian, Hmong, Thai, Portuguese, and Farsi. Many of the individual R&R agencies had more than one bilingual staff person, and in several cases, all of the major language groups in the R&R's service area were represented.

Staff of several different R&Rs recounted times in the past when particular populations, Vietnamese families for example, were not calling for referrals. But as soon as the R&Rs hired a Vietnamese staff person, fluent in Vietnamese, calls from Vietnamese parents increased dramatically, solely based on word-of-mouth within the Vietnamese community that the new staff person was Vietnamese.

We found that R&Rs are extensive consumers of data. They use multiple sources of demographic data to learn about the populations in their service areas, plan programs and make staffing decisions. They most frequently use Census data, county population data, school district data, R&R Network data, and data collected in-house. Half of the R&Rs said they reviewed this information annually, and the remainder said they reviewed it either every 6 months or as needed. By regularly reviewing demographic data, R&Rs can predict population trends for many useful purposes. For example, when a staff position opens, the director can know what language and cultural skills would be most valuable at that point in time, and possibly in the future. And, when the opportunity for training on diversity issues arises, the focus can be on the new populations in the area.

Although R&Rs tended to employ more than one bilingual staff member and sometimes reported as many as 9 languages spoken by staff, the next challenge appeared to be how to take full advantage of these language capabilities. The presence of a bilingual staff person did not always yet translate into formal services provided in languages other than English. For example, three of the agencies that reported at least one Chinese-speaking staff person did not yet actually offer any services or written materials in Chinese. The same was true for three of the agencies that reported a Tagalog-speaking staff person.

According to the R&Rs surveyed, the challenge of fully utilizing bilingual staff seemed to be affected by both lack of resources and difficulty finding bilingual people who also had the requisite early childhood background. Several of the R&R staff we spoke to wanted to increase the languages spoken by referral counselors to reach more parents; strategies included cross staffing (to allow for translation) and cross training, either between agency departments or for specific tasks. Some R&Rs hoped to do more targeted planning around hires to make the right matches for families served. However, there clearly was not sufficient time or money for the training needed.

Translating Materials

R&Rs are known for creating excellent written materials for parents and providers. We found that they showed strong commitment to translating materials into many different languages for families. However, we found that not all R&Rs had the capacity to translate the materials they wished to offer parents. Some had translated great numbers of documents, calling on staff, parents, community organizations and school districts to help them in the work. Other R&Rs wanted to offer translated materials but did not have the resources or support to do so. We saw tremendous potential for R&Rs to share translated materials across programs, as well as to share translation services.

Training for R&R Staff

R&Rs are expected to provide increasingly diverse and complex services to parents and providers, and do so with fewer and fewer resources. Staff felt overwhelmed by the growing demands from apparently all sectors of the ECE field. They must provide all services through blocks of funding, rather than on a fee-per-service basis. In this context, as for child care programs, devoting time and resources to diversity issues may not take precedence when there are so many competing forces. Leadership appeared to be key; R&Rs that regularly provided professional development on diversity did so because of the director's prioritization of these issues.

The type and amount of diversity training varied widely. Some R&Rs brought in panels of community members to discuss the values and parenting styles of different cultural groups. Others sent staff to trainings by outside groups, such as "TODOS" or the Anti-Defamation League's "A World of Difference." Others set aside several professional development days to focus solely on diversity issues.

Some training needs particular to R&R agencies focus on the interaction with parents during referral calls. According to our interviews, it is not uncommon for an issue related to race, language or culture to arise during a referral call. Sometimes a language minority parent will ask about the availability of child care in the home language of the family. Sometimes English-speaking parents will request bilingual child care because they believe that this would be an important educational experience for their child. Almost a third of the R&R staff interviewed reported incidents where they felt parents demonstrated signs of racism or prejudice. For example, parents rejected some providers because they had accents, had Latino or Asian surnames, or were located in a neighborhood of an ethnic group different from themselves.

However, the R&R staff we spoke to had received few guidelines or training for discussing issues of race, language or culture when speaking to parents. For example, many referral staff routinely discuss quality issues with parents during an initial phone call. However, few make the explicit connection between quality care and the implications of race, language and/or culture in the care setting and what that means for family's choices. Many staff we surveyed said they did not always feel comfortable raising issues of race, language or culture with parents during a referral call. Half of the R&R staff surveyed said that they did not raise these issues with parents, but could give the information if asked. A few others said that they would raise the issue with parents only if the parent did not speak English. Several R&R staff believed it was not appropriate to raise these issues at all over the telephone; rather, they believed diversity issues should be addressed in workshops or more intensive educational situations. If supported with the proper resources and professional development, R&R agency counselors could have tremendous potential to assist families in weighing questions of race, language and culture before making decisions about child care.

Resource and referral agencies have also been known to play active roles in promoting and providing professional development opportunities. For some groups, such as family child care homes, R&Rs are among the few institutions with which they interact. Professional development issues are slightly different for family child care homes, which tend to operate more like small businesses. The director and the primary provider in a family child care home is often the same person. In this situation, professional development is useful for improving the care setting, but not for obtaining a promotion since no career ladder exists.

One of the most important shifts a family child care home can make is moving from being unlicensed to licensed. The California Child Care Resource and Referral Network developed the Child Care Initiative Project (CCIP) precisely for this purpose. Recognizing the growing need for Spanish-speaking child care facilities, a crucial element of the program is "El Comienzo," an effort specifically focused on recruitment of Latino professionals. ❧

El Comienzo

EL COMIENZO is an outgrowth of the California Child Care Resource and Referral Network's California Child Care Initiative (CCIP), a public/private partnership that has been recruiting and training family day care providers in communities throughout California since 1985. The Initiative has pioneered a model for building the number of family day care providers and was a response to the great need to develop culturally and linguistically appropriate services for families and providers of color, and for non-English-speaking children and providers. One of CCIP's top goals has been to train Spanish-speaking caregivers.

According to CCIP's *Developing Family Day Care in Latino Communities*, "Recognizing that California's Latino population is itself very diverse, a Latino-based project would also need to reflect this "internal" diversity. The Network and its member agencies launched El Comienzo, a multi-year program that has focused on the family day care needs of California's Latino communities. El Comienzo has developed a coordinated package of Spanish language recruitment and training materials." The project has now conducted numerous community-based demonstration projects throughout the state, recruited several hundred new licensed Spanish-speaking providers, and created new child care spaces for thousands of children.

California Tomorrow attended two El Comienzo trainings at the Canal Community Alliance, a community-based organization in a primarily Latino and Southeast Asian neighborhood of San Rafael. The coordinator of the El Comienzo project at the Alliance was Nancy Ducos, a Latina whose first language is Spanish. According to *Developing Family Day Care in Latino Communities*, El Comienzo's guiding principle is "that the project must not be yet another effort directed at the Latino community, but rather a process that as much as possible is based within it...we saw that the model would have to be carefully adapted, in partnership with the community, to particular values and needs." The development of leadership among Spanish-speaking providers has been a strong benefit of the Initiative.

The 30 participants on the day of the training represented the diversity of the Latino community, including Mexican, Dominican, Puerto Rican, Argentine and Salvadoran. The level of participation and excitement was inspiring. The group of providers had already been training together for a while and had gotten to know each other, evidenced by the friendliness and laughter that filled the room. Had the training been conducted in English, they would not have had access to this experience as learners and holders of knowledge.

The focus of the day was on the usage of language and how providers could support children's language development. For example, the group reflected on the common Spanish expression, "Los Niños son un milagro de dios," which means "Children are a blessing from God." The coordinator pointed out that while this expression is very loving of children, it can imply that everyone agrees on the same concept of God. Since usually a program serves a variety of families who may have different religious beliefs, she suggested using instead, "Los Niños son una benedición divina"—"Children are a divine blessing," a compromise that expresses the same essence.

Later the group did an experiential play exercise, building structures with Legos while talking about what they were doing. During the exercise, participants reflected on how the play activity was an opportunity to encourage language in young children. The guest presenter also presented a range of information regarding the development of bilingualism.

At the second training, the focus was on cultural diversity and child rearing. Participants discussed how their caregiving styles were influenced by their cultures. For example, should cereal be mixed into infants' milk bottles—or not? In some Latino cultures this practice is accepted as nourishing and comforting. In the United States, parents are told not to feed infants solids in their bottles because it is considered over-nourishing.

Many of the providers spoke about the importance of recognizing one's own prejudices around child rearing, for example around cleanliness or dressing. The speaker guided participants in a discussion of the reasons a child may arrive at the program wearing the same clothes for several days. Participants talked about how parents may not have access to a washer or may have to take two buses to the laundromat. Or, a family many not have enough clothes in the house to change often.

Finally, the group talked about establishing open communication with parents. Through role playing, the speaker offered techniques for resolving differences. The role playing sparked animated conversations among the participants about how they might apply the techniques to their programs. ❧

Challenges to Recruiting, Retaining and Promoting the Advancement of a Diverse Workforce

Although these examples of professional development are encouraging, there are still some significant challenges to recruiting, retaining and promoting a diverse workforce. Many of these challenges are problematic for the field for a variety of reasons, not only because they inhibit diversity.

Inadequate Compensation

The average hourly wage for a child care teacher nationwide is $6.89 and in California it is $8.07. For directors, the corresponding figures are $12.70 and $14.94. According to the Cost, Quality and Outcomes Study, teachers earn $5,238 per year less than a person who works in another field and has a similar educational and professional background. Directors lose an average of $3,198 in foregone wages. Clearly, low wages deter some people from contemplating a career in early care and education even when they feel a strong commitment to working with young children and their families. Wages in the field are so low that some may leave the field, or at least move out of working directly with children and families, because they cannot earn what they need to survive.

While low wages are a problem for everyone, they are an even more serious one for some women, especially those who are the primary wage earners for their families and have greater financial responsibilities. Women of color tend to earn the lowest wages of all. According to NBCDI, in 1988, the Council for Early Childhood Professional Recognition surveyed 4,081 individuals who had received a Child Development Associate Credential. Those who had left the field were asked why. All African Americans cited low salaries, as did 84 percent of the whites. Sixty-one percent of African Americans cited lack of benefits in contrast to 48 percent of whites. NBCDI hypothesizes:

> *African Americans may experience more difficulties surviving on low wages and poor benefits. Because a higher proportion of Blacks than whites are single mothers supporting their own children and contributing to the support of parents and other family members, African Americans may not be as able as whites to tolerate low benefits and salaries.*

The child care field is highly fragmented in terms of professional development, as well as service delivery.

Given discriminatory trends in salaries, it is likely that low wages will prevent more people of color than whites from taking low-paying jobs for their intrinsic value. Consequently, while people of color may be more likely to find a job in child care than in other fields because of the barriers to entering other fields, they may also be more likely to leave once they gain the qualifications that make them marketable for higher paying jobs outside the sector.

According to the National Center for the Early Childhood Workforce, the only way to raise salaries for the profession is to break the link between parent fees and the amount of money available to cover the costs of care (Bellm, 1994). While some programs are subsidized through state and federal funds, many programs are heavily dependent upon parent fees to cover their expenses. Since salaries and benefits comprise the biggest cost of operating a child care program, maintaining low fees involves keeping compensation at a relatively low rate. Otherwise, it is not economically viable for parents to work. Not surprisingly, programs which receive public subsidies tend to have more highly trained staff with lower turnover rates.

The low wages are compounded by the fact that the field lacks any type of coordinated system which clearly defines career paths and rewards individuals for their skills and educational backgrounds. As mentioned, the field is highly fragmented in terms of professional development, as well as service delivery. Consequently, a person who has received training in one sector or type of program may not be able to get that training recognized by another sector. Under the current system, staff do not necessarily receive financial rewards for additional education or responsibilities even if they continue to work in the same program. A participant at California Tomorrow's retreat with providers said:

> *There's not much difference between a teacher, entry-level teacher position and a head teacher position, in terms of experience and education. The amount of difference in pay is nothing compared to the outside world.*

> *So, if I were a smart person of color and I went to college to get all of these degrees, why am I going to work in a classroom for nine dollars an hour? Even if I wanted to do it, why would I do it??*

One of the issues this comment raises is that the field needs to find ways to reward those teachers who seek out additional professional development so that they have an incentive to use their newly developed skills in the classroom. Otherwise, once they acquire additional education, their only option for being compensated is to move out of direct work with families into administrative positions or sometimes leave the field altogether. Liz Forge-Chapman, a vice president of Drew King Child Development Corporation, states:

> *If you have been an assistant teacher, a teacher and then a director, where do you go? I had been the director of the child development center at Southwest College for nineteen years. Now the only place for me to go is outside of the system. If I had wanted to stay on campus, I would have had to become a dean and then I would have been away from child development where I wanted to be. We need to develop more layers.*

The creation of a career ladder with a salary schedule for the field is one of the fundamental recommendations of the recruitment and training task force staffed by the National Center for the Early Childhood Workforce and convened under the Pacific Oaks California Child Care Professional Development Project. Some progress on creating such a system has been made in other states. The TEACH program in North Carolina is an excellent example of an effort to link early childhood training with improved compensation. Funded by a $100 million appropriation from the North Carolina state budget, TEACH brings together a variety of scholarship programs. It includes a credentialing program which offers participants wage bonuses, training options under which community college credits result in raises, a mentor teacher program, and a new four-year college degree program which began in Fall 1994. Operating in 74 of the 100 counties in the state, the program serves approximately 1,000 providers working in family child care, as well as center-based programs (Russell, 1994). While such a program is not directly aimed at increasing recruitment and advancement of providers from under-represented communities, it is the type of program which helps to create a basic infrastructure which will address issues which inhibit the retention and advancement of low income and minority individuals.

The Lack of Professional Recognition

Low wages in the field also reflect the failure of the larger society to recognize the value contributed by people who engage in the increasingly important work of caring for the young children who represent our future. Professionals in the field have for many years been struggling to counteract that caring for children is a job that "anyone can do" and does not deserve a particularly high level of compensation because, in the past, it was primarily provided for free by women working in the home. The lack of professional recognition is not only a monetary issue. It also presents morale problems because low-paid providers are less likely to stay in a profession if their contributions are never valued, praised or even noticed. Professional recognition, while not a substitute for adequate compensation, is also essential to providing staff with the motivation to stay in the field.

Patti Hnatiuk, director of Child Care Trainings at Wheelock College, believes one way of recognizing teachers is providing them with opportunities to interact with colleagues on a professional basis. She shares:

> *A worker once told me that the distinction between director and people who work directly with children is that directors carry date books and have a calendar which they use for setting up meetings with other people. People who work directly with children do not have that privilege. That's not truly professional. We need to reshape job descriptions so they include working with other adults as well as children. People need training opportunities with those who work with children. Doing so would serve to retain a high quality and more diverse workforce at the same time.*

Increased retention is one of the benefits cited for Mentor Teacher Programs which create opportunities for new teachers to work with experienced professionals. Such programs are now being established throughout the country. They help to meet the professional development needs of incoming providers while also offering status and professional recognition to experienced, skilled veteran teachers in the field. Mentor Teacher Programs can also create opportunities to recognize the skills and talents of a more diverse group of professionals.

Opportunities such as the Mentor Teacher Program are essential because they create ways to recognize and enhance the professional development of experienced classroom teachers. These teachers want to stay in the classroom but they also want to be fairly compensated for their expertise. One teacher we interviewed expressed heartfelt frustration with the lack of support she felt for continuing to remain in the classroom where she believed she could make the strongest contribution. And, indeed, this teacher had developed an extremely exciting repertoire of activities and strategies. On the other hand, teachers must also be able to access ongoing professional development in order to ensure that their strategies and skills do not stagnate.

Mentor Teacher Program

Since I became a mentor teacher I feel that I am a professional person, not a babysitter, and I have decided to complete my B.S. and get my M.A.

—Mentor teacher evaluating the Mentor Teacher Program

THE CALIFORNIA EARLY CHILDHOOD Mentor Teacher Program has pioneered an innovative, successful approach to identifying and retaining highly-skilled child care providers and to increasing training opportunities for those entering the field.

Founded in 1988, the Mentor Teacher Program was developed to meet four goals:

- To retain skilled and stable child care teachers through advanced training, professional recognition and financial reward
- To increase the opportunities for novice and/or untrained teachers to improve their caregiving skills through participation in a high-quality supervised teaching experience
- To increase awareness in the community on issues related to quality
- To involve the community college with others to improve standards of quality in the community

Working with community college faculty, the program directors on 28 campuses utilize community outreach to identify highly-skilled teachers who work in various types of child care programs. Interested, experienced providers, who themselves have had a student teaching experience, take a course in adult supervision skills, do a self-assessment and site assessment, and then are able to apply for mentor status. A committee of community early childhood leaders visits the teacher on-site and, utilizing a formal assessment scale, makes recommendations for improvements or accepts the teacher to be a mentor.

All mentors receive an annual stipend, plus additional stipends for each mentee who trains with them. This $500 annual base stipend, although small, has been highly significant. Thirty-one percent of the mentors report that the stipend is essential to their ability to meet basic living expenses.

Once selected, the mentors meet as a team on a regular basis, discussing the "mentees," increasing their own supervisory skills, building a professional support network, and developing advocacy strategies for their communities.

Breaking the isolation of teachers, recognizing their skills, rewarding their competence, and creating another step on a career ladder have all had an important impact on the mentors. In written comments evaluating the program, the mentors were clearly enthusiastic about the experience. "Teaching someone to teach makes you re-evaluate and improve your own methods," said one. "This was the first time I felt that there was a reward for being a good teacher," commented another.

The program has not only helped with retention, but has increased the diversity of trainers available for entry-level students. Almost half the mentors in the state are members of ethnic minorities, the most diverse training pool in the state. Although there are program and regional variations in terms of where those teachers work, the overall impact provides a significant model for beginning teachers and an important recruitment approach.

The novice teachers, assigned as mentees, are enrolled in community college classes and placed in community mentor sites for full-credit student teaching experience. As is typical in the field, most mentees are already employed while they receive their training, and almost 20 percent of the mentees are able to student teach at their own worksite. Compared to lab schools, the mentor sites often offer more flexibility in scheduling student teaching hours. Interestingly, mentees tend to be older and more diverse than students who have only lab school experience.

Although lab school students score higher on competency skills, both groups score more highly than community teachers without a supervised student teaching experience. And as mentors develop more experience supervising students, the gap in competency skills becomes smaller.

Michael Modesko, a student teacher from Watsonville, selected Neighborhood Child Care, a bilingual mentor site for his supervised placement. "Getting teaching experience in the Mentor Program is great because I got to choose the hours I could work each week. Colleen Murphy (the mentor) made the transition from textbook-learned knowledge to experiential teaching wisdom a lot easier for this aspiring student! She's great!" Sandra Blanchard, newly hired at the Santa Cruz Toddler Center, commented, "The best aspect of the placement was that I had just started working there and I was given the opportunity to be observed and to discuss my teaching and improve my skills."

Part of the quality impact of the Mentor Program is the ripple effect caused by having a broadly representative mentor selection committee drawn from throughout the child care community. The directors and teachers who visit programs and assess the potential mentors and their sites are engaged in discussion of child care conditions, teacher competency and other quality indicators. These issues include consideration of the program's approaches to multicultural and language development.

Developed by the National Center for the Early Childhood Workforce (NCECW), then known as the Child Care Employee Project, and Chabot Community College in Hayward, the California Early Childhood Mentor Teacher Program was funded by the David and Lucile Packard Foundation and the United Way. Today, still administered by Chabot, the program is overseen by the Child Development Division (CDD) of the California Department of Education, and is funded by federal Child Care and Development Block Grants in conjunction with private monies. ❧

Inadequacy of Traditional Measures of Staff Quality

Traditional measures of staff quality do not adequately recognize the assets of people who have informally gained critical skills and knowledge through their life experiences in the communities served.

A staff person's reflection of the linguistic, cultural or racial demographics of the community being served should be taken into account in hiring. While many in the early childhood profession agree that these characteristics are desirable, there seems to be little agreement about how they should be balanced against the more traditional measures of professional competence, namely formal education, English-language literacy and credentialing. Some fear that giving a higher priority to language and cultural skills leads to a lowering of standards for staff quality. Others feel that too much credence is placed on traditional measures of staff quality, causing an exclusionary impact on people who are low income and from communities of color. This controversy appears to be arising in a number of different forums throughout the field.

For example, during California Tomorrow's retreat with center directors and staff, participants debated what it meant to take race, language and culture into account when hiring staff. One participant immediately raised the concern that this concept implied that programs should place a higher value on a person's ability to speak the language of the family or reflect the cultural beliefs of the community than on experience level or professional preparation. Should a center only hire candidates who reflect the children, even if they have lower levels of education or experience? The participant was clearly uncomfortable with this proposition and felt that it constituted a form of reverse racism. Another participant took a slightly different view: a program could not afford to overlook the need for staff reflective of the community, particularly if they were not represented within the existing staff. Her belief was that programs should keep positions open until they could find someone with the broader qualifications for the job, as well as the appropriate linguistic skills or community experience.

Some people in the field believe that language skills and cultural understanding should, in fact, be a higher priority than credentialing, because they are harder to find in candidates. While people with this perspective still value professional development, they tend to emphasize hiring staff with the right set of community skills and then to provide opportunities for them to gain professional education. Carol Brunson Phillips, executive director of the Council for Early Childhood Professional Recognition, comments:

> *The most effective strategy is to start with teachers who are a cultural and linguistic match with kids and then teach them about good early childhood practice. They can then make the modifications for all of this to make sense to children and families. It is a lot harder to take people who know early childhood and teach them the culture and even the language of the families in care.*

In fact, this viewpoint was fundamental to the staff development approach developed by the Foundation Center for Phenomenological Research. This program, which is described in this chapter, was designed to work with people who may not have even had the opportunity to complete elementary school or acquire basic literacy skills. Its intent was to ensure that program participants would, over time, gain basic educational skills as well as the necessary background in child development. The results in the short-term were that program quality on traditional measures went up. Staff turnover dropped dramatically to approximately 4 percent per year. Parent involvement and satisfaction grew tremendously. The founders of the program even entertained the idea of eventually creating a process by which participants could earn a Bachelor of Arts degree. A continual tension existed, however, between pursuing the goal of hiring from the community and meeting state regulations around educational requirements for staff.

Questions around the appropriate balance between community representation and formal qualifications also arose among Head Start programs. The National Center for the Early Childhood Workforce completed an analysis of Salary Improvements for Head Start. The analysis discussed issues stemming from the $470 million set aside in salary increases for approximately 100,000 Head Start employees as part of the 1994 reauthorization. Decisions about allocating this money among staff were left to the discretion of the approximately 2,000 local grantees and delegate agencies who administered the program at the community level. Grantees could allocate the amount equally among all of the staff, use it to increase the salaries of incoming staff, or any other formula of their choosing. But what would be a proper balance between rewarding a credential versus community background? One grantee shared:

As salaries got better, it was easier to get people with a Bachelor's degree. Those people tended to be Caucasian middle class people. We did not want our program's multiculturalism to be lost, so we really had to stop and look at that and say that is not what we want to become. We've made a commitment that 50 percent of our staff will be recruited and enrolled from the Head Start parent population (Whitebook, 1995).

Institutions of higher education also need to reflect on what qualifies a person to be an instructor or faculty member. To what extent should qualifications be limited to people with academic degrees such as a Master's or Ph.D? In the past, vocational credentials allowed people who had seven years of experience in a field and two years of college to apply for California Community College teaching positions. But, some six years ago the Vocational Education credential was abolished and a Master's degree became the minimum qualification. Some believe that this shift in credentialing has negatively impacted the recruitment of diverse faculty. Like child care facilities, institutions of higher education must ask how they can appropriately acknowledge the expertise gained through experience. Unnecessary credentialing requirements can inhibit colleges from drawing upon the knowledge and skills of individuals who could serve as role models and impart tremendous knowledge to students based upon their connection to practice and community. Life experience should be more strongly recognized as a measure of professional qualification.

Low wages reflect the failure of the larger society to recognize the value contributed by people who engage in the increasingly important work of caring for the young children who represent our future.

How Can Professional Development Equip Providers to Offer Quality Care in a Diverse Society?

A reflective workforce and opportunities for workers of all backgrounds to advance would be an essential foundation for the child care profession in a diverse society. But, it would not be sufficient by itself. The professional development imparted to providers must help them to implement the five Principles of Quality Care in a Diverse Society described in this book. Otherwise, people may obtain credentials and advance without the skills and knowledge to support the healthy development of children and families in a diverse society. California Tomorrow has identified a number of ways early childhood professional education can help to prepare providers to effectively address issues of race, language and culture. We believe these suggestions apply to the general early childhood curriculum as well as efforts specifically aimed at increasing understanding of diversity.

Increase awareness about the critical importance of issues of race, language and culture.

As early childhood educators have grown more aware of the demographic changes reshaping the field, some institutions have launched important efforts to increase awareness about diversity issues. While the efforts described in this chapter should not by any means be considered a comprehensive listing of the innovations in California, much less the country as a whole, they do provide a glimpse of the promising approaches different institutions can take.

California's community colleges are the primary source of professional development for most providers. A quick glance through the course listings reveals that at most community colleges, the child development or early childhood education departments offer at least one course related to diversity. Topics range from anti-bias to multiculturalism to working with children and families from particular ethnic communities. Majors that offer no such courses on diversity are the exception. Some colleges, such as Contra Costa College, have made a course on diversity required for graduation. Other community colleges have developed in-depth programs such as the bilingual/bicultural credentialing program at Santa Barbara City College. Yuba College is developing modules about the religious practices, beliefs and attitudes about child rearing among the diverse cultural groups in the area. Most community colleges also at least embrace a philosophical commitment to infusing attention to diversity throughout their courses.

Another exciting initiative is the Program for Infant/Toddler Caregivers, collaboratively developed by the California Department of Education and the Far West Laboratory for Educational Research and Development, now West Ed, with funding from the state and private foundations. The training program consists of four modules: (1) social emotional growth and socialization, (2) group care, (3) learning and development, and (4) culture, family and providers. Modules include educational videos and resource guides. Issues of diversity are covered explicitly in module four, and both agencies are working to infuse attention to diversity throughout the training program. The video on diversity, *Essential Connections: Ten Keys to Culturally Sensitive Child Care*, is considered by many to be the best of its kind.

The California Association for the Education of Young Children has also taken important steps to make professional development more available through its sponsorship of the Leadership in Diversity (LID) Program. Begun in January 1992, the program, which is described in more depth later, was created in order to increase the number of individuals who could provide quality pro-diversity and anti-bias education to the CAEYC membership and the field in general. LID receives substantial financial support from the California Association of Education for Young Children and the local chapters. The Board established the LID program even though it initially required making hard decisions about reallocating resources away from other projects, including some which had been running for years.

On the national level, the National Association for the Education of Young Children (NAEYC) has recently produced a position statement entitled, "Responding to Linguistic and Cultural Diversity: Recommendations for Effective Early Childhood Education." Adopted in November 1995, this statement offers recommendations for programs working with children and families and for professional preparation. Widely disseminated through NAEYC's annual conference and magazine, *Young Children*, this statement is an important foundation for increasing the awareness and knowledge of child care providers across the country.

Provide participants with a basic understanding of the five Principles of Quality Care in a Diverse Society and their interconnections.

Professional development should provide practitioners with information about each of the five principles. To reiterate, these principles are:

- One: Combat racism and foster positive racial identity in young children.
- Two: Build upon the cultures of families and promote respect and cross-cultural understanding among children.
- Three: Preserve children's family languages and encourage all children to learn a second language.
- Four: Work in partnership with parents to respond to issues of race, language and culture.
- Five: Engage in dialogue and reflection about race, language and culture on an ongoing basis.

Practitioners need an understanding of the theoretical underpinnings of these principles as well as how to put them into practice. And, while these principles may be applicable to children and youth of all age groups, practitioners need to understand how to support these principles among young children. For example, a class on the policies and practices to promote bilingualism and second language acquisition among children in elementary school will not necessarily equip a provider to understand these concepts among infants and toddlers, given the enormous developmental differences.

Participants need an opportunity to grapple with how the principles are interrelated and interwoven. Consider, for example, the connection between race and culture. On one hand, it is a mistake to assume that people share a common culture simply because they appear to be of the same racial background. Any given racial group includes many different cultural groups, because culture is influenced by a number of factors including national origin, socioeconomic background, degree of exposure to other cultural groups, etc. On the other hand, people of a racial group are likely to share some traits because they share a common experience of being treated in particular ways by virtue of their skin color and appearance. The connection between culture and language also offers important insights. As discussed earlier, language is a vehicle for the transmission of culture. Often, a language contains culturally embedded concepts and terms which cannot be easily translated into another language. Knowing a language is both a source of knowledge and an important connection to a larger community. However, two individuals may both identify as being part of the same cultural group even though one may still not

speak the language traditionally spoken by that community. Broadly defined cultural groups may include speakers of different languages or dialects.

Understanding these interconnections can help caregivers see the importance of addressing all of the principles—that addressing one can not substitute for addressing another. For instance, hiring a person who speaks Spanish but does not come from the community being served does not fill the same need as would hiring a person who both speaks the language and grew up in that community. Similarly, a person from the community who only speaks English will not fulfill the need to communicate easily with parents in a home language other than English. Understanding the connection between race, language and culture helps a program make more strategic decisions.

Acknowledge the cultural foundations of prevalent child development theory, such as Piaget, Freud and Erickson, and of prevalent curriculum frameworks, such High Scope, Reggio, Developmentally Appropriate Practice and Montessori.

People with formal training are likely to be exposed at some point to the major theories of how children develop and the most commonly used curricular frameworks. A deep understanding of these concepts and theories is important in professional development, along with the recognition that they are themselves a reflection of certain cultural norms. Ron Lally, director of the Center for Child and Family Studies of the Far West Laboratory for Educational Research and Development, explains:

> *Much of the cross-cultural research conducted over the last ten years has led us to the conclusion that things considered necessary to early childhood development were, in fact, universal only to the European-American culture in which it was based. In child rearing, we have to learn to be particularly suspect of the current proclaimed universals of American practice that have to do with: (1) the early attainment of individuality*

and independence, (2) the necessity of early and free exploration, and (3) the critical importance of the early stimulation of intellect and language. These are three areas which previous research has seen as universal which cross-cultural research has shown not to be.

The controversy over *The Developmentally Appropriate Practice in Early Childhood Programs Serving Children from Birth to Eight*, published by NAEYC, illustrates why it is important to understand and acknowledge the cultural foundations of child development theory. These guidelines are well recognized as defining for the field what constitutes appropriate care in early childhood programs. They represent a valuable effort to establish standards within a field which previously lacked a written consensus over what constitutes "quality" child care. As with many public reports, however, the document generally reflects the norms and beliefs of the surrounding society and the people who developed it. The document, as originally written, does not acknowledge that many of its premises are derived from the child rearing practices of the dominant culture, nor does it specifically discuss how culture or bilingualism should be taken into account in the development of appropriate teaching strategies and curriculum. As these guidelines have grown in popularity, a growing number of people in the field have expressed concern about their suitability for children who do not come from the dominant culture. NAEYC is now in the process of producing a revised version of *The Developmentally Appropriate Practice*, informed by the concerns expressed.

Staff development can help to make practitioners in the field more aware of the cultural foundations of the current theories of child development. Intisar Shareef of Contra Costa College states:

When I was looking for a new textbook for my child development class, I really knew that I had to find a book that at least asked questions about Freud's experience and Erickson's experience so that these experts weren't just seen as a voice from on high—these were men who were raised in a cultural context. As we become more mindful of that and write from that perspective, we begin to examine some of the notions we have.

Education and professional training can sometimes more strongly impact an individual's approach to child rearing than the values and beliefs they learned from their families and communities. Learning to question these frameworks is essential to better understanding why we hold the beliefs we do.

Help providers understand concepts of institutional as well as individual oppression and racism. Take into account the fact that participants may be at different levels of development with respect to their awareness and openness to issues of race, language and culture.

My first premise about staff is that everyone is at different stages of awareness and development as adults, with their own experiences of

discrimination. It is a given that adults are at different stages. Everyone is not at the same place at the same time. Acknowledging that is key.
—PATTI HNATIUK, WHEELOCK COLLEGE

Most people think about racism or oppression in terms of the actions or words of an individual. The concept of institutional racism, or institutional oppression, is typically much more difficult for people to grasp, even though it is just as prevalent, if not more so. Institutional oppression is found where practices, norms or policies of an organization or institution lead to or justify a particular group receiving better or worse treatment or opportunity—along lines of language, culture, gender, ability, etc. It becomes institutional racism when the impact falls along racial lines. Institutional forms of oppression can be elusive because they do not seem to stem from an intentional effort to discriminate or exclude people. Sometimes, institutional oppression arises out of ignorance or adherence to the status quo, without individuals realizing the institution has been shaped by the norms of a dominant culture that may not be appropriate for other groups. Providers must understand concepts of institutional racism and oppression, as well as of individual prejudice. This will help ensure that they are equipped to actively combat racism and to prevent unintentionally promoting discrimination.

Participants are likely to be at different stages and levels of awareness. Staff development needs to take this into account through the array of available activities and strategies used by the trainers. The article by Phyllis Brady beginning on the next page begins to explore this.

We must be able to piece together the knowledge possessed by people from diverse backgrounds to develop strategies for affirming and adapting to our changing environment.

Jointly construct knowledge by drawing upon the perspectives of diverse participants.

We must be able to piece together the knowledge possessed by people from diverse backgrounds to develop strategies and approaches for affirming and adapting to our changing environment. By the very nature of diversity, no one person has all of the knowledge, skills and experience to be "right" in all situations. The evolution of culture and the variations within racial and linguistic groups make impossible a standard recipe for how to work with people from particular ethnic backgrounds. These dynamics mean that staff development should not be based upon the traditional assumption that only the teacher will transfer knowledge to the student. Rather knowledge should be generated through interaction among teacher and participants, as is promoted by Popular Education and other models of empowerment.

Many people we interviewed stressed the importance of tapping into the knowledge of participants in a training, whether it be a community college class or a workshop specifically devoted to diversity. Kate Rosen, an instructor at City College of San Francisco, explained:

The population of community colleges is extremely diverse. When I held open discussions about child rearing, I became very aware that within every culture there were different models and values around caring for children. I learned from listening to students when they brought up a conflict between what they heard in class and what they knew from their own experience.

The Leadership in Diversity Program (LID), sponsored by the California Association for the Education of Young Children, is a model designed for participants to learn from one another. LID is building a network of leaders who can promote understanding of diversity issues throughout the broader field. The LID curriculum

The Journey Towards Anti-Racist Awareness and Identity for Multiracial People, People of Color and Whites

by Phyllis Brady

Phyllis Brady is a co-trainer of the Leadership in Diversity Project of the California Association for the Education of Young Children, along with Louise Derman-Sparks and Cecelia Alvarado. She recently completed directing the Early Equity in Science and Mathematics Project for California pre-K, primary and early childhood educators, funded by the National Science Foundation. Phyllis' racial and cultural identity is diverse. Her mother is Mahican, Cherokee, Creek, African American and Western European. Her father was a first-generation American of Irish and Australian descent. She lived, worked and raised her daughters in Africa for a decade. This is an adaptation of a longer article that can be found in The Web *(please see bibliography).*

LOUISE DERMAN-SPARKS, Cecelia Alvarado and I, for many years, have been working with adults as they develop their cultural and racial identity, awareness of racism, and participate in pro-diversity and anti-racist pursuits. Individually, and as partners, we have observed predictable patterns and learned some lessons about implications of these issues for adult training. The following lessons and strategies are also based upon the teaching and observations of Carol Brunson Phillips and Louise Derman-Sparks when they taught Racism and Human Development courses together at Pacific Oaks College in the late 70's and early 80's. Other trainers and researchers, such as William Cross, Beverly Daniel Tatum and Janet Helms, have also recognized patterns of responses in the anti-racism development of adults, and have developed similar conceptual systems.

Developing an understanding of cultural and multiracial identity, and learning how to pursue anti-racism goals, takes time and hard work. To look at oneself—to examine who I am in the context of family and institutions—requires a process that is lengthy and often painful. It is also hard to examine who they are, and to survey our painful history of privilege and exclusion. This journey of examining family, cultural communities and institutions, however, starts to answer the question of *why* and allows us to move on to *how*.

We have observed three general categories of responses to anti-racism education: Denial and Resistance, Disequilibrium and Struggle, and Reconstruction. These responses, described in more detail below, represent a continuum of characteristics describing people's awareness of racism and connection to an anti-racism commitment. We have often seen individuals experiencing the responses as passing through stages. Not everyone will exhibit every response or manifest all of the characteristics of a particular response. Nor will people necessarily have the same response to all of the "isms." A person may be in a "reconstruction" mindset regarding multiracial identification and awareness of racism, but in "denial" regarding understanding heterosexism and awareness of their own homophobia. However, transfer of insights usually occurs from working through each area to other "ism" areas.

Another very important lesson we have learned is that people from different racial experiences respond somewhat differently as they are exposed to anti-racism education and learn about their cultural and racial identities. Race is a socially constructed concept, not based in biology or genetics. However, it has power as a social and political construct in that a person's experience and opportunities are shaped by the racial category they are part of or look like. Therefore, it is important to explore the similarities and differences in responses among people from different racial backgrounds.

We describe some of these variations by referring alternately to "white people," "people of color" and "multiracial" people. The term "white people" includes all people who are solely of European descent. The term "people of color" includes all people who are not of European descent, including multiracial people. The term "multiracial people" is defined here as specifically those people who have either a blend of two or more ethnic groups of color, or a blend of one or more ethnic groups of color plus one or more ethnic groups of European heritage. Multiracial people are sometimes referred to as biracial (although this implies two races only), interracial or of mixed heritage.

We have found that there are predictable differences in needs among people from particular racial groups who exhibit particular responses to racial awareness and anti-racism work. Identifying some of the patterns of responses has helped us design and execute effective diversity and anti-bias training with adults. It has also helped us to identify and be prepared for particularly challenging group dynamics and "pitfalls." After we describe the responses to anti-racism education, we talk about some of the general strategies educators may use when faced with these complex dynamics.

Responses:

Denial and Resistance

For most people, a response of Denial and Resistance is characterized by a lack of awareness, knowledge, and sense of personal responsibility regarding racism. Fear, guilt, a sense of alienation and defensiveness may be part of the response. People in this category may think or say such things as, "I don't know what the big deal is; I don't see people's color." "Everyone is the same to me." "Why do you bring this up?" "Racism has nothing to do with me." "I don't treat people differently based on their color." This defensiveness exhibited by many people is often connected with fear. The feeling is "Let's not get into this. Don't rock the boat."

Some white people may feel that "Slavery was in the past, and I am not responsible for history" and use this as a reason not to try to understand deeper the effect of the past on the present. A person of color may feel that "I personally am not aware of being discriminated against." and so will not engage in deeper exploration of the dynamics and effects of racism. For a multiracial person, forming a sense of multiracial identity is complicated by many variables. Some of these variables are physical appearances, degree of exposure to different cultures, the nature and proximity of the multiracial mixing, the historical interplay between the different races, and the legal definitions of different races at various historical periods. Faced with such complexity, some multiracial people do not attempt to explore the history of their complex heritage, or to examine the labels and assumptions of a racist society.

Disequilibrium and Struggle

Disequilibrium is a response which represents a beginning of facing the realities about institutional racism and about each of our roles in perpetuating racism. As a result, feelings of pain, sorrow, grief, shame or anger may arise.

Feelings associated with Disequilibrium for white people may stem from a growing realization that they benefit from privileges that keep racism alive. White people may be struggling between maintaining their privileged position in the stem of racism, or accepting the changes they must make if they are to stand up against racism. For people of color, there may be a feeling of opening up of old wounds and anger. Anger may turn into rage, directed at white people in general. One of the most painful struggles for people of color is facing the ways in which people of color have internalized the oppressive messages and behaviors of the dominant society and, in so doing, have played a part in keeping racism rampant.

Reconstruction

Reconstruction represents the ability to take responsibility for personal, professional and institutional change and to channel pain, loss and anger into the work of dismantling racism and reconstructing an anti-racist society. Through Reconstruction, people may engage in an analysis of the past losses and potential gains that clarify the issues and make reclaiming of heritage and new alliances not only possible but necessary. They have developed an understanding of the impact of racism on their own social-psychological development and are able to recognize themselves as cultural beings and take pride in their own ethnic and cultural heritage. Increased knowledge of history, struggle and cultural strengths lead to a stronger sense of activism. The identities and roles of white people, people of color and multiracial people in doing anti-racism work becomes more clear and distinct. At the same time the possibilities for alliances between the activist groups are stronger and their goals become more similar.

General Strategies for Application in Training:

Assess audience variables as accurately as possible to tailor professional development goals and activities. It is important that diversity training be as relevant and closely linked to the needs of a specific group as possible. Use activities such as sharing of personal backgrounds, identifying the community(ies) people serve, and inviting individuals to express their concerns for fine-tuning the agenda to make the training more relevant to their needs. Maximize time for people to reflect on the process and apply the training information to their lives and work. Shared talking and listening time between pairs, small group discussions and planning, journal-type writing, and role playing are some facilitation processes that help participants integrate and apply information to their own needs.

Be prepared for diverse and possibly conflicting needs on the part of learners. Audience members will likely demonstrate a range of the responses to racial awareness and anti-racism work described above. Each group is also unique in the representation of racial, cultural and linguistic backgrounds of learners. The challenge for the facilitator is to help everyone articulate and explore their feelings and to guide them in understanding the underlying dynamics created by the power relationships of racism.

Racially specific caucus sessions provide opportunities to examine some of these issues separately and to explore reactions toward other racial groups. For all groups, it may be useful to spend time with others from the same racial group—with those who are similarly labeled in our society—to explore their own journeys, to learn from each other, to challenge each other, and to create alliances. At different times, multiracial people may want to meet separately with other multiracial people to safely explore the complexities of their mixture and to define their commonality with other multiracial people and people of color. At other times, some may want to connect closely with one or more specific identity groups. In any training which uses racially specific caucuses, there should also be a time to come back together as a whole group before the training ends. This may be a time for sharing with the whole group, planning of next steps or a unity building activity.

Identify the audiences you work best with and focus your work on them. Co-train in cross-racial teams when possible. The key as a trainer is to know yourself—your areas of strength and areas where you need growth—and to recognize when someone else may be a more effective trainer for the needs of a particular audience. If the participants are racially or ethnically specific, it can be very helpful if the trainer, or one of the trainers, is of that same race or ethnicity. If the participants are fluent in a language other than English or are bilingual, it is important that one of the trainers also is fluent in that language. If the audience is mixed racially, culturally or linguistically, it is important for the trainer to be experienced and effective at working with all of the groups represented, and to know what cross-racial or cultural conflicts may arise. We have learned that whenever possible it is generally preferable to work in cross-racial teams. This allows for content and activities to be broader and more diverse in scope. And, cross-racial teams can model dialogue and cooperative work.

Know what your reactions are personally to each "ism" and who and what pushes your buttons. It is important for trainers to have done—and continue to do—the internal work that leads to emotional as well as cognitive clarity. We need to continue honestly reassessing where we are in the developmental journey toward anti-racism, as well as in the other arenas of anti-oppression work. ❧

includes three extended retreats during the first year and a half. Throughout the retreats, participants are encouraged to share views and analyze issues of diversity, from the personal to the institutional. For example, at one retreat, participants wrote and then talked about: (1) their goals in their work on diversity issues, (2) their experiences as children and adults that propelled them to do the work, (3) how their cultures gave them strength in their work, and (4) their burning issues with respect to diversity. Later, participants discussed articles and readings and worked through exercises on topics from institutional racism to strategies for adult learning. Cecelia Alvarado, one of the lead trainers of the first LID class, recalled:

> *We used the group ourselves to learn by raising issues and questions that everybody should be asking in the field.*

Participants' own voiced experiences raised information for the group which was not covered in the planned reading. For example, the first class of LID interns only included one immigrant to the United States. Nonetheless, Rosalie Wasef, who immigrated from Cairo, Egypt, felt that her experience was still recognized because she herself was able to articulate it at the appropriate times.

Create opportunities for putting theory into practice.

For staff development to be meaningful, participants must be able to connect theory and practice. Theory is not useful unless participants know how to apply it to change their day-to-day work and lives. This is key when dealing with sensitive and challenging issues such as race, language and culture—which are much more easily discussed than acted upon.

Staff development can provide opportunities to apply theory in a variety of ways. At a minimum, programs can provide participants with concrete ideas and strategies, and time to think about and discuss the implications of theoretical frameworks for their own work. When professional development is held over a series of meetings, providers can practice implementing ideas they are learning between sessions and then discuss how it went in the following class. Interns who completed the initial LID retreats were expected to practice their knowledge by developing workshops on diversity along with other participants. These were then critiqued by the faculty of the LID program.

In-house staff development programs are in a strong position to connect theory and practice. When the entire staff is exposed to a concept, implementation is enhanced because: (1) a broader base of support has been created, and (2) staff knows that their efforts to change practice are condoned by the administration.

Emphasize the need for ongoing professional development on issues of diversity.

Clearly, a single workshop or training session on the complexities of race, language and culture in child care can not transform the practices of an individual or

group. In fact, the introduction and ongoing exploration of these issues will probably require greater professional development time than many other topics. Time is required to cover the content, as well as to reflect on the underlying premises and the critical nuances. Practitioners need time to digest the information and connect theories to their own practices.

Learning is lifelong. People will meet families and providers who come from backgrounds different from their own, and they must learn to work with them. And, as cultures and even languages evolve, professional development should remind us that our understandings, awareness and knowledge must also evolve.

Build advocacy skills.

How diversity is addressed by child care providers is significantly influenced by broader policies within the profession and the public at large. Public policies—from laws, policy positions to program guidelines—widely influence the field and individual programs. Policies can support or obstruct the efforts of individuals and organizations to address race, language and culture in early childhood education.

Practitioners must be prepared to assess and advocate for policies that will support their efforts. First, they must be willing to take a hard look at how current policies might need to be modified. Cecelia Alvarado, past president of the California Association for the Education of Young Children, has set aside time in professional development workshops for participants to assess the cultural relevancy and consistency of key policies in the field, such as the accreditation guidelines produced by the National Association for the Education of Young Children, or the program quality review guidelines used by the California Department of Education. Close analysis of such documents is essential because often they will include helpful, as well as less constructive, elements.

What these guidelines do or do not say about issues of race, language and culture impacts the operation of child care programs across the country and within California. For example, one predominantly Chinese program we visited had a difficult experience with the NAEYC accreditation. The NAEYC reviewer used the guidelines to cite the program for having too many Asian staff members. In the reviewer's mind, cultural appropriateness was equated with an ethnically diverse staff. In this case, the director felt that the NAEYC guidelines were not broad or clear enough to recognize the goals and strategies of an ethnic-specific program.

On the other hand, providers also must be ready to support policies which address concerns about race, language and culture, such as NAEYC's 1995 position statement, "Responding to Linguistic and Cultural Diversity." A positive reaction to this effort from NAEYC members is essential to ensure further work in this direction.

The ability of individuals, as well as organizations, to support the healthy development of ethnically diverse children and families is greatly affected by local, state and national policies. In recent years, the political environment has grown more and more polarized. Scapegoating of people of color and immigrants is pervasive, resulting in a wide array of policies that will hinder efforts to positively address issues of race, language and culture—from proposals to dismantle affirmative action, to initiatives seeking to exclude undocumented and, in some cases legal, immigrants from educational opportunities or human services. Providers need to become aware of the potential impact of these proposals on the child care profession and advocate for fair and equitable policies.

Challenges to Effective Professional Development Related to Race, Language and Culture

The knowledge base is growing as to what it takes to ensure that child care workers are equipped to work effectively with children and families in a diverse society. The broadening efforts in professional development speak to this inspiringly. However, much of this exciting work is occurring piecemeal. In this chapter, we discuss the major challenges to professional development that we identified in this research.

Professional development opportunities for people who work directly with children and families are limited.

We found that many of the providers in centers had experienced limited in-depth staff development related to the Principles of Quality Care in a Diverse Society. They may have attended a one-shot workshop or been exposed to diversity briefly as part of a community college course. At one center, a provider revealed that she had first heard about anti-bias work in her class on Child, Family and Community, but she knew the "tourist" approach to cultural awareness being promoted in the course was not sufficient. Once she returned to her classroom, she felt at a loss as to how to approach diversity in a more authentic way—she had the desire but not the knowledge, tools and support to do this work.

Staff with strong backgrounds in bilingualism and second language acquisition were the exception in the programs we visited, except in a few that had taken extra pains to develop the staff's language expertise. We hear many staff members say

A Parent and Child Care Provider Thinks about White Privilege

by Julie Olsen Edwards

I DON'T OFTEN think of myself as having privilege. I work in one of the most underpaid, unacknowledged professions in the country. I struggle as a parent with lack of support, lack of recognition, isolation. But after reading Peggy Macintosh's articles on White Privilege, I realize, as a white woman, raising white children, there are many privileges I have just taken for granted. Here are just a few that have become visible to me.

- I can assume if I am called into the principal's office to discuss my child, chances are pretty good s/he will be the same color as I am.
- If my kids excel at school or activities, they are unlikely to be called a credit to their race and expected to speak for white children everywhere.
- If my kids get into trouble, their behavior is unlikely to be counted as due to their skin color, and my parenting is unlikely to be called into question due to my skin color.
- I can generally assume the books, history stories, films, etc., that my children will be exposed to in school will mainly reflect the lives of people with my children's skin color.
- If I go to a therapist or counselor to seek help with my children, marriage or work relationships, I can assume the therapist will speak my language and share my skin color, and furthermore, s/he will not assume my struggles are due to my race.
- If I am hired at a new center, or receive a promotion, I do not have to wonder if other people presume I got the job only because of my skin color.
- If the Fire Marshall, or Licensing Officer comes to visit my center, I can presume s/he will share my skin color, and if they find something wrong I can be fairly sure they will not presume the problem is due to my racial background.
- If I mess up at work, it is unlikely people will presume it is the nature of my entire racial group to make that error.
- If I speak up at work, chances are people will credit my ideas to the quality of my experience and intelligence, rather than presuming I am a spokesperson for white folks in general.

In general, I can presume that most of the time in my dealings with the world, my children and I stand a good chance of being responded to as individuals, not as representatives of a racial group, and people in positions of authority and power in my life will most likely share my skin color and perceive me as a member of their particular human group. ❧

that supporting the home language was important and that they should find ways to validate language in the classroom. But, as discussed in our Principle on Language, once again they felt ill-equipped to implement these concepts appropriately. Family child care providers were even less likely to have accessed professional development in general, or studied issues of diversity in particular. Some operated in relative isolation with little connection to a larger infrastructure that could offer them these opportunities.

Directors are more likely than staff to have been exposed to concepts related to diversity through staff development, but they still often do not have access to the supports they need.

Directors of center-based programs were more likely to have been exposed to concepts related to diversity through staff development than teachers or teaching assistants. This is not surprising, given that directors typically have more opportunities for professional development in general than their staff. Many earned Bachelor's or graduate degrees to obtain or retain their positions. Typically, the greater flexibility of their schedules also permits directors more access to ongoing professional development opportunities such as workshops and conferences.

Throughout our research, we found widespread consensus about the important roles directors play in the entire staff's professional development. Directors serve as role models and set the tone for the entire organization. When the director encourages open expression of opinion and facilitates information exchange across staff, providers have greater opportunity to draw upon each other's knowledge and expertise. By virtue of their leadership positions, directors determine whether a program consistently pays attention to diversity throughout the organization. They heavily influence whether new staff who can foster the racial, cultural and linguistic identities of children will be sought through the recruitment and hiring process. Directors heavily influence whether staff development opportunities will be aimed at promoting a greater understanding of race, language and culture. A director's leadership can determine whether the program draws strength from the diversity of children and staff or ignores these issues, leaving the program paralyzed by division. As one experienced director said:

> *If you haven't addressed it systematically with your staff, it's going to happen because it's percolating up there—issues of race, bias, cliques, etc. At some point, it either gets so bad that it comes to a head and you have to pull somebody in, or you can be proactive and try to bring it out systematically.*

In spite of the power of leadership, it was still clear from our interviews that directors generally lacked access to professional supports which would help them address diversity effectively through their positions as administrators. We found directors struggling with a number of different challenges for which they desired outside support. These include:

- How to facilitate a staff discussion about differences in child rearing approaches.
- How to reach out to parents across differences in culture and language.
- How to develop strategies to more effectively recruit and retain staff of color and staff who are bilingual.
- How to find the resources to fund staff development on issues of diversity.
- How to identify appropriate high quality diversity consultants.
- How to negotiate tensions among staff which arise because of cultural, racial or linguistic difference.
- How to create the time and the support to reflect upon how their organizations may inadvertently work against goals of promoting diversity.
- How to ensure that their efforts to promote diversity are supported by policies and practices of the larger institutions within which they work.

Many administrators reflected on the personal conflict inherent in trying to balance their own authority with the desire to create an environment where staff feel empowered to help shape practice. For any person who possesses power, learning to use it effectively is a challenge. In child care, this challenge is compounded by dynamics of race and gender. Child care is one of the few fields where women, who have traditionally been denied power, are in charge. However, the women with most authority are usually white, even when most of the staff are people of color.

Marcy Whitebook, the founder of the National Center for the Early Childhood Workforce, observes:

> *Women aren't always comfortable about being in positions of authority. I think a lot of directors mess things up because they don't want to own their authority. They act like they don't have it and then pull it out at the wrong time.*

All directors need opportunities to understand and analyze the role race and power play in their interactions with other people.

Our research suggests that all directors need opportunities to understand and analyze the role race and power play in their interactions with other people. We spoke with one Chinese director about her frustration in working with her board of directors. She felt board members would pay more attention to the advice of a white administrator than herself, even though the board members were also Chinese. In this case, she felt the prestige of the dominant culture would outweigh her racial and linguistic connection to the board. On the other hand, this director also acknowledged that tokenism and "reverse racism" can create situations where a board does not appropriately question the actions or decisions of a director of color.

A strong consensus emerged among the directors we interviewed: they longed for opportunities to identify and meet with colleagues in similar positions to discuss and share their respective approaches, lessons learned and ideas about diversity as a program administrator. This consensus held across racial backgrounds and program types.

Staff do not always have support within their program to implement concepts and strategies they have learned about.

When providers return to their program excited about the new concepts they learned in a professional development training, they often find that they still don't quite know how to fully implement an idea. Or they cannot move ideas forward because other staff or the director do not support them. Professional development offered to the staff and directors of an entire program, or a network of programs, helps alleviate this challenge. Group staff development promotes greater buy-in and consistency throughout a program.

In-house staff development may include presentations or facilitated discussions by outside consultants, or designated time in regular staff meetings to discuss diversity. Staff should be encouraged to use those times to raise burning questions, share teaching strategies and seek the advice of other staff about how to work with a particular child.

Unfortunately, consistent staff-wide professional development was not the norm among the centers we visited. Financing greatly impacted this. For example, staff development is core to the Head Start approach and supported through federal funding. A few other centers creatively accessed or set aside funds for staff development. For example, one church-based program was able to use some discretionary funds for staff development because they did not need to pay rent and so their overhead costs were low. Some programs created discretionary income by offering some subsidized and some fee-paying slots for the families served. Income from fee-paying slots is typically more easy to allocate to professional development since it is not as restricted by government regulations. All programs, however, appeared hard-pressed to generate the financial resources needed for professional development.

Finally, some in-house staff development efforts can be loaded. Dialogue can be stifled if participants are not comfortable expressing their true emotions and opinions among the people they work with, some of whom might be the subject of a concern. Skilled facilitation and commitment to a long-term trust-building process are essential to the success of this type of professional development.

There is no system for ensuring that providers receive any professional development on issues of race, language and culture.

No coherent system or credentialing incentives exist to encourage providers to pursue courses and classes related to diversity. Credentialing requirements are relatively minimal and traditionally do not require students to take any specific courses on concepts of race, language or culture.

The early childhood profession suffers from the absence of a shared vision about the skills and knowledge practitioners need to work effectively in diverse settings. Currently, most professional development offers information about only one aspect of diversity. For example, in community colleges, classes typically focus on the culture of one ethnic community, or the development of an anti-bias curriculum, or cultural continuity, or bilingualism and second language acquisition. Students are not encouraged to study a full range of these topics, and a comprehensive array of classes is often not even available. Our discussions with providers reveal serious gaps in the topics covered in professional development.

On another level, professional development instructors are expected to "infuse" some attention to diversity into the general coursework, but this approach does not appear to be comprehensive enough as currently practiced. Within the early childhood profession, we have seen growing advocacy for "infusing" or "integrating" issues and concepts related to racial, cultural and linguistic diversity throughout a course or program. This approach has gained particular popularity among community college instructors. To some degree, the growing emphasis on infusion may indicate that more people realize the field must pay greater attention to diversity and its implications for the profession. It is a recognition that issues of diversity are integral to any discussion of early care and education, given the demographic composition of children in care. Some promote infusion because of their frustration with the way diversity has traditionally been addressed. Diversity has often been covered as a separate topic, strand or course without any acknowledgment of its connection to the core curriculum. Diversity issues have long been marginalized in this way.

Still, trainers interviewed by California Tomorrow expressed deep reservations about the current movement toward infusion. Their chief criticism is that infusion assumes that concerns of race, language, or culture can be "added on" to the existing framework and philosophy of child development and early childhood education. But, the existing framework remains a Eurocentric model based upon the norms and beliefs of the dominant society. Tinkering at the edges will not change the fundamental structure which continues to exclude different points of view about how children develop. Some fear that the infusion approach creates an appearance that the field is addressing diversity, when, in fact, these issues are still often glossed over. A participant at California Tomorrow's trainers retreat said:

> *In theory, infusion would mean inclusion of all children's culture. It would lead to an understanding of home language use, engaging in power analysis, becoming community based. It would help people to value and use conflict. In practice, infusion seems to have resulted in tokenism, ESL rather than bilingualism, a Eurocentric early childhood education base, an emphasis on nonviolent conflict resolution, color-blindness and "celebrating diversity." The infusion model in California doesn't seem to have worked because, by default, it gets lost.*

Some believe that the solution for now is to address diversity separately, as well as to infuse it throughout the curriculum. Joan Waller, director of Family Studies and Early Childhood Education at the College of the Canyons, echoes this sentiment:

> *How do we get away from the superficial approach? Is a three-unit class the answer? Can we (we must!!) integrate these concepts and issues in all the classes we teach? How else can we model what we preach for our students? Both are necessary.*

The "Advancing Careers" initiative spearheaded by Pacific Oaks College has called for new standards for professional development programs that require issues of multiculturalism and bilingualism to be addressed throughout. At this point, however, these standards to improve the overall design of child development programs are voluntary. Community college faculty need information and support to successfully integrate these standards into their courses. Nonetheless, the attention paid to diversity issues through the new program standards is promising.

Not enough support and attention are being paid to ensuring that the individuals who provide professional education have the skills and knowledge to effectively address issues of race, language and culture.

California Tomorrow staff and consultants met with many community college faculty teaching child development courses. Our discussions with these faculty members were revealing. On one hand, faculty expressed a passionate interest and commitment to developing providers who could support the healthy development of diverse children. They were hungry for information and strategies. But, it was clear that these instructors felt unprepared for this challenge. Community college instructor, Liz Regan, coordinator of Early Childhood Studies at Allan Hancock Community College in Santa Maria, captured this feeling:

> *The field of education balloons with increasing needs. There are so many social issues that teachers need to train students to meet, and we, teachers ourselves, have never had that training.*

Echoing a theme we have raised several times in this book, another instructor told us:

> *I'm really excited about cultural diversity, but I have never included information about language acquisition. I don't know enough about why speaking a child's first language is so important. This feeling colors how I teach language development. The question is, how to train the trainer? Where am I going to learn about bilingualism?*

Sharon Hawley, director of the Child Development Training Consortium, discussed some of the impediments to offering faculty this kind of professional development:

Finding time for training is a very real barrier. Time and funds are needed to promote change. Faculty need time to devote to work on making changes in the curriculum, time to discuss those changes with one another and to learn from one another. They need support from local administration to make those changes. People would like to do what's right and appropriate, but it takes time. And, the community college faculty are stretched so far already.

To compound the challenges, many community college faculty are part-time and not compensated for meeting time. Meanwhile, full-time faculty are typically expected to teach fifteen units per semester (usually five courses), covering a broad range of courses within the major. Such busy schedules leave limited time for discussions about anything, much less volatile issues such as race, language and culture.

Too often, the investment needed to adequately prepare people to teach about issues related to race, language and culture is underestimated.

For an instructor to be able to teach about diversity requires more than an understanding of the implications of the issues for working with children and families. He or she must develop the skills and the expertise to help others understand and create strategies for addressing race, culture and language in child care. The work will be volatile and emotional. Trainers must be prepared to facilitate discussions among people who may have conflicting viewpoints. Students must have opportunities to explore the issues from the personal to the professional level. Ron Lally, the director of the Training Program for Infant/ Toddler Caregivers, explains:

A trainer must be prepared for the fact that what will come up is not necessarily what they expect. Trainers must be people who have already dealt with issues around their own identity and are experienced enough so that their own buttons won't get pushed. It is too easy for trainers to end up dealing with their own cultural and emotional reactions.

Two Promising Models of Professional Development

California Tomorrow examined two different programs designed to increase the ability of trainers to teach about diversity. These two approaches reveal what may be required to develop professionals who can offer staff development on issues of diversity. The Program for Infant/Toddler Caregivers (PITC) was developed collaboratively by Far West Laboratory for Educational Research and Development and the California Department of Education to increase the quality of care to infants and toddlers. A hallmark of PITC is its high quality training manuals and videos accompanying each module. The video, *Essential Connections: Ten Keys to Culturally Sensitive Child Care*, a collaborative project with the Department of Education, convened experts in child care to discuss a range of issues. At the time California Tomorrow observed PITC, the training was built around four subject modules covered in two seven-day sessions. "Culture, Family and Providers" was covered primarily during a one-and-a-half day session of the fourth module. Diversity issues were covered in some other parts of the training as well. Most of the information covered related to the implications of cultural and linguistic diversity for working with children and families as opposed to anti-racism work.

Trainers must be prepared to facilitate discussions among people who may have conflicting viewpoints.

Participants in the PITC program primarily attended out of an interest in expanding their knowledge of high quality care for infants and toddlers, not necessarily to further their ability to help providers work more effectively in diverse settings. To graduate from PITC, participants were expected to develop and write training plans for a workshop based on each module. Staff from the Far West Laboratory for Educational Research and Development evaluated the plans.

The reach of PITC is impressive. As of October 1995, over 440 individuals, including 236 in California, had completed all four modules. In addition to California, Far West currently offers this training in three other states and for the national Head Start. The trainings in California are funded by the California Department of Education with federal Child Care and Development Block Grant funds. Staff from the Far West Laboratory and the California Department of Education participate as faculty in the training.

The Leadership in Diversity Program (LID), sponsored by the California Association for the Education of Young Children, seeks to develop more trainers who can provide quality pro-diversity and anti-bias education to CAEYC membership and the child care profession in general. The first pilot of the LID program began in January 1992 and continued for over three years. The participants from communities throughout California were identified in part for their strong personal commitment to diversity. During the first two years, LID participants spent approximately two weeks in intensive training sessions and also conducted trainings in their local communities and local CAEYC chapters. Most interns formed local monthly support groups of colleagues who shared their interest in diversity. By the end of the LID program, graduates were to have gained a stronger sense and awareness of their own identity, a deeper understanding of the dynamics of institutional racism and cultural oppression, and a strong grasp of how children develop their ethnic identity and attitudes. They were also to have developed specific skills for working with adults on issues of bias and racism. The 15 interns to complete the first round were certified in March of 1995. Since the first pilot test, the program has been somewhat modified. Training is now offered regionally and lasts only two years.

The PITC and LID approaches are clearly enhancing the field of ECE trainers. The extent to which the programs cultivate trainers equipped to address issues of diversity is different. Interviews with PITC graduates suggested that the program helped to raise awareness. For participants with little prior exposure to issues of diversity, PITC offered some introduction and new understandings. One participant said afterwards that she now realized that there was no one recipe for working with families of different cultural backgrounds. For others with more extensive personal or professional experience, the session served as a review of familiar concepts. One person who had already been teaching about diversity in her classes prior to attending the training was able to use activities presented in the manual to expand her classroom techniques. Recognizing the limited nature of the information they can cover, PITC administrators encourage interested participants to seek out additional anti-bias training.

LID explicitly seeks to develop trainers skilled in addressing issues of diversity. Every graduate interviewed referred to LID as a life-changing experience that offered skills and techniques for helping other adults to engage in anti-bias work. A year after the first class of LID interns graduated, program administrators estimated that LID interns had conducted approximately 75 workshops for 1,500-2,000 ECE practitioners and parents. And, nearly four years later, LID interns remain firmly committed, promoting a pro-diversity agenda wherever they work. The LID model, however, is resource-intensive and, thus far, only a limited number of interns have gone through the program.

These two programs offer important insights. First, more than one kind of professional development is necessary. The field needs trainers who understand the implications of race, language and culture, even when not specifically teaching these themes. We also need trainers who have the skills to help child care professionals deeply explore these issues. These two kinds of trainers cannot substitute for each other.

Sustaining financial support for staff development aimed at increasing the ability of the field to provide high quality care to an increasingly diverse child population is essential.

Sustained financial support is essential to developing effective professional development programs. The thinking about what constitutes effective professional development related to diversity continues to evolve. For the Far West Laboratory for Educational Research and Development, the nearly 10 years of financial support for the Training Program for Infant/Toddler Caregivers has been critical. This sustained support from state, federal and private funds has allowed the program developers to continually revise the training modules and materials. A great strength of the program has been its ability to continually rethink the approach—a major reason staff have reached a decision to shift their design in order to interweave diversity issues throughout the curriculum.

The field of early childhood education is clearly far from institutionalizing professional development strategies that ensure issues of diversity are addressed for the long haul. Eleanor Clement Glass, San Francisco Foundation program executive and LID graduate, said:

> *We simply don't have a sufficient number of qualified, well-rounded diversity trainers. We need more people who do different pieces of training and they need to know what they are doing. We need ongoing training so people can get better and better, reflect upon what they do and have an opportunity to share and identify best practices. This still needs to happen.*

Chapter 8
A Call for Ongoing Research on Issues of Diversity and Their Implications for Early Care and Education

***Looking In, Looking Out** raises as many questions as it answers. To begin to understand these important questions will require both longer-term, more quantitative forms of analysis, as well as shorter-term qualitative research that stimulates relevant policies and effective practices. Society must make a major investment toward ongoing research on the implications of racial, cultural and linguistic diversity for early care and education. Such research needs to be taken up by institutions of higher education, government agencies, nonprofit organizations and other research institutions—and it needs to incorporate knowledge, expertise and experience from various cultural communities. Embarking upon such research will require the commitment of individual researchers and their institutions, as well as the financial support of private and public funders.*

In the course of developing this book, California Tomorrow identified a range of research topics that, if explored, would contribute enormously to the field of early childhood education.

- What are the implications of the changing nature of child care, and of the families who utilize child care, for current definitions of quality care? How do traditional measures of quality need to be redefined for a diverse society?
- What are appropriate measures of how effectively programs are engaging in the proposed five Principles of Quality Care in a Diverse Society?
- What are the implications of these five Principles of Quality Care in a Diverse Society for existing guidelines for accreditation and program quality review?
- What would alternatives to a Eurocentric approach to child development look like? What aspects of child development are truly universal across cultural groups? What aspects are different?
- How can concepts and practices related to the five principles be effectively incorporated into the basic educational requirements for child care professionals?
- How can race, language and culture be effectively incorporated into all early childhood education courses?
- What is the impact of placing infants and toddlers in the care of providers who do not speak their home language or who come from a different cultural background? What are the best strategies for promoting the development of the home language as well as English among children under five years of age?

- What is the process of racial identity development among infants and toddlers?
- What is the appropriate role for providers in supporting the identity of children of mixed racial and ethnic backgrounds?
- How are issues of race, language and culture connected to other dimensions of diversity, such as gender, economic class and sexual orientation? How are the strategies which need to be employed for addressing these concepts among young children different or the same?
- What are successful strategies for teaching young children in homogenous settings about diversity beyond surface or "tourist" views of other people and communities?
- What factors should be taken into account in determining whether to place individual children in ethnic-specific or multiethnic programs? In home language, bilingual or predominantly English-speaking programs?
- How can parents be best informed about the implications of race, language and culture for their selection of child care programs and in their ongoing involvement in care settings?
- How can early childhood education and K-12 education connect more closely? For example, how can K-12 education build upon early childhood strategies to address race, language and culture?

For these questions to be pursued, some major challenges must be addressed that impede the ability of the research community to effectively expand the knowledge available to early care and education. The challenges we have identified include broadening the research base, strengthening the connection between research and practice, and improving coordination of existing research efforts.

Broadening the Research Base

In the book, *Diversity and Developmentally Appropriate Practice*, Rebecca New observed that child development theory is built upon research conducted on white, middle class American children. In the late 1970s, a five-year review of major child development journals (*Child Development*, *Developmental Psychology*, and *Merrill-Palmer Quarterly*) found that less than 10 percent of the studies discussed anyone other than white American subjects. Studies of children in non-Western societies—Asia, South America, Africa and Oceana—constituted less than 3 percent of research (Levine, 1980). A more recent analysis from 1986 to 1990 in *Child Development* suggested that this trend remained unchanged, with only 9.3 percent of research devoted to subjects other than non-whites (New, 1992). Peter Mangione of the Far West Laboratory for Educational Research, asserts:

> *We need to support academic research which will provide us with a broader knowledge base. Much of the cross-cultural research available in the United States has been conducted by European Americans. Their cultural perspectives still overlay their work. We need to create opportunities for knowledge to be created and generated by people who are from different communities.*

Broadening the research base requires supporting the work of researchers from non-European/white cultural and linguistic backgrounds within the United States and internationally. Researchers and practitioners also must have access to existing relevant research outside the confines of the United States.

Creating and Strengthening Connections Between Research, Especially University-Based Efforts, to the World of Practice

More often than not, research, particularly the studies conducted in university-based settings, are not designed to answer the questions of child care providers and trainers. Few mechanisms exist for university researchers to talk to practitioners about their perspectives of pending issues, and for practitioners to talk to researchers about topics they would like to see researched to inform their work. Very few resources are ever allocated to this type of practice-connected research. The National Association for Bilingual Education "No-Cost" Study (Wong Fillmore, 1991), which called for researchers to interview parents about the impact of their children's language loss, is one of the few times that researchers and practitioners joined together to address a burning issue for the field. Critical to this effort was the leadership of researcher Lily Wong Fillmore, who pushed for the study to be conducted in a timely fashion. But the effort suffered from extremely low resources, and only succeeded because of tremendous levels of volunteer time.

Increasing Coordination Among Researchers

Research is currently carried out by a range of entities ranging from universities and government agencies to nonprofit organizations. Unfortunately, however, no mechanism or forum exists for connecting researchers working within the same sectors or across sectors so that they are aware of one another's work and how they might support each other. Few opportunities exist for researchers to draw upon data collected by other sources. Scenarios where researchers collaborate in the design of data collection instruments—so that the same instrument and data might be used for multiple research projects—are even more unusual. Yet, in this time of fiscal austerity, collaboration is even more crucial in order to make the best use of limited research dollars.

Conclusion

This book has been a journey for California Tomorrow. Along the way we've met many friends and allies among child care providers, parents, trainers, community college faculty, advocates, researchers and others. The collaborative research and writing process allowed us to "look in and look out"—to deeply explore our own experiences and assumptions about caring for children, and to seek to understand those of others. The process gave us great faith that it is possible to find common ground even in the difficult arena of race, language and culture. We worked to craft a vision for the early childhood field that represented our own voices and those of the many, many people who contributed to our research and analysis. Now we urge others to join us in working to realize this vision.

More families than ever before are sharing the responsibility of raising their young children with child care providers. At the same time, families are more racially, culturally and linguistically diverse than ever in history. As the caregivers, teachers and role models for very young children, early childhood professionals are uniquely positioned to contribute to a strong and equitable multiracial, multicultural and multilingual society. The children in their care are our future.

California Tomorrow envisions an early childhood education field where:

- ***Children grow up believing in the equality of all people.*** They learn to respect difference and that discrimination is wrong. Their self esteem is strong because they are cared for in a nurturing environment where they see adult role models of many different races, including their own.

- ***Children are proud of their racial and cultural heritage.*** They learn about their culture at home and in the child care setting, sharing their traditions with families of other backgrounds. They grow up open and curious about learning the values, customs and beliefs of other cultures.

- ***Children are exposed to linguistically rich environments at an early age.*** They develop fluency in their home languages and learn that bilingualism or trilingualism are highly valued. The sounds and meanings of different languages are part of their world, and offer them a deeper understanding of other cultures. They are proud to speak the languages of their families.

- ***Practitioners have developed as many innovative approaches to addressing racial, cultural and linguistic issues in child care programs as there are***

communities. Whatever the approach, programs support infants, toddlers and young children in developing healthy identities and skills to thrive in a diverse society.

- ***Child care providers as a group are as racially, culturally and linguistically diverse as the children in their care.*** They come from all educational and socioeconomic backgrounds, and they are valued for both personal and professional experience. They are well grounded in child development theories, anti-bias concepts, primary and second language development, and skills for working with families of diverse backgrounds. They respect the different cultures, languages and experiences each brings to a program, and they find ways to learn from one another.

- ***Caregivers and family members have the words and confidence to talk about race, racism, differences and bias—and they help children learn to speak about these issues also.*** Adults learn to reflect on their own experiences and reactions, to identify what is effective and ineffective, and to act when they see injustice. They work to overcome their fears, and to say the sometimes difficult but necessary things. They feel supported to raise issues of race, language and culture in planning and policy discussions.

- ***Caregivers seek out parents' expectations and concerns about how race, culture and language will be addressed with the children.*** Families are asked to share their cultural knowledge and bring up concerns and ideas at any time.

- ***Caregivers choose the field because of their commitment to children, and they stay in the field because they are well respected and fairly compensated.*** Turnover in the profession is low because there are opportunities for advancement and personal growth.

- ***Parents, when choosing child care, look carefully at program philosophies on diversity.*** Information about all elements of quality in child care is readily available to parents in different languages from a variety of sources, including prenatal and parenting classes, written materials, libraries, resource and referral agencies, children's stores, high schools, community colleges and others.

- ***Faculty who teach future child care professionals fully incorporate issues of race, language and culture into their courses, workshops and other professional education.*** Faculty themselves expand and apply their knowledge about diversity issues on an ongoing basis.

- ***Researchers throughout the country explore the implications of race, language and culture for the development and care of young children.*** The findings are made accessible to a wide range of audiences and begin to answer questions arising among providers and parents. Programs apply the research to their practice.

- ***Society recognizes the critical role child care fulfills in fostering the healthy development of young children.*** This respect is demonstrated by an ongoing investment of adequate resources.

The full potential of the early childhood field to contribute to a strong and equitable society is far from being realized. We need a movement in early childhood education to take on this challenge.

Building a movement begins with individuals—providers, trainers, parents and others—each looking at themselves and their environments and deciding to make change. At every level, we all must work towards a child care field that draws strength from our diversity and offers the next generation the skills to thrive in a multiracial, multicultural, multilingual society. Individual caregivers and trainers cannot bear the weight of this responsibility alone to advocate for the policies and practices that will make this vision a reality. Parents, researchers, family support organizations and agencies, policymakers and many others need to join in. Only through individual as well as collective action will change be possible. We must break down the isolation of child care professionals and form an alliance that works to overcome fears of diversity. The child care profession can model for California and our nation how equity can be achieved.

Looking In, Looking Out is California Tomorrow's effort to contribute to such a movement—but we know it is just a piece of the work, and that many others have pioneered the way for us. We hope that ***Looking In, Looking Out*** launches deep conversations about hopes, fears and expectations among providers in individual programs or between parents and providers. We hope the principles will be absorbed, analyzed, personalized and implemented in programs, community college courses, professional workshops and conferences. Finally, we hope the stories of the people and programs in our book will inspire others to act, and to keep the avenues open for dialogue about race, language and culture in child care.

Methodology

The methodology for the research behind ***Looking In, Looking Out*** includes:

I. A general explanation of the action research approach.

II. Specific information about the types of data collected.

III. An overview of the process used for analysis and writing.

IV. A description of the multiracial, multicultural, multilingual, multidisciplinary team involved in the research, analysis and writing of the book.

I. Action Research

For this project, California Tomorrow utilized an action research approach which simultaneously allowed us to explore issues, hear diverse perspectives, contribute to the knowledge base and help to build constituencies for emerging ideas. This action research assumes that the knowledge of families, practitioners and programs should be documented, that practitioners should be involved in analyzing data and that diverse perspectives should always be sought.

Documenting and Building Upon the Knowledge of Families, Practitioners and Programs

Families and child care practitioners are the people most familiar with caring for racially, culturally and linguistically diverse young children. Therefore, through our interviews and site visits, we sought to ground our research in the day-to-day reality of what happens in programs with families. Site visits offered a wealth of information about what is possible in practice and the challenges which must be addressed. Synthesizing information from the site visits was useful for identifying the types of policy that might be crafted to support good practice, and we also hope it will offer new insights to programs grappling with similar issues.

Involving Practitioners in Analyzing Data

Where possible, we sought to engage practitioners in analyzing our data and findings. For example, in some cases, we met with lead staff at individual sites to discuss our perspectives of what we had observed during our visits to their program. This type of sharing required that we not violate the confidence of our individual interviewees. But the debriefings were valuable for both the practitioners and ourselves. We were able to share our impressions regarding what we found exciting or innovative about their work, as well as raise any new questions or concerns. The practitioners were able to receive some feedback regarding their efforts, and to help us more deeply understand their motivations and challenges. The purpose of these debriefings was not to provide an assessment, but to allow us to engage the directors, planners and, in some instances, staff in a dialogue about our observations.

We also looked for ways to bring together people from the various programs we were researching to help us analyze the information we had gleaned. Often, California Tomorrow calls on practitioners to help us refine our analysis and to contribute further information to our knowledge base.

We believe engaging practitioners in the analysis is important for several reasons. First, sharing our own thoughts is critical for ensuring that the interpretations of our observations and interviews are accurate. While extensive interviews and in-depth site visits can glean important information, they do pose limitations. For example, they may not capture historical information or all of the key perspectives. We also find that sometimes outsiders are able to offer program staff and directors a fresh perspective regarding their work. As in any field, it is easy for staff to become immersed in day-to-day program details, with little chance to fully appreciate their accomplishments or to realize that their own challenges may well mirror those of other providers in other programs. We have also found that sharing our observations can help programs become more aware of their own strengths, as well as alert them to emerging issues. Sometimes simply hearing the data collected by California Tomorrow allows practitioners to use their individual as well as institutional influence to take immediate action.

Engaging Diverse Perspectives

California Tomorrow believes that the implications of diversity must be explored through many different "lenses" of racial, linguistic, cultural, professional and personal experience. People's experiences based on their skin color, home languages, cultural backgrounds, community in which they were raised, education, economic class—and a myriad of other factors—profoundly influence how they view the world. Our experiences can make us sensitive to particular situations or cause us to interpret incidents completely differently than the next person might. For researchers to portray a full picture of any situation requires the ability to gather and synthesize diverse perspectives and knowledge. This helps to identify common ground and pave the way for a deeper understanding of important differences between groups.

In this research, as in all the work of California Tomorrow, we strove to seek out diverse perspectives of a broad variety of stakeholders: parents, providers, trainers, researchers, etc. The large majority were interviewed during the process of data collection. Many were project advisors and reviewers of our draft report.

Finally, we tried to bring together a racially, culturally, linguistically and professionally diverse project staff so that we would be better equipped to solicit information and understand what we heard. We knew that some interviewees would feel more comfortable confiding in a person who spoke their home language or who shared a similar cultural background. We also knew that people's professional training and experience impact their world views and understandings. A researcher who is a child care provider, for example, would likely come away from a visit to a child care program with a different set of insights than a researcher with a background in public policy. To benefit from such diverse perspectives, we teamed project staff from different disciplines to conduct the site visits. We also found that throughout our research and writing, it was important for the project team to invest significant time for discussing and exploring our different interpretations of the data.

II. Data

Looking In, Looking Out is based on extensive research conducted beginning in early Spring 1994 and ending in Summer 1995. It includes data drawn from a variety of sources: (A) site visits to child care centers and family child care homes, (B) interviews with and surveys of resource and referral agencies, (C) interviews with individuals involved in the professional development of child care providers, and (D) documentation of professional development and recruitment programs.

A. Program Site Visits

Site visits to 23 child care centers and 10 family child care homes represent the largest body of data. While we think the experiences of the programs researched for this report are applicable to other programs, readers should keep in mind that the information gathered is not necessarily representative of child care programs in general. We intentionally visited programs that had been called to our attention for their work related to issues of race, language and culture. Given our selection bias, we suspect the extent to which the average program currently addresses race, language and culture is less than what we observed. In addition, while we were impressed by the commitment and energy of the programs visited, we are not suggesting that any program, by itself, represents "the answer." Every program had both strengths and areas in need of further development. We are also aware that the programs visited are not the only ones working on issues of race, language and culture; our resources limited us to visiting only 33. We continue to hear about the exciting work of many other programs which are not described in this book.

The site visits provided California Tomorrow the opportunity to speak with a total of 247 people, including interviews with 126 center-based staff (directors, administrators, teachers and aides), 91 parents with children in centers, 10 family child care providers and 20 parents of children in family child care. See Appendix A for a list of the centers and family child care programs visited.

Site Selection Process

California Tomorrow sought nominations for child care centers and family child care homes from a number of sources: community college instructors, trainers, resource and referral agency staff, and child care program staff. We asked the nominators to recommend programs which, to their knowledge, were innovatively addressing issues of race, culture and language. Described below are the processes we used to select centers and family child care programs. Because of differences in structure and accessibility to researchers, we used slightly different procedures for the two types of programs.

Center Selection

Once nominated, centers were chosen based on: (1) their ability to contribute to the diversity of our sample in terms of the criteria below, and (2) a telephone interview with the director of the program prior to final selection for a site visit. We wanted a program sample that offered a wide variety of populations and contexts. We sought a diversity of programs in terms of:

- Geographic distribution within California (north, south and central, rural, urban, suburban)
- Program population (multiracial, multicultural, multilingual, or predominantly one or two racial, cultural or language groups)
- Racial/cultural group (programs that served different racial/cultural groups; programs that focused the curriculum on one racial/cultural group)
- Language (programs that served different language groups; bilingual programs for different languages)
- Auspices (nonprofit, employer-sponsored, Head Start, church- or temple-based, etc.)

The pre-selection interviews conducted with program directors were designed to gather basic information, e.g., program size, ages served, hours, racial and cultural groups of children and staff, languages spoken by children and staff. They also solicited information about the program's philosophy, goals and experience working on issues of race, language and culture in early childhood education.

Family Child Care Program Selection

Identifying family child care homes and obtaining permission to visit them proved more complicated. Family child care programs are much smaller and employ fewer staff than centers. Many seemed to have less staffing capacity to respond to our requests and were less accustomed to outsiders observing their programs. We found that the most effective way to make contact with family child care programs was to be introduced by a person whom the operators knew well and trusted. Ultimately, because of these challenges, we ended up visiting programs primarily in the San Francisco and Los Angeles areas. The programs visited represented a diversity in terms of racial and linguistic background of the providers (please see Appendix B).

Site Visit Structure

Site visits to centers and family child care homes involved interviews as well as some observation. The process used to conduct the visits varied slightly due to differences in program structure.

Site visits lasted approximately one and a half days for child care centers. During each center visit, we interviewed four to six teachers and aides, four to six parents, the director and occasionally other administrators or program board members. We gave the directors the option to organize our visit in whatever way would be least disruptive to the program. Generally, we interviewed the director once upon arrival at the program, and then again at the very end of the visit. Typically, California Tomorrow used the final interview as an opportunity to share and confirm our observations with the director. Interviews with teachers and parents were organized around their schedules. We spent time observing classrooms as well. Site visits were typically conducted by a multicultural team of California Tomorrow staff involving two or more people.

Family child care program site visits lasted from a half day to a full day. With the exception of the first visit which involved a team of three, these site visits were conducted by a project staff member. The interviews took place somewhat informally throughout the day as the provider at the family child care home carried out her regular responsibilities as a caregiver. A significant portion of time was spent observing what occurred in the child care home. Interviews with parents were conducted at their convenience—at the program, in the workplace or at their homes. Some parent interviews were conducted over the phone. Occasionally, the researcher returned to programs to clarify observations or questions.

Interviews

Generally, the interviews lasted about 45 minutes. But interview length varied according to the time the interviewee had available. Some parents could only spare 15-20 minutes, while many of the administrators or family child care home providers spent two or more hours speaking with us. All interviews were conducted by project staff, and, when possible, in the language the interviewee preferred. Project staff spoke English, Spanish and Mandarin Chinese. When we did not have in-house language capacity to interview a subject, we tried to hire translators. Specifically, we utilized Cantonese Chinese and Vietnamese translators. In two instances, we unfortunately did not have the language capacity to interview parents and needed to rely on program staff to help us communicate. We avoided that approach as much as possible because we were concerned that the presence of a staff person might inhibit a parent(s), particularly if they had concerns about the program.

While we brought certain research questions with us, the interviews were designed to be open ended and to encourage reflection, examples and stories from the subjects. We did not want to limit the responses of interviewees by using an overly restrictive instrument, and we wanted the freedom to follow the natural course of a conversation when it seemed relevant to our research questions and to the interviewee. The outcome of this approach was that not every interview addressed every single question, and the content of each interview was unique. Interview questions were first piloted at two centers and one family child care program by four researchers. This piloting process allowed the team to hone the questions and gain a better understanding of how to work together as a team. Taken as a whole, the interviews laid out a multitude of implications regarding race, language and culture for early childhood education and care.

Research Questions

The categories and questions listed below were used as guidelines for interviews with family child care home providers and with center teachers, teacher aides and administrators. Not every question was appropriate for every interviewee—administrators and staff of centers and family day care home providers were asked appropriate variations of the research questions.

At each site we learned about the context of the program (structure and philosophy) and community and program demographics. We also asked each provider to tell us about his or her professional background and reasons for entering the field.

Research Questions for Center Staff and Administration and for Family Child Care Home Providers

- ***Race, Culture and Language in the Classroom.*** What are the joys and challenges of a diverse program? What are the advantages and disadvantages of a homogenous program? How do you incorporate the cultural and ethnic backgrounds of the children into the environment and curriculum? What resources or materials do you use to incorporate culture or language into classroom activities? What languages are used in the classroom? What is your approach regarding supporting the children's home languages and/or helping them learn a second language? Where do you go for help in addressing issues of language and language acquisition?
- ***Role of Program.*** What do you think the role of the program is in reinforcing a child's cultural and racial identity? What is the role of the program with regard to the child's home language, or second language learning? What do you think the role of the program is in teaching children the necessary skills for getting along/understanding others in a diverse society?
- ***Culture and Child Rearing.*** In what ways does your culture influence your child rearing style? Have you ever faced a conflict between your own culture and the philosophy and practices of the program? Have you ever had conflicts with parents regarding child care/child rearing practices? What is the nature of the conflict? How do you resolve these conflicts?
- ***Staff Development.*** What types of staff development have you had regarding race, culture and language in early childhood education? Do you ever have in-service trainings regarding ethnic or linguistic diversity, or cultural differences in child caregiving? Who does the training, if there is any? Who decides that training is needed? What about outside of the program—what other opportunities have you been able to take advantage of? Do you ever use the local resource and referral agency for training or technical assistance? Are there opportunities outside of staff meetings for staff to discuss issues around race, language or culture? What kinds of issues do staff have discussions about? Is there any dialogue about issues of diversity? If so, what kinds of issues? Do you ever turn to another staff member to get information/advice on how to approach/handle a child of a background other than yours?
- ***Partnerships with Parents.*** What are the formal and informal ways in which parents are involved in the program? What are the formal and informal opportunities to meet with parents? Do parents ever ask questions or voice concerns about language or cultural issues? About other child rearing issues? How do you respond? How do you commu-

nicate with parents who speak another language other than your own? What are the challenges of communicating with parents who are of a different cultural background?

- ***Staffing Structure.*** What is the hiring process at this program? Who does the hiring? What qualities do you look for in a staff member (personality, experience, training, race, culture, language)? How do you find applicants/how do applicants hear about open positions? If you are looking for diversity, have you faced problems in finding qualified staff of diverse backgrounds?

Research Questions for Parents

Questions for parents followed many of the same themes as the staff and director interviews, but of course were more specific to the parents' experiences.

- What were you looking for in a child care program? Where did you get information about child care? Why did you choose this program? What are your other experiences with child care (with this or another child)?
- What language or languages does your family speak at home? What language do you want your child to speak at the center? Why? Do you ever worry about your children maintaining their home language? Why or why not? What is the role of the center in promoting language skills? English? Home language?
- Do you feel that you understand the curriculum and policies of the program? How did you learn about the program curriculum and policies? Do you have an opportunity to contribute, get involved in activities, planning or decision making?
- What do you think the role of the center is in reinforcing the traditions, values and language of your family to the children? What do you think the role of the center is in teaching the children the necessary skills for getting along/understanding others in a diverse society?

B. Resource and Referral Agency Interviews and Surveys

Resource and referral agencies are an important part of the child care infrastructure. They are a critical source of information about child care options and financial support for parents, and they often offer a wide variety of services to providers as well. In order to explore the impact of diversity on their work, California Tomorrow conducted telephone interviews and written surveys of 33 resource and referral (R&R) agencies located in 28 California counties. See Appendix D for list of programs.

Early in the project, California Tomorrow presented our proposed research at regional R&R meetings and asked for agencies to volunteer to be interviewed. For those agencies that volunteered to participate, we followed up by sending the directors the interview protocol with a request for them to assign the most appropriate person for California Tomorrow to interview (themselves or another staff person). In addition to these agencies, we identified a few additional R&Rs to interview to round out the geographic representation of our sample. The R&R interviews were conducted over the telephone by California Tomorrow staff and lasted 30-60 minutes. Data from these interviews were supplemented with information from a follow-up written survey we mailed out that was returned by 19 agencies.

The interviews and the follow-up survey were designed to provide us with information about the following topics.

- A basic understanding of the types of services offered by the R&R agency.
- Whether and how R&R agencies tracked the changing demographics of the communities served.
- The racial and linguistic composition of staff and the extent to which it reflected the demographics of the community served.
- The extent to which the services were offered in the home languages of the parents and the child care providers located in the community served.
- Whether and how questions or concerns about race, language and culture arose during conversations with parents and how the R&R agency interacted in such cases.
- The extent to which the R&R agency provided staff development on issues of diversity to its own staff and/or to child care providers.
- An understanding of the challenges faced by R&R agencies in ensuring appropriate care and education for an ethnically and linguistically diverse population.

After we analyzed our data, California Tomorrow presented our initial findings to the staff of the statewide California Resource and Referral Network. Their review and questions helped us to hone and improve our information. We also solicited reactions from staff of local R&R agencies by making a presentation of our findings at their 1994 annual statewide meeting.

C. Individual Trainer Interviews

We interviewed 28 individuals who were trainers of early childhood providers, including consultants, community college instructors, university faculty, R&R staff and center directors. Individuals were selected based on California Tomorrow's staff knowledge and contacts in the field. The criteria for selecting individual trainers were as follows: (1) their work in early childhood education included a focus on diversity issues, and they had experience in helping adults better understand the implications of diversity in early childhood education; (2) they represented a variety of training programs and formats; and (3) they themselves represented a variety of racial, cultural and linguistic backgrounds and experiences.

Each interview was conducted over the telephone and lasted about 90 minutes. The interview format was a series of open-ended questions designed to elicit the lessons learned, examples and experiences of the interviewees. The interviews were conducted by consultants Marcy Whitebook and Dan Bellm, both of whom brought tremendous experience and knowledge about early childhood education, training and issues of diversity.

Trainer Interview Questions

The interview questions were developed jointly by California Tomorrow staff and the consultants. They included the following:

- What have you seen or done that's successful in training teachers/providers to work with children of different cultures and linguistic groups? What do teachers, providers and directors need to know and do in relation to children's home languages? What role does the age of the child play? What role does the family play?
- What have you seen or done in child care settings that is successful in reducing children's biases and expanding their views about the diversity of cultures and languages? How does one train teachers/providers to implement such a program?
- What have you seen or done that is successful in training teachers/providers to work with parents of different cultures and linguistic groups?
- What have you seen or done that is successful in helping teachers/providers work in an environment with diverse staff?
- Teachers and providers may often be unaware of the ways in which their program itself proceeds from a context of cultural values and assumptions. What needs to change in training in order to raise this kind of self awareness? What works?

  At a broader level, such widely-used curriculum frameworks as High Scope, Montessori or NAEYC's guidelines for *The Developmentally Appropriate Practice* also proceed in various ways from particular cultural values and assumptions. What do you think teachers/providers need to understand and consider when using such models?
- How can child care program directors best be trained to take leadership on diversity issues—setting a tone for their program that diversity is a high priority?

  How can directors be trained in the ability to navigate possible cultural conflicts among staff and also to encourage staff to use each other as resources for cultural information?
- What are the barriers to recruiting more diverse staff? What are some effective strategies? To what extent does diversifying the staff of a program to reflect the diversity of families it serves address the major issues here?

  Beyond recruitment or hiring, how can child care programs most effectively retain a diverse staff (i.e., entry level recruitment may not be a major issue, but rather the extent to which people of color and other staff are able/unable to access training, advance up a career ladder and remain in the field)?
- Can you tell us about how you were able to gain the skills to work in the area of cultural and linguistic diversity? Do you see any implications in your own experience for possible career pathways for other trainers?
- How do you think your own cultural and linguistic background affects your approach to training? What implications might this have for the field?
- Have you been able to influence other trainers to do more work in the area of cultural

and linguistic diversity? What does it take to equip child care trainers to effectively address issues of diversity in their work? What are the barriers?

- What do you feel has been your own greatest success in bringing others to a new level of awareness or practice in the area of cultural and linguistic diversity in child care programs
- If you could design the ideal training or recruitment program to address issues of diversity, what would it be?

D. Documentation of Professional Development and Recruitment

California Tomorrow also documented in-depth the experiences of four early childhood professional development and recruitment programs in California. The programs were: (1) the California Child Care Initiative Project (CCIP), an initiative of the California Child Care Resource and Referral Network; (2) Leadership in Diversity (LID), an initiative of the California Association for the Education of Young Children; (3) The Foundation Center for Phenomenological Research; and (4) the Program for Infant/Toddler Caregiving sponsored by the Far West Laboratory for Educational Research and Development and the California Department of Education. ***Looking In, Looking Out*** also briefly profiles the California Community College Training Consortium and the California Mentor Teacher Program. The profiles for these programs were, however, based upon already existing written materials and the knowledge of Julie Olsen Edwards, director of the Early Childhood Department at Cabrillo Community College.

Selection Process

The programs were again identified through contacts in the field, recommendations from child care professionals, and California Tomorrow's own body of knowledge. Once we had a list of possible programs, we conducted pre-selection interviews with a representative of each program. We were interested in two types of programs: (1) professional development programs which explicitly addressed the implications of race, language and culture in their curriculum; and (2) programs which specifically recruited an under-represented group to the early childhood profession (non-whites or individuals who spoke a language other than English).

Documentation Process

In general our documentation process included interviews or focus groups with the program director or developers, teaching staff, program participants and/or graduates, observations of the instructional program, and a review of any available written materials. In one program, Leadership in Diversity, we also spoke with individuals who had received training from program graduates. The specific design of the documentation process and interview questions was tailored to each program. The number of people interviewed per program ranged from 4 to 14. At times, we also drew upon a California Tomorrow staff person's prior experience and knowledge about the program.

While the emphasis of our questioning varied depending upon the specific focus of the program (e.g., recruiting a particular population of providers or building the capacity of trainers to teach providers about diversity), most of the underlying questions explored were largely the same since we felt issues of recruitment and professional development are highly interconnected. Our questions included:

- How did the program develop and evolve? What people or organizations were key to its development?
- What are the major goals of the program? How do issues of race, language and culture fit into those goals? To what extent do program graduates, faculty, administrators and people who have received services from program graduates articulate similar goals?
- Who is served by the program? Does it seek to recruit ethnically diverse participants? What are its recruitment strategies? What are the barriers to recruiting a diverse pool of participants?
- What is the curriculum? To what extent does it seek to prepare participants to address racial, linguistic and cultural diversity? How are those issues addressed through the curriculum? What are the lessons learned about what is effective and ineffective? How has the programming with respect to diversity evolved over time?
- What are the skills and qualities of the faculty involved? How has their own racial, cultural, linguistic or professional background prepared them to engage in this work?
- What are the benefits that program participants report they have gained from attending the program? How do they feel that the program could be strengthened?

Community College Consortium Meetings

With the help of the Community College Child Development Training Consortium, California Tomorrow held focus groups with community college educators throughout the state. Offering 90-95 percent of the available professional development in California, community colleges bear the largest responsibility for training child care providers. These focus groups were held as part of the Training Consortium regional meetings. They allowed California Tomorrow to present and discuss our findings about the inadequacy of currently available professional development opportunities to prepare providers to work in racially, culturally and linguistically diverse settings and to explore the implications of these findings for the work of community colleges.

III. Data Analysis

While California Tomorrow staff have been responsible for the analysis of the data collected, we also sought to engage key groups in reviewing our findings and honing the analysis. We believe such an approach deepens the analysis and broadens feelings of ownership for the report throughout the profession. Described below are the variety of ways we sought to do this.

Retreats with Providers and Trainers

California Tomorrow solicited the insights of practitioners through two two-day retreats. One retreat was held with a cross-section of directors and teachers from the centers we visited and the other was held with trainers, community college faculty and others involved in staff development. Both retreats allowed California Tomorrow to present and hone our findings, and to stimulate participants' interest in further exploring the issues. Effective professional development and strategies for recruiting a more diverse workforce were topics of discussion at both retreats.

Draft Review Process

We conducted an extensive review process of the first two major drafts of our book. Project advisors were brought together to review and discuss the first draft (see page 7 for a list of advisors). Our second draft was sent to more than 80 reviewers, including members of our national advisory board, participants from both retreats and other regarded experts in the field. Reviewers approached this task with unanticipated enthusiasm and tremendously influenced our final report.

Incorporating Feedback from Conference Presentations

During the final months of the report writing, the primary authors were concurrently giving presentations about the research findings at child care related conferences across the country. The feedback gathered from the national audiences, and the experiences of presenting the information to a wide variety of audiences, were also very useful in fine-tuning our final product.

IV. The Research Team

All of the research, analysis and writing of ***Looking In, Looking Out*** has been conducted by a multiracial, multilingual, multidisciplinary team. Our team process compelled each of us to take time to clarify our own beliefs and world views, as well as to try to better understand each other's perspectives. Our team is described in greater detail in our Acknowledgments.

Bibliography

Anderson, M. Parker. "Frequently Asked Questions about NAEYC's Linguistic and Cultural Diversity Position Paper," *Young Children*, Vol. 51, No. 2, Washington, D.C., January, 1996.

Bellm, Dan. *Breaking the Link: A National Forum on Child Care Compensation*, National Center for the Early Childhood Workforce, Washington, D.C., April 29-May 1, 1994.

Bernhard, Judith K. "Child Development, Cultural Diversity, and the Professional Training of Early Childhood Educators," *Canadian Journal of Education*, 20:4, 1995.

Bernhard, Judith K., Marie Louise Lefebvre, Gyda Chud and Rika Lange. *Paths to Equity: Cultural, Linguistic, and Racial Diversity in Canadian Early Childhood Education*, York Lane Press, Toronto, Canada, 1995.

Brady, Phyllis. "The Journey Towards Anti-Racist Identity for Multiracial People, People of Color and Whites," *The Web*, April 1996.

Brendekamp, Sue, ed. *Developmentally Appropriate Practice in Early Childhood Programs Serving Children From Birth Through Age Eight*, National Association For the Education of Young Children, Washington, D.C., 1987.

Brunson Phillips, Carol. *Early Childhood Reform: Innovative Approaches to Cultural and Racial Diversity Among Families*, paper presented to the National Association of State Boards of Education, 1993.

Brunson Phillips, Carol and Dwayne A. Crompton. *Best Practices for Black Children: Discussion Points on Developmentally Appropriate Practice in Early Childhood Education*, paper presented at the National Black Child Development Institute Annual Conference, Washington, D.C., 1995.

Carter, Margie and Deb Curtis. *Training Teachers: A Harvest of Theory and Practice*, Redleaf Press, St. Paul, MN, 1994.

Cazden, Courtney, ed. *Language in Early Childhood Education, Revised Edition* (originally published in 1972), National Association for the Education of Young Children, Washington, D.C., 1981.

Cazden, Courtney, Betty Bryant and Melissa Tillman. "Making It and Going Home: The Attitudes of Black People Toward Language Education," *Language in Early Education*, National Association for the Education of Young Children, Washington, D.C., 1981.

Chang, Hedy Nai-Lin and Laura Sakai. *Affirming Children's Roots: Cultural and Linguistic Diversity in Early Care and Education*, California Tomorrow, San Francisco, CA, 1993.

Cohen, Abbey and Carol S. Stevenson. *Caring for the Future: Meeting California's Child Care Challenge*, Child Care Law Center, San Francisco, CA, 1992.

Cost, Quality and Outcomes Study Team (1995). *Cost, Quality and Outcomes in Child Care Centers, Technical Report*, Center for Research in Economic and Social Policy, University of Colorado at Denver, 1995.

Cost, Quality and Outcomes Study Team (1995). *Cost, Quality and Outcomes in Child Care Centers, Executive Summary*, Center for Research in Economic and Social Policy, University of Colorado, Denver, 1995.

Cummins, Jim. *Empowering Minority Students*, California Association for Bilingual Education, Sacramento, CA, 1989.

Derman-Sparks, Louise and the ABC Task Force. *Anti-Bias Curriculum Tools for Empowering Young People*, National Association for the Education of Young Children, Washington, D.C., 1989.

Diaz Soto, Lourdes and Jocelyn L. Smeaker. "The Politics of Early Bilingual Education," *Reconceptualizing the Early Childhood Curriculum: Beginning the Dialogue*, Early Childhood Education Series, 1992.

Gallinsky, Ellen and Bernice Weissbourd. "Family Centered Child Care," *Yearbook in Early Childhood Education*, University of Illinois, Champagne-Urbana, 1992.

Gallinsky, Ellen, Carollee Howes and Susan Kontos. *The Family Child Care Training Study: Highlights and Findings*, Families and Work Institute, New York, NY, 1995.

Gonzalez-Mena, Janet. *Multicultural Issues in Child Care*, Mayfield Publishing Company, Mountain View, CA, 1993.

Gonzalez-Mena, Janet. "Taking a Culturally Sensitive Approach in Infant/Toddler Programs," *Young Children*, Vol. 47, No. 2, January, 1992.

Hakuta, Kenji. *Mirror of Language: The Debate on Bilingualism*, Basic Books, Inc., New York, NY, 1986.

Hale, Janice E. *Culturally Appropriate Pedagogy*, paper presented at the National Black Child Development Annual Conference, Washington, D.C., 1995.

Harding, Edith and Philip Riley. *The Bilingual Family: A Handbook for Parents*, Cambridge University Press, Cambridge, Great Britain, 1986.

Heath, Shirley Brice. *Ways With Words: Language, Life and Work in Communities and Classrooms*, Cambridge University Press, Cambridge, MA, 1983.

Katz, Phyllis A. "Development of Children's Racial Awareness and Intergroup Attitudes," *Current Topics in Early Childhood Education*, Volume 4, pp. 17-54, Ablex Publishing Co., Norwood, NJ, 1982.

Kendall, Frances E. *Diversity in the Classroom: A Multicultural Approach to the Education of Young Children*, Teachers College Press, New York, NY, 1983.

Kontos, Susan. *Family Day Care: Out of the Shadows and Into the Limelight*, National Association for the Education of Young Children, Washington, D.C., 1992.

Lally, J. Ronald. "The Impact of Child Care Policies and Practices on Infant/Toddler Identity Formation," *Young Children*, Vol. 51, No. 1, Washington, D.C., November, 1995.

Larner, Mary. *Linking Family Support and Early Childhood Programs: Issues, Experiences, Opportunities*, Family Resource Coalition, Chicago, IL, 1995.

Lee, Deborah. *An Evaluation of Six Parent Services Project Programs in San Francisco*, Parent Services Project, Inc., Fairfax, CA, August 8, 1995.

Lee, Lisa. *Working with Non-English-Speaking Families: Foster a Climate of Equality and Inclusion*, Parent Services Project, Inc., Fairfax, CA, 1995.

Levine, R.A. "Anthropology and Child Development," *New Directions for Child Development*, pp.8, 71-86, 1980.

Lynch, Eleanor W. and Marci Hanson. *Developing Cross Cultural Competence: A Guide for Working with Young Children and Families*, Paul H. Brookes Publishing Co., Baltimore, MD, 1992.

Mallory, Bruce L. and Rebecca S. New, et al. *Diversity and Developmentally Appropriate Practices: Challenges For Early Childhood Education*, Teachers College Press, New York, NY, 1994.

Mangione, Peter L., ed. *Infant/Toddler Caregiving: A Guideline to Culturally Sensitive Care*, California Department of Education, 1995.

McLauglin, Barry. *Second Language Acquisition in Childhood: Volume One, Preschool Children, Second Edition*, Lawrence Erlbaum Associates, Inc., Hillsdale, NJ, 1984.

Miller, Darla Ferris. *First Steps Towards Cultural Difference: Socialization in Infant/Toddler Day Care*, Child Welfare League, Washington, D.C., 1989.

Mistry, Jayanthi. "Culture and Learning in Infancy: Implications for Caregiving," *Infant and Toddler Caregiving: A Guide to Culturally Sensitive Care*, California Department of Education, 1995.

Morgen, Gwen and Sheri L. Azer, et al. *Making a Career of It: The State of the States Report on Career Development in Early Care and Education*, Center for Career Development in Early Care and Education, Boston, MA, 1993.

National Association for the Education of Young Children. "Position Statement: Responding to Linguistic and Cultural Diversity—Recommendations for Effective Early Childhood Education," *Young Children*, Vol. 51, No. 2, Washington, D.C., January, 1996.

National Black Child Development Institute. *Paths to African American Leadership Positions in Early Childhood Education: Constraints and Opportunities*, Washington, D.C., 1993.

Neugebauer, Bonnie, ed. *Alike and Different: Exploring Our Humanity with Young Children*, National Association for the Education of Young Children, Washington, D.C., 1992.

New, Rebecca. *Babies and Bathwater: Uses and Abuses of Child Development Research and Developmentally Appropriate Practice*, paper presented at the American Educational Research Association, San Francisco, CA, April, 1992.

Nieto, Sonia. *Affirming Diversity: The Sociopolitical Context of Multicultural Education*, Longman Publishing Group, White Plains, NY, 1992.

Ozer, Emily J. *Bay Area Hispano Institute for Advancement Parent Survey Report*, Department of Psychology, University of California, Berkeley, CA, 1994.

Parent Services Project. *Serving Families, Building Partnerships*, Fairfax, CA, 1996.

Program for Infant and Toddler Caregivers. *Infant/Toddler Caregiving: A Guide to Sensitive Care*, California Department of Education Child Development Division and Far West Laboratory for Educational Research and Development, December, 1990.

Ramsey, Patricia G. *Teaching and Learning in a Diverse World: Multicultural Education for Young Children*, Teachers College Press, New York, NY, 1987.

Russell, Sue. "North Carolina: The TEACH Program," described in *Breaking the Link: A National Forum on Child Care Compensation*, National Center for the Early Childhood Workforce, April 29-May 1, 1994.

Sandoval-Martinez, Steven. "Findings From the Head Start Bilingual Curriculum Development and Evaluation Effort," *National Association of Bilingual Educators Journal*, Vol. VII, No. 1, Fall, 1982.

Siederman, Ethel, Lisa Lee and Jesse Lienselder. *Sharing the Vision*, Parent Services Project, Fairfax, CA, 1996.

Smitherman, Geneva. *Testifying and Talking: The Language of Black America*, Wayne State University Press, Detroit, MI, 1986.

United States Department of Health and Human Services, Head Start Bureau Administration on Children, Youth and Families, Administration for Children and Families, *Multicultural Principles for Head Start Programs*, Washington, D.C., 1992.

Whitebook, Marcy. *Salary Improvements for Head Start: Lessons for the Early Care and Education Field*, National Center for the Early Childhood Workforce, Washington, D.C., 1995.

Whitebook, Marcy, Carollee Howes and Deborah Phillips. *The National Child Care Staffing Study: Who Cares? Child Care Teachers and the Quality of Care in America*, Child Care Employee Project, Oakland, CA, 1989.

Whitebook, Marcy and Laura Sakai. *The Potential of Mentoring: Assessment of the California Early Childhood Mentor Teacher Program*, National Center for the Early Childhood Workforce, Washington, D.C., 1995.

Willer, Barbara, Sandra L. Hofferth, Ellen E. Kisker, Patricia Divine-Hawkins, Elizabeth Farguar and Frederic B. Glantz. *The Demand and Supply of Child Care in 1990: Joint Findings from the National Child Care Survey 1990 and a Profile of Child Care Settings*, National Association for the Education of Young Children, Washington, D.C., 1991.

Wong Fillmore, Lily. "When Learning a Second Language Means Losing the First," *Early Childhood Research Quarterly* 6, pp. 323-346, 1991.

York, Stacey. *Developing Roots and Wings: A Trainers Guide to Affirming Culture in Early Childhood Programs*, Redleaf Press, St. Paul, MN, 1992.

Zinsser, Caroline. *Born and Raised in East Urban: A Community Study of Informal and Unregulated Child Care*, Center for Public Advocacy Research, Inc., New York, NY, 1990.

Resources

Videos for Staff Development

Diversity
Four Early Childhood Training Videos by Janet Gonzalez-Mena
Magna Systems, Inc.
(800) 203-7060

Essential Connections: Ten Keys to Culturally Sensitive Child Care
Available in English, Spanish and Chinese
Far West Laboratory, Program for Infant/Toddler Caregivers
Distributed by the California Department of Education
(916) 445-1260

Anti-Bias Curriculum
Pacific Oaks College
(800) 831-1306

The Color of Fear
Stir Fry Productions
(510) 419-3930

Books for Staff Development

Anti-Bias Curriculum: Tools for Empowering Young Children
by Louise Derman-Sparks and the ABC Task Force
National Association for the Education of Young Children
(800) 424-2460 or (202) 328-2604

Roots and Wings: A Trainers Guide to Affirming Culture in Early Childhood Programs
by Stacey York
Redleaf Press
(800) 423-8309

Multicultural Issues in Child Care
by Janet Gonzalez-Mena
Redleaf Press
(800) 423-8309

Language in Early Childhood Education
Courtney B. Cazden, editor
National Association for the Education of Young Children
(800) 424-2460 or (202) 328-2604

Affirming Children's Roots: Cultural and Linguistic Diversity in Early Care and Education
by Hedy Nai-Lin Chang and Laura Sakai
California Tomorrow
(415) 441-7631

Helping Children Love Themselves: A Professional Handbook for Family Day Care
The Children's Foundation
(202) 347-3300

Training Teachers: A Harvest of Theory and Practice
by Margie Carter and Deb Curtis
(206) 325-0592

First Steps Toward Cultural Difference: Socialization in Infant/Toddler Day Care
by Darla Ferris Miller
Child Welfare League
(800) 407-6273

Trainings

Assessing and Fostering First and Second Language Development in Early Childhood
Child Development Division
Contact: Marcia Meyer
(408) 476-0178

Healing Racism, Inc.
Leadership training
(847) 492-0123, (800) 322-4122

Leadership in Diversity Training Project
Offered through the California Association for the Education of Young Children
Contact: Mary Norman
(213) 265-8869 or CAEYC State Office at (916) 442-4703

Oyate
Anti-Indian Biases Resource Center and Clearinghouse
Workshops, resource library, resource materials by and about Native peoples for children and adults
(510) 848-6700

TODOS: Sherover Simms Alliance Building Institute
Diversity training
Contact: Hugh Vasquez
(510) 444-6448

Ujamaa Family Life Project
Counseling and consulting
(770) 981-7261

Unlearning Racism
Stir Fry Productions
Contact: Laura DeFrey
(510) 419-1094

World of Difference
Anti-Defamation League
Anti-racism/anti-bias training
(212) 490-2525

Resources for Young Children

Cultural Connections
Anti-bias and multicultural books
(510) 538-8237

Global Village, Inc.
Anti-bias and multicultural books
(310) 204-4018

Shen's Books and Supplies
Multicultural/multilingual books for children
Books in Asian languages
(818) 445-6958

Appendix A
Profile of Child Care Centers Interviewed

The demographics refer to racial and cultural groups in programs at the time of our visits. "Primarily" refers to cases where most children were of one racial/cultural group, but children of other backgrounds were also enrolled. Most programs enrolled some or several biracial children.

Alpine Children's Center, Markleeville
Auspice: Nonprofit
Demographics: Primarily white and Native American
Monolingual English
Number of children: 63, ages 0-12 years

Centro de Niños, Riverside
Auspice: Nonprofit
Demographics: Primarily Latino
Bilingual Spanish and English
Number of children: 64, ages 3-5 years

Centro VIDA, Berkeley
Auspice: Nonprofit
Demographics: Multicultural/multiracial
Bilingual Spanish and English
Number of children: 55, ages 2-5 years

Davis Children's Center, Davis
Auspice: School District
Demographics: Multicultural/multiracial
Monolingual English
Number of children: 74, ages 3-7 years

Delta Migrant Children's Center, Courtland
Auspice: Nonprofit
Demographics: Latino
Monolingual Spanish
Number of children: 24, ages 2 months-5 years

Discoveryland, San Francisco
Auspices: Church-based
Demographics: Primarily Chinese
Bilingual Cantonese Chinese and English
Number of children: 70, ages 3-6 years

Drew Child Development Corporation, Los Angeles
Auspice: Nonprofit
Demographics: Primarily African American
Monolingual English
Number of children: 120, ages 2 mos-6 years

Hilltop Nursery, Los Angeles
Auspice: Nonprofit
Demographics: Multicultural/multiracial
Monolingual English
Number of children: 38, ages 2-5 years

Hintil Kuu Ca, Oakland
Auspice: School District
Demographics: Primarily Native American
Monolingual English
Number of children: 140, ages 3-12 years

Hoover Intergenerational Child Care, Los Angeles
Auspice: Nonprofit
Demographics: Primarily Latino and African American
Monolingual English
Number of children: 53, ages 2-1/2-5 years

Las Casitas Head Start, San Jose
Auspice: Head Start
Demographics: Vietnamese and Latino
Multilingual Spanish, Vietnamese and English
Number of children: 20, ages 3-5 years

Live Oak Migrant Head Start, Live Oak
Auspice: Head Start
Demographics: Latino and East Indian
Multilingual Spanish, Punjabi and English
Number of children: 40, ages 3-5 years

Marie Kaiser Infant Center, Tri-Cities Children's Centers, Fremont
Auspice: Nonprofit
Demographics: Multicultural/multiracial
Monolingual English
Number of children: 30, ages 0-3 years

Marin Learning Center, Marin City
Auspice: Nonprofit
Demographics: Primarily African American
Monolingual English
Number of children: 36, ages 3-8 years

Native American Child Development Center, Fresno
Auspice: Nonprofit
Demographics: Multicultural/multiracial
Monolingual English
Number of children: 30, ages 2-1/2-5 years

Plaza Child Development and Observation Center, Los Angeles
Auspice: Nonprofit
Demographics: Latino
Bilingual Spanish and English
Number of children: 65, ages 2-12 years

Rancho Los Amigos, Downey
Auspice: Employee-sponsored
Demographics: Multicultural/multiracial
Monolingual English
Number of children: 120, ages 6 weeks-6 years

Second Baptist Child Development Center, Los Angeles
Auspice: Nonprofit
Demographics: Latino and African American
Monolingual English
Number of children: 98, ages 1-6-1/2 years

Simcha, Santa Cruz
Auspices: Temple-based
Demographics: Primarily Jewish
Monolingual English
Number of children: 60, ages 1-1/2-6 years

Step One School, Berkeley
Auspice: Nonprofit
Demographics: Multicultural/multiracial,
Monolingual English
Number of children: 135, ages 2-6 years

University of Southern California/Health Science Campus Child Care Program, Los Angeles
Auspice: Employee-sponsored
Demographics: Multicultural/multiracial
Monolingual English
Number of children: 58, ages 6 weeks-6 years

Wool Creek Head Start, San Jose
Auspice: Head Start
Demographics: Vietnamese and Latino
Multilingual Spanish, Vietnamese and English
Number of children: 20, ages 3-5 years

Yerba Buena Child Development Center, San Francisco
Auspice: School district
Demographics: Multicultural/multiracial
Monolingual English
Number of children: 193, ages 33 months-8 years

Appendix B
Profile of Family Child Care Homes Interviewed

The demographics refer to racial and cultural groups in programs at the time of our visits. "Primarily" refers to cases where most children were of one racial/cultural group, but children of other backgrounds were also enrolled. Most programs enrolled some or several biracial children.

Anita Surh, Oakland
Demographics: Primarily Chinese
Bilingual Mandarin and Cantonese
Number of children: 9, ages 2-6 years

Elsa Muñoz, Berkeley
Demographics: Primarily white
Bilingual English and Spanish
Number of children: 9, ages 1-3 years

Faina Weinstein, San Francisco
Demographics: Multicultural/multiracial
Monolingual English
Number of children: 10, ages 1-1/2-5 years

Families Working Together Child Care, Los Angeles
Demographics: African American
Monolingual English
Number of children: 11, ages 1-1/2-4 years

Jose and Celia Gomez, Watsonville
Demographics: Primarily Latino
Bilingual Spanish and English
Number of children: 6, ages 1-7 years

Lari Chouinard, Pasadena
Demographics: Multicultural/multiracial
Monolingual English
Number of children: 4, ages 1-1/2-5 years

Little Engines, Rohnert Park
Demographics: white
Monolingual English
Number of children: 6, ages 3-6 years

Little Rascals, Torrance
Demographics: Multicultural/multiracial
Monolingual English
Number of children: 11, ages 2 months-10 years

Maria Maravilla, Berkeley
Demographics: Primarily Latino
Monolingual Spanish
Number of children: 6, ages 1-4 years

Sweet Dreams Family Child Care, Oakland
Demographics: Multicultural/multiracial
Monolingual English
Number of children: 11, ages 2 months-5 years

Appendix C
Trainers Interviewed

Leo Bonner
Carol Brunson Phillips
Mary Cardenas
Margie Carter
Agnes Chan
Eleanor Clement Glass
Ardella Dailey
Jerlean Daniel
Louise Derman-Sparks
Toni Denton
Yolanda Garcia
Janet Gonzalez-Mena
Maria Gutierrez
Patti Hnatiuk
Nancy Johnson
Lisa Lee
Marie Lee
Beatriz Leyva-Cutler
David Longaker
Julie Olsen Edwards
Chris Peralta
Intisar Shareef
Mary Smithberger
Melinda Sprague
Bonnie Waterer
Yolanda Torres
Lily Wong Fillmore
Marlene Zepeda

Appendix D
Resource and Referral Agencies Interviewed

4 C's Council of Santa Clara, Santa Clara County

4 C's of Sonoma County, Sonoma County

4 C's of Alameda County, Alameda County

BANANAS, Alameda County

Child Action, Inc., Sacramento County

Child and Family Services of San Fernando Valley, Los Angeles County

Child Care Information Service, Los Angeles and San Bernadino Counties

Child Development Resource Center, Santa Cruz County

Children and Family Services, Los Angeles County

Children's Council of San Francisco, San Francisco County

Children's Home Society, Orange County

Choices for Children, Alpine and El Dorado Counties

City of Davis Child Care Services, Yolo County

Community Resources for Children, Napa County

Contra Costa Child Care Council, Contra Costa County

Crystal Stairs, Los Angeles County

Family Resources and Referral Center, San Joaquin County

Infant/Child Enrichment Services, Mariposa and Tuolumne Counties

Community Connection for Child Care, Kern County

Marin Child Care Council, Marin County

Children's Services Network of Merced County, Inc., Merced County

Modoc Child Care Resource & Referral, Modoc County

HRC Child Care Resources (formerly Mountain Family Service Agency), Amador and Calaveras Counties

OPTIONS, Los Angeles County

Placer County Office of Education Child Care Services, Placer County

Resources for Family Development, Alameda County

Riverside County Office of Education, Coordinator for Child Care, Riverside County

4 C's of San Mateo, San Mateo County

Valley Oak Children's Services, Butte and Glenn Counties

Wu Yee Children's Services, San Francisco County

YMCA Child Care Resource Center, San Diego County

List of California Tomorrow Publications

For information about these publications, call (415) 441-7631 or fax your request to (415) 441-7635. Prices do not include taxes and shipping costs. Discounts of 20% available on orders of 10 or more of the same title.

Drawing Strength from Diversity

1994 / $21.00 / 126 pages

This report examines how the current service system, which fails to work for many families, can be transformed to yield positive outcomes for all families. *Drawing Strength from Diversity* is a valuable resource for public agencies, schools, community organizations, families, policymakers, funders and anyone dedicated to creating services and supports that are culturally appropriate, accessible and effective for a diverse and pluralistic society.

California Perspectives, Vol. 4, Special Issue: Community Canons

1994 / $17.00 / 109 pages

Community Canons documents the efforts of parents, community groups, public libraries, churches and independent small presses to create a curriculum for children to help them grow up strong, proud and informed. This anthology includes profiles of community programs, interviews with leaders in the field, and a resource list.

California Perspectives, Vol. 3

1992 / $15.00 / 82 pages

Topics of articles in this anthology from California Tomorrow range from the movement to create African-centered education to how growing anti-immigrant sentiment and misinformation threatens our future.

California Perspectives, Vol. 2

1991 / $12.00 / 58 pages

With articles on student teachers working in diverse classrooms, this anthology provides an analysis of California's debate over the social studies curriculum and the broader issues of power, knowledge, national identity, growing up biracial and bicultural, and more.

The Unfinished Journey: Restructuring Schools in a Diverse Society

1994 / $27.00 / 360 pages

This book reports on school restructuring and reform in California. It relates the efforts of teachers, school principals, parents and community members who see that the old ways of schooling aren't working for many students, as they dare to try to invent better ones in their place. The challenge is to focus creative energy on addressing the challenges of a multicultural, multilingual educational environment.

Embracing Diversity: Teachers' Voices from California Classrooms

1990 / $20.00 / 115 pages / ISBN 1-887039-03-1

Meet 36 California teachers doing remarkable work in mainstream classrooms with students of diverse cultural, national and linguistic backgrounds. Through in-depth interviews, the educators share their strategies to inspire their students to bridge the gaps of language, culture and national backgrounds which often separate them. The teachers send out an urgent call to policymakers, staff developers and teacher trainers to support and prepare teachers for the reality and challenges of California's diverse classrooms.

Affirming Children's Roots: Cultural and Linguistic Diversity in Early Care and Education

1993 / $17.00 / 101 pages

What are the implications of cultural and ethnic diversity for early childhood care and education? This report presents research documenting the impact of California's demographic changes on child care centers, exploring questions about the implications of our growing diversity for early care and education through a review of the literature and profiles of sites and training programs. Includes recommendations for policy and practice, and an annotated bibliography.

Crossing the Schoolhouse Border: Immigrant Students in the California Public Schools

1988 / $16.00 / 128 pages

A groundbreaking report based on interviews with more than 400 immigrant students and hundreds of educators, community workers and parents about the needs and experiences of newcomers in California's classrooms. Crossing the Schoolhouse Border provides information about the backgrounds of students, their academic and social needs and adjustments, the political climate and funding.